BORED BEAGLE: MY WINTER OF DISCONTENT

Russell The Beagle

FOREWORD

I am Russell. I'm a 5 year-old Beagle, and this is the story of my daily struggles in living with my family. If your household has a dog, teenagers, working parents and a cavalier attitude towards the cleanliness of the kitchen, some of my thoughts might strike a chord with you.

I started writing down my perceptions of life as a blog. This was to cheer up a young friend of mine who was having Nasty Things done to him in the Marsden Hospital. It came as a surprise to me that other people enjoyed reading this nonsense, and I was encouraged to write a book. So here it is. Of course, if you enjoy the book (I think the chances will be slim), you can always read the blog which has carried on and is updated every couple of days. I know, I don't know how I do it all, either. It's at boredbeagle.wordpress.com.

There's an important message right at the end of my book. I would have a look at that first, if I was you. It's the only sensible part of the whole thing.

DEDICATION

Really? I have to dedicate this nonsense to someone?

Well, She and I have argued long and hard about this. I want to dedicate my book to dear Ebony and Pippa's Pack Leaders, who save me from a life of complete boredom. She wants to dedicate my book to Friends Who Have Propped Her Up Over Tricky Years.
So we've compromised.

To Sicknote.
Because I wouldn't be living this life, if it wasn't for you.

CHAPTER ONE

First Attempt

November 13th

Excellent. A decomposing mouse on the drive this morning, and a pile of weekend vomit by a lamp-post. I didn't get quite near enough the latter, but I did have a chew of the former.

Well, bowing to HUGE public demand, I'm turning my blog into a book. I don't quite see why my blog wasn't enough for some people, but apparently we're now writing a book. Don't hold your breath, Friends – She is useless at this sort of thing. Fully expect it to be an epic fail. We've needed an awful lot of help to get this far and I can't see this catching on.

For any new Friends, here is what you need to know. I'm Russell and I'm five, which surprises many people by the river as they think I'm an old dog. This is due to my weight and lack of interest in puppies or playing, plus a rather dour demeanour. I live with She (Pack Leader, or so She thinks), He, Lad and Young Lad. They are not a normal family. It worries me at times.

Here are the good things about me:
- I'm very affectionate. Especially if you are holding a piece of food.

Er. That's it.

Here are some other facts about me. I roll in fox poo, cow pats, decomposing rats and fish by the river, and anything else truly vile. (I have occasionally excelled myself by finding human excrement in the bushes.) I fart a lot and have trouble with my anal glands. I snore loudly. I steal food. I raid bins. I eat things from the bathroom waste bin that you wouldn't think could be eaten. I bark at:
- people with dark skin
- people in wheelchairs
- old people
- the neighbour over the back (I've really got a problem with him)

She says I'm the most un-PC dog ever, but I've no idea what She's on about. She also says I have a weight problem, but frankly that's a bit rich.

I don't like being left on my own when they all go to school/work. She tried working full time recently for a few weeks – that REALLY cheesed me off. No amount of dogwalking (thanks to Pippa's Pack Leader and Ebony's Pack Leader) made up for it. So I had to show them all. I emptied bins, I ate a whole chocolate birthday cake. (Ha! A £300 vet bill). I threw potato peelings all over the lounge floor. But She still didn't get the message, so I had to escape through the back fence (into the back neighbour's garden so I barked a lot) and run round the estate and over the Rec, with Builder and Retired Neighbours chasing me. By the time She was telephoned and came back from work (muttering that She was in the middle of Something Important), I had come home and was back in my armchair. She then had to run round the estate to find the Builder and Retired Neighbours and let them know I was back thankyouverymuch bldydog.

Anyway, it worked because She's now part time again, and I just ignore the moaning about needthebldymoney.

It's a strange house to live in. She seems to swear a lot these days, often at me, and has a friend called Gordon who often has an ice cube and slice of lemon with him. They all seem to argue a lot, and speak in code; "Xbox/COD/GCSEs/getoffyourbloodyphone," seem to feature a lot in these arguments. I do love them all, but sometimes I do wonder about them. A new duvet cover was recently bought from somewhere called John Lewis – She seemed very smug and middle England about this, even though I know it was in the sale – but I could have TOLD her what a stupid decision that was! Yes, white looks nice the first time you make the bed, but if my glands leak a bit or it's been raining outside, it's not going to stay white, is it? It's no good shouting at me.

Apparently, I'm a disappointment because She can't go running with me. We've tried it a few times but it just doesn't work as She'll be up one end of the river waiting for me while I'm rolling in fox poo. Anyway, I'm saving her from a lot of indignity – some people just aren't built for running, and She's one of them. So we "power walk" (don't make me laugh) for three miles up the fields.

To thank her for this morning's "power walk" I'm now letting off some particularly fresh smells. The house did smell of cleaning spray earlier, but this is much better.

Anyway. I really can't see that this book thing will work – we could just about cope with a blog, but this really will be a step too far. So if you are managing to read this, well done. Please mention it to anyone else who might be vaguely interested. I realise that will be a small pool of people.

CHAPTER TWO

Birdseed

November 14th

Whoa!! It worked! You're still reading my book! She is looking as self-satisfied as the time She bought her first North Face jacket (from a reduced outlet store) to replace her Tesco jacket. I chewed holes in the NF one so She didn't look self-satisfied for long.

Now before I go on, a special shout out to my young friend J, who is spending time in the Marsden. Sorry to hear about the Incident in The Night Time last night, and I do hope your Pack Leader gets it together soon. They are an embarrassment at times. Some dogs are used in hospital as Therapy Dogs, but I don't think I'd be let in on hygiene grounds.

So, it was an exhausting day yesterday what with the power walk and everything. I managed to stagger out of my armchair when She went off for school pick up, however, to find a couple of spearmint polos in the bedroom and a tissue in Lad's bin. Yesterday I ate a pack of silicon earplugs, but they haven't come through my system whole yet, which makes me wonder if I've had some particularly strong gastric acid going on that's broken them down. It could explain the smells.

She seemed a bit disorganised at teatime and started to make a Jamie Oliver roly-poly with some vegetable suet She found at the back of the cupboard – I suspect out of date. It was a shame She only started this at 5.30 and then discovered it takes two hours to steam. Nobody liked it much anyway. I think it was the stress of losing a pack of silicon earplugs that distracted her. Hopefully better service will resume tonight, and they'll be given a tin of peaches and a yogurt.

After dinner last night it was the usual Quiet Hour. This involves a lot of argybargy about something called homework; have you got any/ no I haven't/ check your bag/ I have checked my bag /you must have something it's Year11 for God's sake.

Eventually they all settled down and I slept while She tested Lad on Irreversible Reactions. It was dull. Then She and Young Lad read about Alex Rider. That seemed quite dull too. He read the paper and did the crossword.

This morning She was more stressed than usual due to standing outside the Dr's surgery for twenty minutes before it opened to get an appointment for Lad. Lad has health issues which I suspect are an excuse to get out of PE. There was a lot of moaning about stupidruddytelephonebookingsystem which is why She left early to stand in the cold. I think the Dr is a bit like the Evil Vet, but there is never a problem getting an appointment at the Evil Vet to have my anal glands squeezed, Bastards. (Though She does have to check it's not a Pregnant Vet on duty as it's not nice for Pregnant Vets to squeeze anal glands. And I can tell you it's not great for me either.) While She drove round like a bluearsedfly delivering Lad and Young Lad to schools, I had a look in the cupboard under the stairs, found a packet of bird seed and chucked it on the lounge floor for good measure. I didn't bother opening it though, so they should be grateful.

Our walk today was only for two miles as there isn't bldytime to walk three miles and write a bldybook and get to work, so I did one of my favourite tricks – waited till she was half a mile ahead and then took a comfort break, so She had to stomp all the way back to me with the poo bags. This is good for her Exercise Quotient and doesn't require all the tutting. It was a nice walk – the Bastard Swans weren't there today, only their offspring who are still grey, but She says will turn white soon and become Bastard Swans like their parents. We have a strong mutual dislike. I saw my friend Lexie down there and a new chocolate lab puppy that wanted me to play, but I don't do that. There is no point if there is no food involved.

Despite the fields being a bit muddy, I'm still very white and clean. Lad bathed me on Sunday, and he does a lovely job of it. He takes time and care, and doesn't shout LOOK AT THE STATE OF YOU like She does.

Apparently She has to go to work now. How selfish. So I will pretend to be asleep in my chair, but actually plan what I'm going to do in the next four hours... She may think all bases have been covered by putting the bin out and shutting bedroom doors, but I usually find something to do. Dognextdoor has the radio left on for him when his family go out, but oh no, not me. GingerCat and I have no comforting voices.

I can't believe anyone's reading this; who would have thought it!

Oh well. She says GodKnows WeAllNeed ABitofALaugh Sometimes so maybe it'll brighten someone's day. I'll do my best.

CHAPTER THREE

Poor Standards

November 15th

Today is Wednesday. Wednesdays are rubbish because they've all left home by 7.45 am and nobody gets in until 5.30pm. They are very wrapped up in themselves on a Wednesday.

Anyway. This could be an interesting chapter as apparently you can write a book and cook asparagus risotto at the same time. I think we all know this isn't going to end well. My prediction is burnt onion, dried-out rice and overcooked asparagus. It will go down as well as the Jamie Oliver steamed pudding; if She'd stuck to fish fingers and chips like most working parents, they would all be much happier. She never learns.

Hello to my young friend J in the Marsden again, hope you enjoyed Jolly Johnny and his guitar today. We did warn you about enthusiastic music therapy entertainers. When Lad was in hospital the nurses used to tell them that Lad was heavily asleep so that the entertainers left him alone. Music therapy wasn't Lad's cup of tea.

Well, as I said, there has not been much going on today. At least I was left with a bone this morning (guilt issues). That kept me quiet for four minutes. After that I had another look in the cupboard under the stairs; it is disgusting. I cannot believe any of you have a cupboard that looks like ours does. There is an ironing board, hoover, tool box (rarely used), torches that don't work, batteries that don't work, Christmas scented tea lights from four years ago, tins of paint (dried up), three irons, a yoga mat (really?) , weedkiller (ooh that's a safe place to keep poison) and three million carrier bags. There was also a Quality Street tub with various screws, nails, hot water bottle cap, curtain hooks and key tags; for something to do, I chucked this on the floor so it went everywhere. Frankly it might encourage them to CLEAR OUT THAT PIGSTY OF A CUPBOARD.

After that, Ebony's Pack Leader from three doors down came to let me out for a comfort break. I didn't want to go and made it clear that I was comfortable in my chair. She forced the issue. Then a bit later, Pippa's Pack Leader took me out for a walk. It's nice that someone cares about me on a Wednesday, as clearly my own family don't.

Tonight's excitement will be trying to get into the dishwasher when they load it with the barely-touched asparagus risotto plates. I don't care if it's a bit dried up. Last night He shouted at me when I stood on the dishwasher door trying to lick the plates. He rarely shouts at me, and so I usually behave much better for him. To be honest though, the risotto looked awful. One word; stodge.

That said, there is a good mood here this evening because "The Apprentice " is on tonight. She and Lad watch this together, shouting rude, patronising things and laughing. She also texts Colleague to do the same thing over the phone, and Nana aged 86. So you see, multi- tasking can be done when necessary and a much better job could have been made with the risotto. Apparently Lad and Young Lad are "STARVING" (this seems to be a permanent state and I know how they feel) and this is due to being served up a below-standard meal for dinner. Readers, I feel this is Neglect and will be keeping my eye on the situation. Poor Lad has taken to shouting, "there is NOTHING to eat in this house!", pointedly ignoring the bowl of fruit and fridge full of yogurts. I feel for him.

CHAPTER FOUR

Sad Face and Retching

November 16th

I am exceptionally talented at pulling a sad face every morning when they all go out. I sit on the bottom stair and look clinically depressed as they leave. (Seconds after they've gone, I'm going through the cupboards.) Today's sad face was particularly good. It made no difference. They still all went to work and school.

Last night was a bit of a corker. I was in the middle of a lovely sleep (somewhere that many of you don't let your dogs sleep) when I felt a bit queasy. I struggled on until 2.30 am, when I could hold it down no longer, and woke them with the most dramatic retching you can imagine. It started as a low note, deep down in my stomach and built to a crescendo of GLP GLP GLP BLEUGHHH. You'll be pleased to know I had the self-discipline to avoid the John Lewis not-quite-so-white duvet, and made it down to the wooden floor in the hall. I was proud of this.

All that had to be cleared up when She got downstairs was a hard piece of the Guilt Bone that I'd been given yesterday, which hadn't broken down very well. I had cleared up everything else. It was quite nice. I didn't get much thanks, it being 2.30 am, and was chucked in the garden for a while.

Anyway. It's been a dull old day, saved only by Lovelyneighbourontheright who let me out mid-morning, and Pippa's Pack Leader who walked me again later. To be honest, if you haven't got time to have a dog, don't get one. It's not a difficult concept.

There was a conversation over dinner tonight (Smokeroni Cheese; don't ask, but it was more successful than the risotto) that made me uncomfortable. They were discussing what to do on Christmas Day, and apparently we are going to AD's house for lunch. Well. THEY are, but AD has a huge monstrosity of a cat, let's call him Nasty Git, who won't allow me in the house. So I have to be dumped elsewhere. Anyway,

Young Lad said he wanted me to go to AD's house with them, as I always get my lipstick out when I see AD. Much sniggering followed this. I can't help it – AD is a very pretty lady and it's a perfectly normal reaction for a healthy male to find his lipstick has popped out in the presence of beauty. I don't see why they have to laugh. And I'm NOT happy about being dumped elsewhere while they eat Christmas Dinner.

I managed to find a bin today that hadn't been hidden away – the one in the downstairs toilet. She often forgets that one. So I spent a while throwing the bits of paper and tumble drier fluff around, and was pleased to find a muffin wrapper at the bottom. All I'd been left with this morning was my Kong, with a smear of chicken squashed down one end, mashed up with out-of-date hummus.

Quiet Time last night involved more tedious revising and testing – this time something called Greenhouse Gases and Global Warming. I was somewhat annoyed when methane gas was mentioned, as apparently this is the result of animal emissions, and so there was lots of juvenile laughing that I produce enough methane to melt ice caps by myself. They need to focus on what they're doing, if you ask me.

So, tomorrow I will actually have a decent walk as She is not at work, though is already muttering about gotsomuchtodo don'tknowwheretostart. There is a lot of "negotiating" going on here at the moment as Lad wants to go to something called a House Party next weekend, a long way away. There is some doubt as to whether this is a Good Idea, and the discussion becomes a little Heated. I feel this will rumble on for some time.

She is going to the cinema with her good friend Loadsakids tomorrow night, as apparently it's something called Children In Need tomorrow, and Loadsakids reckons it should be called Mothers In Need instead. There was a lot of guffawing at this, so they will go out and probably have Something to Drink. They have been known to compare notes about their teenagers and dogs on these occasions. Not kindly, I feel.

CHAPTER FIVE

Muzzled

November 17th

Unbelievable. Absolutely unbelievable. Today She has been to ToysRPetsRVetsRUs or whatever it's called, and bought a horrid black rubber muzzle. This is so that ear drops can be administered down my sore ears without having one's hand bitten off. Am I seriously expected to sit nicely while a long white thing is poked down my ear and stuff squirted into it? No, I will try to take the hand off that person, and rightly so.

So now I have a muzzle. It was "ridiculously expensive" apparently and She could have saved herself the bother. I tried not to laugh as She read the instructions for "familiarising your dog with the muzzle" – it seems I'm meant to happily walk round the house wearing the hideous thing, if she trains me properly. Instead, some more out-of-date hummus was smeared in it (why don't they just throw that away?) and as I stuck my head in to eat it, I was rugby tackled to the ground, She gripped the muzzle and stuck the thing in my ear. This is not what the pictures in the instruction booklet looked like. It's bad enough being muzzled every time I see the Evil Vet, (because I try to take their hands off too), but when someone that's supposed to love you does it, that's rubbish.

In other ways, things are looking up. The Guilt Bone has gone through my system and firmed things up a lot, which is good for my anal glands as they tend to empty with the extra pressure of hard stuff passing through.

J in the Marsden, are you still being sick? Hope I'm helping with that side of things. Sorry to hear you're stuck there till Sunday now, but to cheer you up, I hear the Therapy Magicians are coming round tomorrow.

I had a decent walk today – I found some unidentifiable brown stuff to roll in, but carefully waited until She was well ahead up the field.

She then had to run full pelt down the hill waving the long pink ball flinger thing at me and shouting. This was very funny. The Bastard Swan Offspring were there, right at my favourite spot for going in for a drink. I hate them. Someone had thrown some bread out for the birds in the usual spot, so it was a race between her and me to see how much I could grab before She got the lead on me. I won.

There is still a lot of arguing about the House Party going on. Also something called an Exam Revision Workshop which Lad doesn't want to attend but is being told it's not his decision. He doesn't seem to agree with this. Loudly.

It's rather cold in here today, Readers – the Boiler doesn't appear to be working and there's been a lot of stressed muttering about "dear God 3grand for a new one." I'm not looking forward to this evening with no heating, and may need to cuddle up on the sofa for warmth. British Gas Man is coming tomorrow; She says, "really is that theirideaofbldyurgent."

I've been told off a lot today for barking. I could see, out of the window, a very threatening 96 year old lady standing at the bus stop. She looked like she meant trouble, so I went ballistic. Not long afterwards, a mother and toddler walked past our car in a sinister way so I let rip at them too. Nobody appreciates what I do to protect this family.

Well it's nearly my dinner time – only another hour to go, so I'll start whining and making a fuss about it now.

CHAPTER SIX

The Gas Man Cometh

November 18th

It was quite a cold night, after no heating for 24 hours, but thankfully there was an extra blanket on the place-that-I-don't sleep. She was up bright and early, dressed and in full make-up (you'd never know) by 8am, ready for the Gas Man. I barked a lot at him as he looked dodgy, so was told to Shut Up and shoved into the lounge.

Anyway. After showing Great Interest in his Gas Engineering Career thus far, nodding and smiling in the right places, and making a "really nice cuppa", She has managed to get the excess for today's call-out waived, and a Fantastic Deal involving 2yearsinterestfreecredit and a halfpriceboiler. Needless to say, She is quite pleased with herself on her clever use of tactics – some would call it flirting.

Today's walk was great! I was feeling a bit feisty – just one of those days – so I took on a large Alsatian first of all. This was an error of judgement. Then I barked shamelessly at a little girl who smiled at me. Next I saw NiceDogWalkerLady and her three hundred dogs, most of whom were barking so I joined in. My beagle bray is much louder and better than any of their barks. NiceDogWalkerLady had Barney the Oh So Adorable Beagle with her – the one that is "oh so lovely, he's so gentle and well-behaved, look how he leans against my legs," blardy blardy blah. We moved on swiftly, and would you believe it, there was a THIRD beagle down there! This really annoys me. I like to be The Only Beagle In The Village when I go out. I cheered up a bit when NiceTallLadywiththeStaffie stopped for a chat – she said I was looking slimmer, which seems to be the main aim in life. Pack Leader seemed really proud of this; if She paid as much attention to her own physique, things would be a lot better. "Power-walking" my arse. I saw Lexie, who looked jealousy at my stick, so I didn't hang around.

Well, Readers, this is a short chapter today as She is about to drive to the Marsden to visit J and take his Pack Leader out for

SomethingToEat. This will also involve SomethingToDrink, at least for J's Pack Leader as six days in hospital drives you insane apparently. She has packed treats (Pimms for Pack Leader and Tangfastics for J if his mother lets him have them.) It will be interesting to see how She gets on driving to Sutton; apparently He hastakenthebloodySatnav in his car, so She will be relying on Google Maps. She only discovered those this week thanks to Colleague. But there will be no internet in the car, something She doesn't appear to have considered. She seems more excited about the £5 Hits of the Seventies CD bought in Tesco this morning, for her to listen to on the long journey.

I know. I'm thinking the same thing.

CHAPTER SEVEN

It's Official

November 19th

I knew it! Beagles are good for your health! It must be true; it was in yesterday's Torygraph. According to obviously highly accurate research, owning a Beagle increases a human's mortality by 35%. So She needs to quit the whingeing about how much work I make, by accepting that "demanding " dogs like me will make her live longer. If She wants to.

Well, much to everyone's surprise the drive to Sutton and back was managed without thebloodysatnav. Apparently the M25 in sheeting rain is much more bearable in the presence of Leo Sayer. I would think this is debatable. I had to make quite a fuss during the evening as there were readymeals from SparksMeanMarks, as She was toobldytiredtocook. It is a known fact that I get to clean out the plastic tray of any ready meals. Though they "practically never have them and have wholesome home cooked food every day", someone is shouting. I wasn't happy to find the said plastic tray in the bin, without being offered it first. Normally I clean it completely so it can go into recycling, which is my bit towards the environment. I had to stare at the bin and whine for AGES until anyone got the message. It was ok, but only a 400 calorie Lite prawn linguine, and really I'd have preferred the full on option. So would She.

Her friend Gordon came to visit last night. Seemed a lot bigger than usual and required extra ice. This is due to "a bit of a week" apparently.

Today is Sunday which meant something of a lie-in, (after breakfast and a comfort break at 6am). I heard some church bells ringing. When Lad and Young Lad were younger they were dragged to Church occasionally, but now on Sundays Lad doesn't get up till lunchtime and Young Lad plays on the Xbox. She seems to worship at the altar of somewhere called Costalotta in town. It's where she goes to be reflective and pray. And get away from everyone. She assuages her guilt about the price of an Americano in Costalotta by taking one to the Homeless Guy outside Sainsburys. (I know for a fact she queues up in Dreggs for his to save 50p.) Today the Homeless Guy went into a lot of detail about his medical problem so She gave him an extra £2 and didn't hang around.

There will be an attempt at a family Sunday lunch in a while, which really just involves shouting about homework. Then Lad and He are going up the pub later to watch something called Wet Sham play football. She and Young Lad are looking forward to this as it will be peaceful here. I've already had my walk; Nicedogwalkerlady said she likes my book so I've told her to tell everyone about it. Incredibly there was yet another Beagle in the far field today; that's three interlopers in the past two days! I wonder if his Pack Leader has read the Torygraph article. But seriously, enough with all the Beagles out there when I go out. Go somewhere else for your walk so that I have everyone's attention.

Mmm, the stuffing smells like it's burning so somebody needs to spring into action. I'll sit by the oven and wait for some bits to drop.

CHAPTER EIGHT

Unloved

November 20th

What a rubbish day. She was called into work so I was left here ALL DAY. Without the kindness of Ebony's Pack Leader Male and LovelyDor, who both let me out for a comfort break, I wouldn't have seen a soul all day. Oh yes, it's all very well leaving me with another guilt bone, but some company might be nice. Gingercat just sleeps. And, would you believe, She had shut every door, removed the bins and blocked off the cupboard under the stairs with a stool. So I threw a bag of potato peelings around as that was all I could find.

Remorseful, She did rush home and drag me out for a walk in the pitch dark. I had to wear this ridiculous light- up collar so I could be seen on the playing field, but I wasn't the only one. In fact there were loads of us out at 5.30pm, all wearing ridiculous light- up collars and chasing ridiculous light-up balls in the dark. All the Working Owners stood around chatting, but really they need to be thinking about their lifestyle choices.

Yesterday I ended up having a second walk and saw my friend Ebony. She is a Pointer, which puts her a few marks ahead of me in the prolonging-your-owners'-life-span results. Her Pack Leader doesn't appreciate this any more than mine does. I rolled in some fox poo and Ebony dug to the centre of the Earth. We had a great time.

Tonight has been the same old dinner/homework/arguing scenario followed by some frantic furniture moving around. Carpet cleaning man is coming tomorrow, and She still hasn't got over the horror of last time, when he pulled out the sofa and asked her if she could possibly clean up before he started... it was grim. So, all the furniture has been pulled out and hoovered behind, with a lot of huffing and puffing, and yet again the area behind the sofa was shameful. Yogurt lids, a knife, a spoon, three biros, a tissue (used), 150 nerf gun bullets and a dice. She muttered something about whycouldntthere besomethingbldyusefullikeatenner and wasn't best pleased. I enjoyed eating up the crumbs but the used tissue was taken away before I could get to it.

Lad has something called a Non-Pupil Day tomorrow. He interprets this as a day to stay in bed and then play on the Xbox. She interprets it as a Going To a Revision Workshop and Tidying Your Room Opportunity. The discussion continues.

I seem to have a fair amount of wind tonight, which is the result of the two guilt bones. As you gnaw/chew for an hour, you take in lots of air, and it has to come out somewhere. She doesn't seem to have realised this. With a bit of luck I might be given some attention tomorrow, but don't hold your breath.

CHAPTER NINE

I Lost my Heart to a Starship Trooper

November 21st

That Hits of the Seventies CD has a lot to answer for. Our Power Walk today was conducted in time to Sarah Brightman and several other such wonders, as She sang them (thankfully) in her head. That is, until the last stretch up the hill towards home, which is always walked extremely fast as one's pelvicfloor is not what it was, due to havingbldykids apparently, and there's a lot of yanking my lead with "not going to make it" muttered.

We made it, just. In case you were wondering. It was a close call.

Carpet Cleaner Man arrived bright and early. However, he managed to pull the sofa out further than She had done, and called her attention to some more cutlery, dried satsuma peelings and a lot of crumbs. He then lectured her in correct sofa moving technique (lift don't drag, foot underneath to tip backwards and never mind if it falls and crushes your foot, at least you will have cleaned up ALL of the crap.) His carpet cleaning machine was horribly noisy and scared Gingercat and I so much we had to retire to the bedroom for a sleep until he'd gone. He did a very good job of cleaning the carpets and sofa, though they are all now soaking wet. He also pointed out a small amount of fabric damage to the sofa" probably caused by your dog." As soon as he'd left, I walked round the study with muddy paws to show him what I thought. I'm not keen on Carpet Cleaning Man.

After he'd gone, She had to 'pop to town', which means half an hour in Costalotta. As usual, the baristas said hopefully, "anything else today?" in the vain hope She might splash out on more than the cheapest possible coffee. She didn't. Homeless Guy wasn't outside Sainsbury's, and now She feels bad for not listening longer to him.

The walk was reasonably good – I chased my ball a few times to humour her, but really what is the point unless you wrap some meat around it? There was a young golden retriever down there, who I could have SWORN was dear, dear Pippa, but it wasn't and I was disappointed. The Bastard Swan offspring were there, and looking much whiter than they did last week. It won't be long before they are launching themselves out of the river and attacking me. Hate them. Once home, I amused myself by emptying one of the recycling bags round the garden. The garden looked a mess anyway, so it hasn't been done any harm by some fish finger and potato waffle boxes ripped up and spat out everywhere.

You'll be very relieved to know that Lad made it to his revision workshop. She drove him there, and picked him up from outside, to make sure he didn't get lost on the way, via KFC. She spent the two hours amusing herself in the big town nearby, which probably involved a cheese scone (that's called splashing out) in John Lewis and wistfully looking at things we will never be able to afford. Occasionally I'm reminded that the gym membership had to go when they adopted me as There Wasn't Enough Money for Both. Actually, I'm reminded of this a lot. I think it's a cause of some resentment.

Well, the sofa is now covered in a waterproof sheet (left over from when Lad and Young Lad weren't very reliable at night) and several blankets. It's still soaking wet and this doesn't bode well for a comfortable evening. Gingercat and I may have to go back upstairs. Tomorrow is likely to be a rubbish day as it's Wednesday which means nobody gives a stuff about me.

Those of you who are old, enough, have you got Starship Trooper going round your head now?

CHAPTER TEN

Oily Fish

November 23rd

All I heard last night was, "eugh, Russell you stink whatisthatgodawfulsmell GETOFFTHESOFA," etc etc etc. They know exactly what the godawful smell is – it's my anal glands. There is no need for all the drama every time they flare up, and certainly no need to frantically light scented candles. Yes, it is a unique smell, like a tin of particularly greasy sardines that has been left out in the sun for a couple of months, but don't go on about it! Plus I was shouted at early this morning (5.15am to be precise) for scooting my bottom along the floor – hello, if you buy a cream-coloured carpet you expect streaks occasionally – as scooting is the only way to relieve the discomfort of over-full anal glands. So I went out in the garden for half an hour to have a good clear-out, as I thought this would help. But no; more moaning at me to hurry up and come back in as it wasn't even six o'bldyclock yet. I cannot win. She has even threatened me today with the Evil Vet if I don't unblock my glands by myself. Reader, I'm trying.

Apart from that, yesterday was BRILLIANT as I went to daycare at dear Pippa's house, and spent the day with people that actually give a damn about me. To top off a day playing and sleeping with one of my besties, we went for a walk and I flushed out a pheasant from the bushes!! Yes! Li'l ol me! I didn't catch it, and it did stick two fingers up as it flew off, but still! A great day all round.

Today's walk was pretty good, too. (3.25 miles according to her app. 288 calories). The usual crew were down there, plus my dear friend Chuck, whom I haven't seen for ages. Chuck and I are very fond of each other, and often go off into the bushes together. Chuck's Pack Leader says it's all very Brokeback Mountain and they laugh, but I've no idea what he means. Chuck is very handsome. I rolled in some stuff in Top Field, and ate something that was decomposing – only a mouthful before

She arrived, panting and shouting, on the scene. Nicedogwalkerlady and her husband stopped for a chat, and were soon discussing whether my anal glands smell better or worse than a dead badger. I wonder about people, at times.

Well, Friends, you'll be glad to know that Lad's Revision Workshop was a great success. He has been talking animatedly about it, something like, "it was the best two hours of his life, and thank you so much for making me go to it." I think that was the gist, anyway. She has been mumbling to herself upstairs this morning as there were four used towels on Lad's bedroom floor – research shows that people of Lad's age have some sort of disability and can't bend down to pick up anything they've chucked on the floor. This is of benefit to me, as it involves food wrappers and used tissues. She often discusses this disability with her Friends who also have offspring of Lad's age, and they share many happy moments, celebrating the Utter Joy involved in Parenting this Age Group. Young Lad will be there before long. He was in trouble last night for playing rugby in the lounge, and the ball (only a soft squidgy one), hit Gingercat on the head. Gingercat didn't like this and ran off. He was soon back, mind you, when they shook his biscuit box.

There is something called The Ashes on the telly at the moment, which He seems very excited about. I can't see the attraction, myself.

She has a Whole Day Off today, which is rare. These occasions usually involve a lot of frantic hoovering and laundry, and sometimes a Scandinavian drama Noir from about 10 years ago that She's trying to catch up with. Dreary.

Those of you still reading my boo; well done. I only started all this to amuse my young friend J while he was in hospital, and I'm glad to say he's back home for a bit now. But I think I'll keep going with my book; I've had some lovely feedback from you – several people have used the words "highlight of their day", which is nice, but to be frank, don't you think that's a bit worrying?

CHAPTER ELEVEN

Tangled

November 24th

Evening all. I've just had a very frustrating few minutes trying to kick the blanket out of my chair – this is a routine that takes several minutes of me kicking and digging at the blanket, growling and barking at it. Sometimes I toss it over my head for variety. It appears this is entertaining, as tonight they decided to video me doing this. Anyway, it was ruddy irritating, as I make it perfectly clear that I HATE having a blanket on my chair, and yet still I have to bark, whine, go round in circles, dig at it, kick it and scratch at it to make my point. Unfortunately tonight I became rather caught up and sat for a while with it over my head. I pretended I had meant to do this, so I didn't look ridiculous.

This was after the usual frustrating Friday evening, whereby they all collapse on the sofa with pizza (and raw vegetables/dip for nutritional balance, just so that you know). Now, bear in mind I haven't seen them all day, and the pizza smells pretty good, so naturally I want to sit with them, and I whimper/wail/bark until they give me a crust. I do feel it's a bit harsh that I'm told off and ordered to sit in my chair. I might, if they wouldn't put the ruddy blanket on it! And a crust of pizza really isn't too much to ask, after I've been neglected all week.

Anyway. Again, my own family were useless today but thanks to Lovelyneighbourontheright I had a little company mid-morning when they came to chuck me in the garden. These people are SO nice that they even stopped to play with me for a while. Then I did have a walk later on. It's very peaceful here tonight as He and Lad have gone to watch football – this time not at the pub, but all the way up to Wet Sham. So Young Lad and She are cuddled up with me in front of the telly for the evening and there is no arguing. There is, however, chocolate and sugar-free Lilt for Young Lad, and Gordon has popped round again for her.

I have NO bad behaviour to report from today! This is very unusual. Unless someone has been in while they were at work/school and tidied up, I appear not to have emptied any bins, gone through any cupboards, thrown around any recycling or dragged potato peelings across the lounge floor (recently steam cleaned, as you know). I've been known, if there is NOTHING else to do, to empty Lad's art equipment out of the box and I once chewed a bright blue oil pastel which then went all over the carpet. (She had to do a lot of googling that night, to find out How To Remove Oil Pastel from Carpet. Dishwasher liquid, in case you need to know). And there was the one REALLY boring day, when I was reduced to chucking a box of paperclips round the study so that they went everywhere. All in all, you would think I deserve a pizza crust tonight, wouldn't you? But no.

Lad has ~~worn them down~~ discussed things in a mature way, and is going to this House Party tomorrow night. There is still the feeling that this is a Disaster WaitingTo Happen, as Lad and his friends seem to attract trouble wherever they go. However, the House Party is being held in a Nice House, and there will be Parents there, so not too much should happen. She is thrilled at the prospect of going to collect him at midnight, because it's abldy40minutedrive and it's meant to be minusbldy4tomorrownight. She and her friends enjoy sitting in cars in the pitch dark, waiting to collect their offspring from House Parties etc. It is living the dream, they say.

Hopefully, it being the weekend tomorrow, I'll get some decent walks and even a little attention. Other than House Parties, it will be the usual round of Homework and arguments about Homework. She may have to "pop into town" several times, and by now you know what that means.

Here's an interesting thing, Readers. While She and I were marooned in the kitchen on Tuesday, because Carpet Cleaner man was soaking the carpets and sofa (and making un-called for comments about fabric damage) She started looking through some recipe books. These don't come out often – we know Jamie Oliver has been used recently, with limited success, but generally these sit on a dusty shelf and She makes it up as She goes along. Well, Readers, the notebook was found that is used for writing down the list of presents received by Lad and Young Lad every Christmas and birthday since they were born. (This is to enable them to write thank you letters, which they absolutely love doing). Anal, isn't it? Also in the notebook was the food plan for Christmas 2008. Friends, how hard can it be? Christmas Eve supper was; "Roasted vegetable lasagne, Caesar salad, French bread," followed by "homemade fruit tartlets with butter pastry, and creme fraiche." At some point after 2008, Christmas Eve supper changed to egg and chips.

Well, Readers, I'm exhausted from begging for food and fighting with the blanket. I'm not sure if I'll be writing much tomorrow due to "bldyridiculous driving to backend of godknowswhere at midnight" to collect Lad. Who, of course, won't have been in any trouble. Watch this space.

CHAPTER TWELVE

Cheap And Nasty

November 26th

Quite a morning, Friends! There was the usual early comfort break at 6am, but I failed to coordinate this with Gingercat wailing to be let in at 5.30am, so She had to get up twice and wasn't happy. However, I've just had a smashing long, eventful walk and I can smell Sunday lunch in the oven. Multi-tasking is being tried again. Fingers crossed.

It's truly beautiful out there today; a day simply made for a long relaxing walk. She didn't find it relaxing. We had a good chat with NiceDogWalkerLady and her husband, and I really wanted to carry on walking with them and the pack. But oh no, we had to go over the bridge and up through the Top Field because it's a more Physical Walk apparently. I took some persuading but eventually followed at a distance. This distance was great because it enabled me to find some fox poo in the bushes (more of that later.)

Anyway, I dutifully followed her from half a mile back. She was singing "Ma Baker" in her head this time, which appears to have a fast tempo judging by the speed at which we were marching. Occasionally I heard my name shrieked and upped the pace a bit, but generally I dawdled behind. Then, from nowhere, appeared two German Shepherds and a Man On A Bike! This was too much intimidation for me, so I took a shortcut through the woods and back to the safety of the more public area. Only I didn't let her know I was going. So She thought I was lost and spent a lot of time screeching, blowing the whistle and frantically looking for me (maybe I am loved, after all). I chose to ignore her desperate calls for, oh about ten minutes, so then She had to run right through the field, along the lane and over the bridge to find me. Not easy in a duffle coat and wellies, apparently. Anyway, it was good for the Exercise Quotient (see previous chapter.) I've no idea why I was called a bad name and put on the lead – I was having a nice time talking to a lady who was worried about me.

We marched home, her complaining about the smell of the fox poo and how late Sunday lunch was going to be because of me being lost. I hadn't wanted to go in Top Field in the first place – why does nobody listen? I've got to have a bath this afternoon, and I'm hoping Lad will do it as he is much kinder. The main problem is the shampoo. When they first adopted me, and gave a damn, I had "hypo-allergenic lavenderscented treatyourdoglikeaprince" expensive shampoo. That ran out ages ago and now I have the Value Range. And they wonder why I scratch all the time. Actually it does smell really nice, and makes my fur very soft (just in case anyone from PetsRVetsRToysRus is reading).

Readers, I nearly forgot; I had a good bark at a fisherman down there this morning. You can add those to the list of minorities that I Don't Like. It's the imposing rods and unnatural stillness that worry me. Though I did steal a fisherman's sandwiches once.

You'll be relieved to know that Lad survived the House Party intact, and apparently it's the Females of His Age that get blathered and are poorly in the gardens. She didn't have to do the midnight pick-up after all, as He was staying up till silly o'clock to watch the cricket, and "there'snobldypoint in both of us being up." So He nobly offered to fetch Lad and she went to bed. She called this a Right Result.

This afternoon will be spent on Homework/laundry/ironingbldyschooluniforms but Young Lad has also suggested playing a board game. They do this about Once a Year to look like a normal family. Gingercat and I love these afternoons – I always lay in the middle of the money (please, please be Monopoly) and Gingercat likes to walk across the board several times, knocking all the pieces over. Quite why they don't get off the floor and use the table, I don't know.

I'm sad to say She has taken on Extra Work this week. If I hear much more of "needthebldymoney," I'll scream. The large vet bill was AGES ago and I can't still be blamed for the economic crisis. Just how much is an Americano? I rest my case. Talking of which, Homeless Guy is still not outside Sainsbury's, and She feels really, really bad now. I'm a bit worried about him. She hopes he's in a Shelter somewhere, and will stretch to a sausage roll in Dreggs next time.

Well, the roast potatoes smell done, but She's completely forgotten to make the crumble topping for the Berry Crumble. (Value range frozen berry mix. You get what you pay for in life.) So dessert will be served at tea time.

Ma Ma Ma Ma Ma Baker, she taught her four sons....... you know you're singing it now.

CHAPTER THIRTEEN

Craft Club

November 28th

Evening Friends – a top day!! I felt highly creative today. Don't know why, just one of those days. I started off by photobombing her Important Picture that She needed to send to an Important Hospital In London for some research project that they've been involved in. She asked Young Lad to take a quick photo of her as they left home this morning – I felt it looked dreary, so I sat behind her with my most miserable face on. Neither She nor Young Lad appeared to notice. Anyway, her Professional Standing won't be at all damaged by having a suicidal beagle behind her.

Once they'd all gone for the day, I wandered round the house. I fancied doing some Art and Craft so grabbed the Craft box in the study and threw it around. This box is chock-a-block full of rubbish/useful things for Art projects, such as card, paper, ripped up jeans, sequins and many other things for collage that are never needed. It didn't take long to pull loads of it out and spread it across the floor. Pippa's Pack Leader found it when she came to walk me; how she laughed. Unfortunately she texted a photo of the carnage to my own Pack Leader at work, and She was not laughing.

I felt the day needed a little more je ne sais quoi, so in the afternoon I pulled Lad's oil pastels out of his Art box. I threw them across the newly-steam-cleaned lounge carpet, and chewed the box up. And guess what! The blue oil pastel leaked again – see previous chapter – and She has to clean it all up later on. But does it end there? No, my friends, it doesn't. I've also ripped up one of the better quality tennis balls (not the cheap ones from the Pound Shop.) Plus two bags of potato peelings distributed across the back porch. Well, it's a simple enough task – don't be so bone idle, take a couple of steps outside and put them IN the recycling bins. (Doh).

So all in all, a satisfying day. It's all because yesterday I thought She had FINALLY grasped the problem, and I spent a great day at Ebony's house. I didn't do much other than sleep in their very comfortable chairs, but at least I wasn't ALONE and UNLOVED. But no, today we're back to the old, "bye Russell we're off to work for 10 hours" type behaviour.

I was far too tired to write last night due to being with Ebony all day. It was all rather stressful at tea time, as ANOTHER gas man came round, this time to Measure Up and talk about boilers. It was incredibly dull. I barked fiercely, as unfortunately he belonged to one of the groups of people I don't like (you work it out). How She expected to make a rational decision between Worcester or Vaillant systems while making leek and potato soup, I have no idea. After tea, Young Lad had to do an Art project which was bldypainful according to his mother, and Lad did a small amount of revision.

Tomorrow She is taking Lad to the Important Hospital in London, as he is having a Large Injection in the back of his head (into a nerve I'm told). This is to try and stop some of his pain, which I think STILL mostly occurs on PE days. I would imagine he's missing PE at school tomorrow. Anyway, Lad is Brave and sits still while the Evil Doctor sticks a massive needle in the base of his head. He doesn't have to be muzzled, or sat on by four veterinary nurses, and doesn't try to bite the doctor's hand off. After that they will go for a snack, then he has to see some different Evil Doctors in the afternoon. Lad has been told he will be taking Revision books with him to do on the train – he looked pleased at this thought. Young Lad and I will be dumped with anyone who will have us – this has happened many times over the years. And they wonder why there are issues.

I'm looking forward to Thursday, as it is Advent Calendar day. She has finally given up making them have traditional Religious advent calendars, and they now enjoy a Cadbury's picture rather than a biblical scene. But I'm looking forward to it, because at some point they'll forget to put them UP HIGH and that will be my lucky day. Plus She is actually at home Thursday morning, so there will be a power walk. I hope the elderly lady isn't down there that I saw the other day – not only was she white-haired and had a stick, but she was wearing Very Dark Glasses!! I was terrified. Readers, she didn't have a dog with her and clearly had No business to be down by the river. I was very worried for our safety so barked hysterically and aggressively at her, from a safe distance.

Well, after all my creativity today I'm pretty exhausted. Tired, but satisfied with an enterprising day.

CHAPTER FOURTEEN

Royal Babe

November 29th

Unbelievable! Harry has clearly made a good choice because the lovely Meghan Markle, who has agreed to become his wife, is.....a Beagle owner. One who loves and cares for her Beagle, and treats it like her child by all accounts. One who is not ashamed to say that her Beagle sleeps on the bed – in fact, publishes photos of her Beagle sleeping in her arms on said bed. Oh you lucky, lucky Beagle..........not for you the life of telling off and reprimands. I bet Meghan Markle doesn't keep dumping her Beagle with the neighbours. If she's got any. Her Beagle has a REASON to smile. Her Beagle isn't made to feel ASHAMED of his smells.

Well, today has been ace actually, because I was dumped with the neighbours, but I love going to Ebony's house. I struggle to keep up with her on our walks, as she is much younger and slimmer than I am, but I give it a go. She and Lad left early for a Long Day in London at the Important Hospital. She says her first mistake of the day was to take some super-strong Cough/Cold/Whatever/Max/Strength stuff (her cough is getting on my nerves,frankly). This stuff knocked her out, and reversing into the extremely small parking spaces at the station was rather a challenge. She then found it hard to stay awake on the train, and Lad wasn't exactly helping with his lack of conversation skills. What did keep her awake, though was the interesting discussion being held loudly by a man behind them. It involved the following; interfacing/in the loop/delivery of programme/transparency/approval of results/ visibility/ working to the original data/ design being stubborn and a need to up the delivery plan. Some people do talk a lot of crap.

Anyway, apparently Lad was very brave and sat still while a large needle was wiggled around in his occipital nerve. If anyone tried to do that to me, I'd have them. There weren't any veterinary nurses with him, but a Playworker did come to see him and offer distraction during the procedure. This usually involves looking at Where's Wally, and as Lad is legally old enough to marry he felt he'd be ok. At least the Giggle Doctors weren't there – they don't try to make children laugh on Wednesdays. I don't get this service at the Evil Vets. Nobody tries to distract me with animated voices and picture books.

Actually, on that point, I've been told I have to stop calling it the Evil Vets. She says they are a fantastic veterinary practice, with kind, caring staff who have the patience of a bldy saint. I suspect She's worried about the next bill.

Well, Friends, it's a short chapter for my book tonight as She is bldywornout. How it can be tiring sitting in hospital waiting areas with a lovely teenager all day, I do not know.

I wish I could live with Meghan Markle.

CHAPTER FIFTEEN

American Hot

December 1st

Evening all; hurrah it's Friday night! Pizza on the sofa, and everyone in their pyjamas by 7pm. Slovenly or what. Well, I've whined and begged, which paid off in that I was given a tiny crust of Margherita and several carrot sticks. Lad has taken his Pepperoni to the study to play on the Xbox (or the bldy Xbox as it's known here). I've spent a while gazing at him and making my eyes go huge, and dribbled on the carpet, but he hasn't let me have any. Yet. I'll wear him down.

Yesterday was a fairly good one, in that we had a lengthy walk even though it was freezing. There's a homeless person camping down by the river at the moment – She was concerned for his welfare and tried to look in his tent. Nosey cow. We saw the usual crew at the river, plus Chloe, who always has it in for me; I can't work out why. She's a retriever, and they're not known for their fighting skills, but she does have a good try with me. Anyway, Chloe trying to take a chunk out of my neck meant she was in Big Trouble with her Pack Leader, and to be honest it makes a change for it to be someone else being told off. I didn't roll in anything yesterday, but still got moaned at for being half a mile behind her when her pelvic floor signalled it was time to Get A Move On.

Once home, I had a little look through the recycling bags while She was distracted, making a Guilt Chocolate Cake (because Young Lad had to walk all the way home from school by himself and be a Latch Key Kid while She was at work.) I rearranged the recycling for her, and spread it out around the garden again. Then some bread was put out for the birds so I sat under the bird table, waiting for some starlings to knock it off for me to eat. They are so thick. Very predictable, are starlings. Before long, She went off to work so I was left with Gingercat for the afternoon. It was boring. Except when Gingercat chased a bottle lid up and down the hall.

Today, however, things were looking up again! Another day at Ebony's house, trying out her bed for comfort and generally making myself at home. I don't throw their craft stuff or potato peelings round the house, because I don't need to make a point there.

Now Readers, here's a thing. I honestly thought I'd got away with this one! While She and Lad were in London all day Wednesday, nobody noticed that I'd chewed through Lad's school bag!! Yep! Epic! It was only when Lad tried to put his rucksack over his shoulder that he realised the strap was in two pieces! It was funny. Bear in mind it was 7.10am and he was late for his bus and he's always in a shocking mood in the mornings, you can imagine how amused Lad was! There were some words that I don't often hear. She received an Angry Text Message from Lad, telling her how comical he found the whole thing. So last night, in addition to alltheotherbldythingsI'vegottodo She had to get out her sewing box, blow the dust off and try to sew up Lad's bag. I had made it as tricky as possible, by chewing right down to the seams. Sewing is not her thing. Lad's designer school bag now has some poking out bits.

I was wrong, Friends, about Thursday being advent calendar day. I had muddled up my dates – imagine my disappointment when I woke up on Thursday and rushed downstairs, only to find it was still November. A whole extra day before the potential not-up-high-enough situation. Today is the day – one Galaxy, one Cadbury's – I have no preference, not that anyone asks. Sadly at the moment the advent calendars are still Up High, but they will Come Down. Fear not. And I'll be ready.

There's been a little huffing and puffing in the last half hour as Young Lad was promised he could go to the cinema with two friends tomorrow. Only, when She went to book the tickets, it was discovered that the film is a 12A so requires an adult with them. As you can imagine, there is much discussion over who will be the responsible adult, i.e. who wants to spend their Saturday afternoon in a loud cinema with loads of tweens. The debate continues.

Well, I'm hoping for a better night's sleep tonight. Someone still has a REALLY annoying cough which involves the whole bed shaking. Have you ever lived with someone when they have a bad cough? It's the pits! It's incredibly irritating. And then when the coughing stops and you think peace has been restored, the snoring starts, and the horrid open-mouthed breathing noises. And to think I get shoved in the ribs for snoring! Plus He forgot to shut Gingercat out last night, which meant Gingercat was prancing around, miaowing and patting everyone on the face at 3am. So I had a terrible night's sleep and hope things are better tonight.

I still want to live with Meghan Markle.

CHAPTER SIXTEEN

Guts

December 2nd

A cracking afternoon walk today. We went to Top Field, passing a Man with Spaniels on the way – he said I looked lovely and white, so She said "don't worry, he'll find some fox poo to roll in soon, he thinks it's Chanel," and the Spaniel Man said, "Shitnel no 5," and they started laughing. So I soon wiped the smile off her face by finding some fox poo and rubbing it all into my neck, under my ears, where it's really hard to get off. Then rolled on my back in it for good measure.

But this wasn't the best bit! Later on I did the toilet thing, waiting till She was right back down by the entrance to the Top Field, so She had to climb all the way back up to find where I'd been. There were lots of leaves down, so it took her ages to find it – I spent this time looking longingly at the rabbits in the next field – but She eventually found it due to the aroma.

But this STILL wasn't the best bit! I climbed up the bank at the edge of the Top Field, and found a massive pile of intestines! Lord only knows whose/what they were. There were loads and loads – more than one animal, for sure. I waited till She was well down along the path before I started tucking into a liver (I think it was, anyway) so She had to scream and run all the way back up the path, and through the field to me (Exercise Quotient, again; Pizza last night!) Reader, I was in heaven. It was like being let loose in Dewhursts. Small intestines, large intestines, kidneys, liver, oesophagus.... you name it, it was there in the bushes. Now, really, Lad ought to come and have a look as part of his Biology GCSE revision, and Young Lad will enjoy it too, as he's a great fan of CSI and the like. So eventually She caught up with me – I grabbed one last mouthful of something grey – and put me on the lead, swearing at me. The swearing got worse as She tried to clamber down the steep bank with me on the lead, pulling her. Honestly, I've never seen so much digestive system – they were big, too. In fact, She thought about checking whether the Homeless Man was still in his tent, on the way back, but his tent was zipped up and even She's not that rude.

Sadly, I vomited up the whole lot on the way back home. I suspect they were beginning to go off. I did my best to recycle what I brought up, but was pulled away sharply before I could reach it. I have to say I don't feel too chipper now, and haven't asked for any dinner since we've been back. I imagine I'll let off some cracking smells tonight.

It's fairly peaceful here at the moment – Young Lad is at the cinema with his friends, and He has gone with them as the Responsible Adult. This means that He'll have a doze for two hours in the warm. Lad is doing some Maths Revision, which seems to require shouting, "How The Heck Can Y = three?" every so often, and some stronger words. Occasionally a pen gets thrown across the floor.

She has been emailing the Gas Man about the boiler quote – does this saga never end – and has done A Lot Of Cleaning because the house is a bldytip. This morning I spent a lot of time running in and out to the bird table, as the Stupid Starlings were back, so I've pretty much ruined all the Cleaning She did anyway.

Good news! She "popped into town" this morning and Homeless Man by Sainsburys is back! He seemed ok. She was going to stop and chat, but another well meaning lady had beaten her to it, and was taking his orders for coffee etc. So no queuing in Dreggs needed today. She did, however, buy some Cadbury's Tree decorations for when they put up the Christmas Tree next week. I have my eye on them – most years I manage to get a couple off, regardless of how high they THINK they've put them. The Advent Calendars are still up high, but it's only day two and it won't last.

Well, Friends, I'm a little tired after the exciting find on the walk, and my stomach doesn't feel great. So it's time to sleep it off in my chair. There is lemonade and treats for Lad/Young Lad tonight and I suspect Gordon might be popping in for her. Hope Gordon stops the bldy coughing.

CHAPTER SEVENTEEN

Run Rabbit

December 3rd

Evening all – well, it turns out that the intestines and guts that I found in Top Field yesterday were probably the result of some shooting that had been going on. Nicedogwalkerlady and her husband were down at the river today, and they said there had been two men in camouflage in the field yesterday. (Nicedogwalkerlady's husband says he didn't see them. Think about it.) Anyway, these men were shooting, and it is reckoned all the intestines were the result of what they shot, as they gutted them on the way down the field. Not nice. Although it was for me. Various suggestions were proffered of what the unfortunate creatures could have been – the large intestine was far too big for pheasants/birds, but probably not Muntjac size, so we settled on Large Rabbits. It was an interesting conversation.

I have to say, those rabbits weren't at their best – I was sick several times. Actually, I was probably only sick twice, but I don't like waste and so it becomes a bit of a cycle. My poor friend Ebony had also been in Top Field yesterday and she had a very bad stomach in the early hours. I think she'd tried rabbit entrails too. Do you know what, Readers, She was in two minds whether to pop into the police station this morning, to let them know about the body parts in the field. She almost did! Thank goodness She thought better of it – can you imagine? How embarrassing. Her attention was diverted by Homeless Guy outside Sainsbury's who told her all about his few days in hospital last week. He said the food was great. I don't think that Dreggs sausage roll can compete.

But listen, today has been a blast. A nice lie-in, and a decent walk this morning. There were loads of friends down there – including Teddy. I haven't seen Teddy for a bit; he is a copper coloured Cockapoo and gets LOADS of attention whenever he's down there. Unnecessarily, if you ask me. All the Pack Leaders say, "Oh look it's Teddy," when they see him, and make a Big Fuss. Teddy is far too Bouncy for my liking – he is young and energetic and sometimes like a thing possessed. She says things like, "why can't you run around like Teddy?" and actually ASKS Teddy to chase me, "to get some of the weight off." Pot. Kettle.

There was a mug outside the Homeless Man-by-the-River's tent but I suspect whatever was in it is cold by now. I thought about cocking my leg against his tent ropes, but She bellowed at me. There seemed to be a huge number of Staffies down there today – I tend to adopt a very submissive position whenever one goes past.

So then it was time to cook Sunday lunch. I managed to steal some pieces of raw carrot, and was delighted to find some Brownies being knocked up. Being a very messy cook, there is brownie mixture all over the place by the time She finishes, and I even licked some off the washing machine door. It needed a tadge more vanilla, if you ask me, not that anyone does.

But Readers! The pies de resistance came this evening. I fooled everyone into thinking I was tired, so imagine their surprise when I went in the garden for a wee, and didn't come back!! Yes! I managed to shove my way through the back fence in the pitch dark, and get into Man Over The Back's garden. It was important that I did this today, being Sunday, as there had probably been Roast, and their bins were full. Not for long! I made light work of tipping them over, and dragging out as much as I could in the few minutes it took everyone to realise I'd escaped. He was very angry and shouted at me, and had to walk round the road to get me back. I didn't care. I've eaten some lovely bits the last couple of days.

It's been rather noisy here this afternoon, with Lad and Young Lad arguing a lot about, ooh, well, everything really. She tried to help both of them with homework but I could sense She was becoming a teeny weeny bit frustrated when She shouted that She might have to pop back into town for a second time!

Well, it's nearly time for something called Blue Planet, which involves lots of oohing and ahhing about the AMAZING colours and AMAZING photography and AMAZING creatures. This bores me rigid every week, so time for a snooze.

CHAPTER EIGHTEEN

Splitting Sides

December 4th

Oh Reader, where to begin!! What a day!! I haven't laughed as much since the Chasing A Stag for Twenty Minutes in HartyFarty Forest Incident. (The Stag only won because I collapsed from exhaustion. Granny said that Stags belong to The Queen, and that if I'd hurt the stag, we would all have been in A Lot Of Trouble. I haven't been back to HartyFarty Forest since.)

Honestly, it's been the funniest day so far. It all started late last night when they shoved me in the garden for a comfort break – forgetting that only hours earlier I'd escaped through the fence at the back! They're so thick! So despite the hour, and the fact that they were in pyjamas, I escaped again and had time to pull out some Roast Carcass from Man Over The Back's bins. It took them so long to work out the torch setting on their mobile phones, and run round the road in their pyjamas and welly boots, that I actually had a fair old tuck in. I growled a lot and snapped at them for good measure though. He shouted at me and made me sit on the bottom stair.

And today has been a corker so far! I snatched a bit of Young Lad's toast when he wasn't looking (mobile phones – such a distraction). It was ok, but spread with Tesco own brand Fine Shred marmalade – there was a time we had Wilkins of Tiptree, but of course thereisnobldymoney at the moment. I sat and drooled while Lad attempted to eat his bacon roll – if he spent more time eating and less time moaning, "I haven't got time to eat this, I TOLD YOU not to do me any breakfast," he would get on quicker. It only takes me one second to eat a bacon roll. (One of Lad's many medical issues involves difficulty lifting his body from his bed at 6am. This is another common disability amongst people Lad's age and usually takes half an hour of nagging and shouting. I think they have a problem with their legs at this age.) Anyway, I snatched a bit of bacon that fell on the (dirty) kitchen floor.

It gets better, Friends! While She was dropping Young Lad off at school and calling in at PetsRVetsRToysRUs or whatever it's called, I had a look in the cupboard under the stairs. Do you remember me telling you about this one in a previous chapter? It is still a tip, and nobody has tidied it out. Well, my new box of food was in there, masterfully hidden behind the ironing board and the hoover again. I had no trouble in dragging it out, knocking the ironing board over in the process, and pulling it into the lounge. I chewed through the box and spat it over the floor, and then it was easy ripping into the bag. Nice. I love that food, and it makes my coat really glossy. When She came in and saw the mess She called me a shocking name and shouted, "WHO did this? Did YOU do this?" Seriously. How patronising. No celebration of the technique involved in negotiating all the crap in the cupboard under the stairs to drag a five kilo box out and along the hall. None whatsoever. And Readers, She is so anal that She actually weighed the remaining package of food to gauge how much I'd stuffed. (Two kg as it turns out. Though the kitchen scales are cheap and rubbish.)

So then we went for my walk, with her moaning about having to clear up the mess in the lounge. A beautiful day at the river today; it makes one glad to be alive and even She cheered up after a bit. A large black Alsatian tried to take me on, so I did a crab-like sideways manoeuvre of which I was quite proud. Homeless Man By the River's tent was interesting – the mug has disappeared, but there was a carrier bag there instead. I would like to have investigated the contents, but was distracted by a wonderful sight.

The sun was shining on his soft grey coat, even from a distance, and I could see the twinkle in Chuck's eyes. He was a vision today! We ran to each other and sniffed each other's backsides happily for ages – blind to the many other dogs around us. I love Chuck. His Pack Leader used to read my blog out over the tannoy at Sainsbury's where he works nights. She was very concerned about this, due to the swearing. He told her not to worry, there aren't any customers in at that time. He also told her that Teddy is an Australian cockapoo – wrong information in yesterday's chapter. I apologise for her ignorance.

Eventually I left Chuck's rear end and we trotted on. Marching homewards ("Brown Girl in the Ring", usual rhythm. I think Boney M worked to a formula), a squirrel was sitting in the middle of the path. It eyeballed me and made the Loser sign with its thumb and forefinger, then ran off. I gave chase but forgot I was on the lead, so it didn't end well.

Since being home, there's been loads of moaning about havingtoblockoffthebldyfence because She has a lot of other bldythings todo. Frankly, piling up the garden furniture in front of the wobbly fence, and shoving an old blue paddling pool on top just looks dreadful. Slum city. And I'm quite sure I can find a way through it.

By the way, the Nice Manager at PetsRVetsRToysRUs or whatever it's called, told her today that Beagles need special handling. We need lots of stimulation and exercise. At last, a sensible man who knows we are special. Let's hope She listens to him. Meghan Markle understands us. It can't be that hard.

She's also huffing about having to wash the white John Lewis duvet cover again today. It's December. The ground is muddy. DEAL with it.

Well, Friends, I'm going to pop out and see if I can knock the blue paddling pool down. It's been a cracking day so far.

CHAPTER NINETEEN

Tannoy

December 5th

It's true, apparently! Chuck's Pack Leader really did read out my blog over the tannoy at Sainsburys on the night shift. His colleagues enjoyed this, because it gave them a brief break from the soddingChristmassongs that are played 24 hours a day. Well I never. I'm quite chuffed about this.

It was a pretty good walk today – Mr Squibb was down there, and I haven't seen him for months. We've always had a soft spot for each other, though not quite as much so as Chuck and I. Excited, I bounded over to Mr Squibb ready for a romp, but he was On The Lead as he had been Running Off. His Pack Leader was cross with him. (Here's a sad fact, Friends. Mr Squibb and I used to be dragged out for a very short walk in the dark over the Rec every Saturday teatime just before Strictly Come Dancing. These were pathetically short walks so they could dash back for the theme tune.) I saw Chuck's Pack Leader in the Top Field, but – no sign of Chuck! He was missing, and I was frantic with worry. He eventually turned up, but it was far too late for me to get anywhere near his rear end today. Then I met a black lab called Holly, whose Pack Leader and She were discussing breeds, and She said that Labradors are far more intelligent than Beagles. How rude. I'd like to see a Labrador that could negotiate the ironing board, hoover, tool box and 3000 carrier bags in the cupboard under the stairs like I did yesterday, So I deliberately had a good kick of the leaves after I'd had a comfort break, which had the added effect of distributing all the things She was trying to pick up in the little black plastic bag. It took a long time to find it all and serves her right.

I suppose I was lucky to get a walk this morning, though. She had intended popping over to John Lewis. She says, and I quote, that when you're in John Lewis, all is right with the world. Everything smells nice, is tidy and calm. There are no builders, Gasmen, kids with medical conditions, heavy workloads, idiot dogs or any other stress. Sitting with a cheese scone and a coffee makes everything right in her life. She can look out at the tidy, well organised, good quality products and feel her mental health improve. Please note the word LOOK. It doesn't say BUY. She did once push the boat out in the Bobbi Brown section, but that was a while ago while She Was Having A Crisis and she's back to Rimmel at Tesco now.

The only time all wasn't calm for her at John Lewis was when She tried to park in the underground car park, forgetting She had the roof box on. The drivers on the ramp behind her all had to reverse back up, to let her out. I don't think all was right with the world on that occasion, but I suppose it doesn't count as She wasn't actually through the glass doors into the inner sanctum.

Anyway, it was decided not to go today because She's going to work in a bit, and it would have been a rush. That went in my favour as the walk was a good long one. He is having a Day Off today, which is unusual, so I imagine this afternoon we will watch The Ashes and Have A Sleep. He and I will enjoy this.

Lad is off school again today with a terribleheadache; let me just check, ooh, yes, double Games this afternoon. The deal was that if he didn't go in, he has to do revision/work at home all day and She has taken his phone away. To people of Lad's age this is akin to removing their kidneys, so the headache must be genuine. It is now 5.15pm and Lad still hasn't asked for his phone back, and this is now quite concerning.

A slight pause there while vegetable curry is being cooked, and there seemed to be a problem getting the lid off the Curry Paste. I don't think I would have had a problem, but anyway She has been tutting and trying to find a rubber glove and elastic band – a trick learned doing House Orderly badge in the Brownies in the 1970s. (This badge also required the task of hand washing Nicola Francis from round the corner's grey/white socks, which took a lot of scrubbing.)

Well, Regular Readers will remember my friend J who was in the Marsden, having some unpleasant treatment, almost up there with having your anal glands drained. J is back in hospital having some more unpleasant treatment. I feel for him, because yesterday afternoon he was having a lovely sleep when he was Rudely Awoken by some Minor Celebrities from the local football team. They were all smiling and posing for photos. This must have been awful for J but probably made the Minor Celebrities feel they are Doing Their Bit for the community.

When Lad was in hospital once, he was visited by Minor Celebrities from CBBC. She was quite upset about this, because they'd missed Johnny Depp by a week.

Well, the curry is turning to mush so I think today's writing must come to an end. Can I just say, to the Doubting Thomases who think some of the things I do have been MADE UP (and you know who you are) – they haven't. Not a single thing mentioned in my book is fabricated. Worrying, isn't it.

CHAPTER TWENTY

Reeesult

December 7th

Oh Readers, another good day yesterday! Very, very satisfying on the food front. It was Wednesday, so I went to Pippa's house for daycare. On arrival, I noticed that Pippa hadn't quite finished her breakfast, so I tidied up her bowl for her. We had a great walk, and I was THAT close to catching a pheasant, but it just slipped past. It made the same Loser sign at me, that the squirrel did the other day. I rolled in some fox poo, but it was fairly dry, so easy to brush off. THEN Readers, comes the clever part. Pippa's Pack Leader took me home in the afternoon and gave me my dinner, but Young Lad failed to notice her written note saying I'd been fed, and gave me another dinner when he got in!! Then I whined and grizzled in the hope that he'd give me the Cat Bowl to lick out as well. He did. So, to recap – my own breakfast, Pippa's leftovers, nearly-a-pheasant, and two dinners. Plus the remains of some Whiskas. Excellent! I did let off some cracking smells in the evening, though.

AND I've just remembered, I emptied the recycling round the garden again and found a Harry Ramsden's box that had some nice batter crumbs in it! Lush.

Last night, He, She and Lad had to go to a "Sixth Form Options Evening" at Lad's school. These options seemed to consist of, "That One's Too Hard, That One's Too Boring, That One Involves Too Much Reading, and That One's for Geeks." They all seemed rather tense when they got in, and She was banging around in the kitchen cupboards looking for her friend Gordon, but apparently he's disappeared. (I know for a fact She drank a couple of mouthfuls of Pinot Blush straight from the bottle in the fridge, despite the no drinking till Friday rule.) So Sixth Form Options Evening wasn't the best couple of hours, I gather. Young Lad and I were dumped with people yet again. LovelyDor down the road had to collect Young Lad from school and feed him. I was just

Home Alone. With Gingercat, who was asleep as ever.

But look, I am truly astonished by the nice things people have said about my blog! Yet again this morning, "the highlight of my day" has been voiced (you know who you are), and, get this – someone has called me "quite the wordsmith"!! Really! Who would have thought that the details of my dreary life would be interesting. Should it be? Maybe you need to think on that.

Well, my walk was a little late this morning as She had to 'pop into town'. She had to sort out Lad's medication and is going to have an x-ray on her ankle. I remember her falling out of a bungalow on holiday, a good three years ago, and we all stood around laughing as it was hilarious. But it seems that her trying-to-be-brave and not-lose-face in front of her brother, nieces and nephews wasn't such a good plan, as three years on the ankle is still swollen. And clicks a lot. I did question at the time whether it was wise to walk round to the park and play cricket after such a nasty fall, but She was trying to be a Good Sport. Anyway, the swollen clicking ankle doesn't seem to slow her down on the speedy march back up the hill when her pelvic floor is about to give way, each time we've been for a walk. I think this is psychological, in the same way that the Library and Indoor Shopping Centres bring on the need for a toilet visit. I must say, today's walk was extra fast-paced, to burn off the Marks and Spencer Mini Mince Pie that had been eaten before we left. (95 calories).

Bastard Swan's Offspring were on the river today – three of the blighters. No sign of their parents, thankfully, but the Offpsring are turning whiter by the day, and one of them gave me the eye. Hate them.

Quiet time on Tuesday night involved Lad revising Quadratic Equations, and Young Lad revising the reasons that the Normans won the Battle of Hastings. There was a debate about how the tactics of standing at the BOTTOM of the hill could possibly have been clever, until Young Lad explained that the army at the top only had swords whilst the army at the bottom had long-range missiles called arrows. This was all pretty dull and I slept through it. The loading of the dishwasher was particularly good, as She had made lasagne so the plates were filthy. It seems to go everywhere. I helped tidy up.

I'm having some broken nights at the moment, as I feel the need to go out in the garden at 3am to eat some grass. It could be that my stomach is still struggling a bit after the intestines episode. It would be nice to have some sympathy, instead of being moaned at for waking people up at such a Godawful time to go in the garden. I generally like to stay out there quite a while munching the long grass, and it's a good job the neighbours aren't looking out the windows, as they would see my family in a various states of night attire trying to drag me in. It's a lovely time of the day – very peaceful out there – and I can't see what the problem is.

Well, I've just noticed the Stupid Starlings knocking some mouldy bread off the bird table, so I'll pop out and hoover up the lawn. There has been no bad behaviour to report in the last couple of days, other than emptying the bedroom bin over the floor, and the usual potato peelings round the back porch scenario. I expect Meghan Markle's Beagle does these things, too, and doesn't get shouted at half as much.

I'm going to let you in on something – at times I cannot believe their stupidity in this house. You know they've put the Advent Calendars up high? Thinking I won't get the chocolate? Well. They've only hung them up under a light fitting, and above the radiator! I know! She only found out her mistake today when raiding the home-filled advent Father Christmas for some chocolate. And then discovered that the Lindt round balls aren't so round any more! They need sucking out of their wrappers now, no way can you peel them off. Dear God. So now the Advent Calendars have to be moved, and I'm hoping it's a bit lower down. (Incidentally, the packet of Cadbury's Tree decorations was broken open in secret the other night. Stress, apparently).

There was an elderly lady with a ZIMMER frame standing at the bus stop outside our window today. She seemed to be there a suspiciously long time, so I felt I had to protect the household and bark like mad at her. I think she might have been casing the joint. This is a bad time of year for barking, as there are so many Amazon deliveries, and elderly people waiting for the bus to go Christmas shopping. Or so they say.

CHAPTER TWENTY-ONE

Deck The Halls

December 9th

Evening all! Last night I was busy whining for some pizza crust (it being Friday Night) though to be honest, I was quite tired after a day with Ebony as I really do try to keep up with her on our walk, and it's exhausting. I'm glad to say it wasn't me being told off yesterday; Ebony was Extremely Bad while we were out, and I sat there as good as gold. Homeless Man by the River has packed up and gone, and had tidily left some bags of rubbish by the bin. Ebony decided to empty these and run around the field with their contents. I didn't, Reader. I just sat there, appalled at her behaviour.

Today I have done my best to be helpful. It is the time of year where the Christmas Decorations are put up, and She has been very stressed and bad-tempered. She decided to put up some pretty icicle lights along the guttering – really, what's the point? – and spent a happy hour up a ladder today trying to putthebldythingsup. This appeared to be tricky, as although the box said 7.4m of lights there were actually 3.0 m of lights and they didn't even reach the front door. She was perplexed and asked Niceneighbourontheleft to have a look and see where She'd gone wrong. It appears She has gone wrong by buying some rubbish cheap lights. So Young Lad and She stomped into town which was bldyheaving (it being two weeks before Christmas) to take thesoddinglightsback and start all over again. They were so exhausted they had to stop off in Costalotta to refuel.

Anyway, Reader, while they were out I thought I'd do my bit by emptying out a box of decorations across the lounge floor. It would save them time when they got back, and you never know, there might have been a chocolate tree decoration from last year in there. There wasn't. But of course, I was shouted at when they got back, for my behaviour.

She has finally managed to put up lights around the guttering (why?) which involved standing on a ladder in unsuitable footwear, and a large tree is now in the lounge. This is a Swedish Nordic Non-Drop, but I've managed to shove my way under it and it definitely isn't Non-Drop. There was a brief hold-up when nobody could find the box of tree decorations. Despite Young Lad having helped to get five boxes of crap down from the roof this morning, there was no sign of the baubles. They had to search the cupboard under the stairs, which still hasn't been tidied out – wouldn't this have been an ideal opportunity? By now in a foul mood, She went back into the roof and found the box of baubles right by the entrance.

The tree is now decorated and leaning at 45 degrees. The chocolate decorations haven't gone on yet – I hope they haven't forgotten about them. I have a feeling She hid them in the cupboard above the oven, so expect they will have gone the same way as the advent calendar over the radiator. Lad is now revising Physics, under duress, He is asleep and Young Lad is watching rubbish on the telly. It's quiet, at least for the moment.

Yesterday was fun, being at Ebony's. Everyone was quite late home as the traffic was bldyawful and the town was gridlocked. She bumped into her dear friend Loadsakids in Tesco after work, but surprisingly not in the Drinks aisle. She and Loadsakids had a good chat which went something like this: "bldyteenagers bldyChristmas bldyhomework bldyteenagers". This is the form, generally, of their conversations but they both feel much better whenever they've met up.

It's very cold here today. There was a sharp frost last night, which is a good thing, apparently, in that it makes clearing up the garden with those little black plastic bags much easier. Things are easier to pick up when frozen, it seems.

I've had TWO walks today, Reader, I've no idea why. This morning was lovely because the sun was out, even though it was freezing, and lots of friends were down there. I need to apologise to Teddy YET AGAIN for her ignorance as She still hasn't got it right. Teddy is an Australian Labradoodle, not a common cockapoo, and it's very hurtful being mistaken for one. She needs to listen to people better. Nicedogwalkerlady and her husband were there, and assured her that the shooting we could hear was a long way away, so there wouldn't be any intestines in Top Field. However, we were taking no chances, and went to Far Field instead. There was some fox poo in that one, so it worked out well. The music we had to march along to today was Bonnie Tyler's "I was lost in France." Nope, I've no idea why that was going round her head, either. It was a toss up between that or Mariah Carey.

Then I've had another walk this afternoon, which I think was to de-stress from the Christmas decorations. I met Ebony and guess what?!! I've been invited there on Christmas Day! Readers, you will remember that I am very upset because They are all going to pretty AD's house for Christmas lunch, but I'm not allowed to go because of their cat Nasty Git. So I was going to be dumped somewhere on my own while they all had a lovely time and drank wine. But Ebony's Pack Leader has taken pity on me, and said I can go there for Christmas lunch instead of being Alone and Unloved. What a wonderful woman

Frankly I'm exhausted by two walks and emptying out the Christmas decorations, so time for a sleep I feel.

CHAPTER TWENTY-TWO

White Stuff

December 10th

Brrr, afternoon Friends. Well, what a day. Loads of snow here, much to everyone's surprise as this part of the world hasn't had any for several years. I really didn't want to go out in the garden this morning to answer the call of nature – She shoved me out the back door, so I ran under the bushes all the way down to the bottom of the garden. It was cold and wet and I don't like it. I then had an unfortunate problem as, having eaten a lot of long grass lately, what was meant to be popping out of my rear end quickly and efficiently, didn't. I don't know how I can put this delicately, but like I said, it's to do with the very long grass. I couldn't get rid of the damn thing, however hard I tried. Young Lad and She were watching out the kitchen window shouting, "PUSH!" as though I was giving birth, and falling about laughing. Reader, it was chucking down with heavy snow and I was freezing. You've no idea how frustrating it was to have a Difficult Toilet Moment right then. I had no option in the end, but to scoot my backside along the thick snow to help move things along. Just imagine what that felt like. I can't see why they found it so funny.

Back indoors I had to have a sleep to recover from this. Despite the heavy snow, She 'popped into town' even though it was very tricky getting the car up the road. Sadly, there had been a power cut in town, so the place She was heading for was unable to open for business. Despite the weather, Homeless Guy was outside Sainsbury's, poor chap. I would imagine people will be more generous towards him today. She couldn't get him a coffee due to the power cut (yes, Dreggs affected too) so just had a chat. I'm sure he appreciated that.

Anyway, Readers, at some point it was decided that a Family Walk in the Deep Snow was called for. I made it clear what I thought about this, but nobody cared. Even Lad made it out of bed before 11.30am to join in the Fun. So I was made to walk for two miles through thick snow while they all threw lumps of it at each other, taking care to pack them into really hard snowballs. It appears this is Funny. They threw a few for me, and I did chase them, hoping there was something to eat inside the snowball. I soon tired of this game and began to hold my paws up pitifully to show them I wanted to go home. There were many families down there today All Having A Good Time. Or so it seemed. None of my friends were there – doubtless they were lucky enough to be curled up asleep indoors. He was wearing his Wet Sham bobble hat and there were other people with Wet Sham bobble hats, so they all stopped to talk to each other. I just wanted to go home. On the bright side, though, I had found a pile of Weekend Vomit in the snow as we started off our walk – I managed to snatch some carrot chunks before She got me on the lead, and I remembered EXACTLY where it was for the way back. Unfortunately She got me on the lead again. I'd had my eye on the sweetcorn.

She made fish pie for lunch today – some romantic notion about what a warming, healthy meal that was for a snowy day. Normally this goes down like a lead balloon, but the walk had made everyone hungry (especially me) and they actually ate the stuff. The bonus for me was that there was salmon and cod skin sitting in Gingercat's bowl – I whined and grizzled for ages until someone gave in and let me have it. I will smell nice tonight.

He and Lad are going up the pub soon to watch a football match. They are discussing whether to walk (He wants to) or take the car (Lad wants to.) It is quite icy and the roads aren't great so common sense says they should walk. I imagine Lad will come up with a strong argument for taking the car as he "can't be arsed" to walk. Lad and Young Lad are both hoping their schools are shut tomorrow, due to a small amount of snow on the ground. She is praying that their schools are open. I'm not sure why. The Swedish Nordic non-drop Christmas tree is still at a worrying angle, and they still haven't hung the chocolate decorations up. Gingercat was told off last night for knocking baubles off the tree, and chasing them around the lounge. Gingercat is the equivalent of 80 in human years, and rather immature if you ask me.

I'm going to have a good nap in a bit – She is already muttering about emptyingthe bldyairingcupboard and ironing the bldyschooluniforms, not to mention tidyingupthebldyhouseyetagain. I will keep my head down in my chair. Although it is now nearly dark, there are still people walking up the road in their thick coats and wellington boots – what possesses people to go out for unnecessary walks in thick freezing slush? Which part of this is enjoyable? It beggars belief. Talking of which, it's Blue Planet again tonight so there will be the weekly oohing and ahhing over some dull fish or jumping squid, and lots of "he's in his 90s you know!" Boring as.

CHAPTER TWENTY-THREE

Distinction

December 11th

Evening Friends, hope you're in the warm. Well, a strange old day today. I was so bored this morning that I was reduced to pulling Lad's Gold Distinction Certificate off the cupboard in the kitchen, then ripped bits off and spat it on the floor. To be honest, it's been blu- tacked on the cupboard door for four years and it's well overdue for coming down. Lad has never received another one of these, so I imagine that's why they keep it up there.

So yes, I was bored this morning. It was very cold overnight, and there is still loads of snow on the ground so I didn't hang about in the garden. He had to go into work very early to shovel snow. Lad and Young Lad were very disappointed to find their schools were open Despite The Snow, and took some encouraging to get going at 6.30am. She very nobly offered to drive them around, to save being on a bus for an hour, or walking. They didn't seem appreciative. It took a very long time to drive all over the place, dropping boys and friends at schools, and She had to pop in somewhere to refuel. By the time She got home there was a blizzard coming down. I had spent this time asleep on Lad's bed, which is what Lad had wanted to do. Blow me down, Readers – no sooner had She got in and had a cup of tea, than the messages came to say schools were shutting and could She drive back to pick them up. She laughed gaily at this. Then got back in the bldycar.

The downside to all this driving, Friends, was that there was ample time for listening to the Hits of the 70s CD. Our walk, when I FINALLY got one this afternoon, was marched to "Jolene" by Dolly Parton. Not easy to walk in time to that in several inches of snow.

So, when Lad and Young Lad were eventually brought home, they were very amused to find that someone had pulled the lights off the Christmas tree. They have no idea whether it was Gingercat or me that did it, and my lips are sealed. So are Gingercat's. We made a pact. However, there was some consternation about Lad's certificate being torn up as they felt this was a Personal Slur. Rubbish. I was bored.

I had a reasonable walk, though it was very cold on my paws again. The Weekend Vomit was still there and not completely covered by snow, but She kept me on the lead. I tried to pull her down the slope towards it – it would have been so funny if She'd fallen over, but sadly there was too much slush. If I'd waited another hour, it would have been sheet ice and She wouldn't have stood a chance. I tried to accelerate round a corner coming back up the hill, too, on what looked like a really icy bit – Reader, I tried so hard to pull her over. I'll try again tomorrow. I'm cross because there was some grumbling about clearing up the garden in the deep snow – I explained to you the other day, that a Hard Frost is a Good Thing when they're out there with the little black bags, but Snow is not, as you can't tell "what lies beneath" or some such rubbish. For goodness' sake.

Dishwasher duty was lovely tonight, as a 'good, warming roast' was in order and so there was loads of gravy, stuffing and cauliflower cheese sauce on the plates. I was VERY determined to stand my ground on the dishwasher door as they loaded and it took a lot of pushing to get me off. It's cold. I'm hungry. Still no sign of the chocolates for the Christmas Tree – I do hope they remember soon. I had a brilliant time last year pulling those off. They even set up the iPad to film what I did when they went out – so as well as climbing up the tree and pulling the chocolates off, I also put my nose on the lens of the iPad. Which was the equivalent of two fingers.

Let's hope that the pavements are more icy on our walk tomorrow, Readers. Nudge nudge, wink wink. I'll let you know. It'll be so funny if I manage to pull her over.

Jolene, Jolene, Jolene, Jo-leeene

I'm begging of you please don't take my man......

CHAPTER TWENTY-FOUR

Revising

December 13th

Evening everyone – have you ever lay down with your head in a GCSE Physics book? This was my chosen position yesterday evening, and it's a good job I was looking at the book, as Lad didn't seem to be. By God it was boring. The electromagnetic system was the page I was on – dreary beyond belief. No wonder I fell asleep, and no wonder Lad didn't seem keen on reading it. She finally got round to writing some Christmas cards which seemed to take most of the evening. They won't be posted for another week, mind you.

Well, yesterday was okayish – there was still a lot of snow on the ground and it was frozen solid into ice. I didn't enjoy my walk at all and made it perfectly clear, that it was hurting my bldy paws. It's all very well marching along in two pairs of socks and boots, but my bare pads stuck to the ice – it was awful. I did my best limping action, and walked as slowly as possible, looking sad, but oh no, we still had to do the two-mile 160 calorie power walk. On freezing cold ice. The only good thing is that She did slip several times – didn't quite go over fully, but there were some undignified slides with arms windmilling in the air to stay upright. I laughed, and momentarily forgot my freezing paws.

While She was "in town" in the morning, I didn't get up to much, beyond the usual throwing the potato peelings round the back porch. (Put. Them. Out. In. The.Green.Bin.) What did REALLY annoy me, readers, is that I was thrown out of the lounge before they left, and the door was Firmly Shut. Do you know why? Yep. At long last, the chocolate tree decorations have gone on the tree. And it was deemed Too Risky to leave me in the same room. They are nowhere near high enough to be out of my reach, and I had already tried standing on the sofa to see how far I could stretch. But no chance yesterday or today, as I was locked out of the lounge. Don't worry, this attention to detail won't last.

It was quite funny last night, Friends. She got in from work, and was conscious that the family would all be cold, and hungry. So She sighed, and set about making lasagne which is, apparently, a rightbldyfaff at the best of times, and requires three hundred saucepans. One hour and a filthy kitchen later, there were two big dishes of lasagne bubbling in the oven. They smelled great! Imagine how She laughed when the penny dropped that Young Lad was at his friend's house for dinner, and He was going out for a curry. So there was only Lad and herself to feed. She could have taken the fish fingers out and saved a lot of work. And all that washing up!!

Today has been great as I've been out with Ebony. It was soaking wet and we got filthy, as the snow has now melted and, as usual in this country, it's now raining hard and turned everywhere to cack. But Ebony's Pack Leader doesn't grumble about the state I'm in and shout "get off the kitchen floor" – no, Ebony's Pack Leader lovingly gives me a bath. Tonight I smell lovely, and am clean. I don't think it was value shampoo, either. Ebony has nice stuff. I'm in luck tomorrow, as He has taken a Day Off so I will have company All Day. I imagine there will be some sleeping involved for both of us.

It's getting a little tense here this evening with lots of the usual argybargy of youmusthavesomehomework and noIhaven't and it'snotthe endofterm yet!! I'm becoming tired of hearing about Mocks and Options and Your Future. Nobody thinks about my options and future. Oh, we're on to getoffyourphone now – this will rumble on all evening.

Reader, She spent ages last night with a needle and cotton, threading monkey nuts (in their shells) into a long line, to hang up on the bird table. She had thought this was a lovely Nostalgic thing to do from back in the day, and that Lad and Young Lad would like to help her relive her childhood. (They didn't have much to do back then. One summer She sat in a wigwam in the garden shaking a jam jar with milk in it until it turned to butter. It took four days.) Lad and Young Lad weren't remotely interested. Neither were the birds, who haven't touched the monkey nuts. But the funniest part is that in her nostalgic fantasy, She had completely forgotten how much it bldy hurts your fingers, trying to shove a needle through nut shells. Stabbed to pieces. Happy days.

Well, I'm fairly exhausted after my walk and bath. Time for another kip. I'll let you know the instant they forget to shut the lounge door, and I reach the chocolate tree decorations. It may well be tomorrow.

CHAPTER TWENTY-FIVE

Drawing Pins

December 14th

Well, a different sort of day today. She and Lad left very early this morning for school/work as He was having a day off. His first mistake was to forget about putting the kitchen bin out when He took Young Lad to school. This is a classic schoolboy error. They had barely left the drive when I had that bin over, lid off it and emptied it across the kitchen floor. Readers, it was fantastic. Not only was the bin completely full (slovenly people) but there were even a few edible bits in there. Some burnt lasagne scrapings, sweetcorn, and yogurt lids. Plus plenty of things that aren't technically edible, such as cat food foil wrappings, soggy kitchen towel and egg shells. Yum. My stomach is somewhat on the chunky side tonight, which shows how much I found. I LOVE days like this. Later on I had a good walk at the river and didn't get as muddy as yesterday so didn't need a bath.

She seems rather harassed tonight. An Xray was done on her ankle from the three year- old injury, on the way home from work, then everyone got stuck in bldytraffic for ages. I was told off for barking a lot in the garden (it was dark, and I sensed something untoward over the back fence), and I was pushed out of the way when I stood up at the kitchen counter to see what She was cooking. Then, and this really made me chuckle, She tried to put up the Christmas Cards. Oh Friends, it was priceless. First of all She dragged a chair into the hall to stand on; the hall has a wooden floor. No sooner had She put one foot on it, than the chair skidded across the floor. Once safely up on the chair and not moving across the hall at speed, She tried ramming drawing pins into the crease where the wall meets the ceiling. Too funny; the drawing pins had a life of their own and just pinged back out and onto the floor. This meant She had to get down off the chair, look for the bldythings before someone trod on them, stand back on the chair, slide across the hall, and start again. Eventually, some ribbon appeared to be secured and sighing with relief, She started hanging the cards on. You've guessed it! Like that game Buckaroo, it was a delicate game of which card will be the heaviest and cause the whole thing to fall down? Brilliant! I sat on the stairs watching all this, and shook my head in disbelief from time to time. The language I could hear was dreadful, Reader, and not at all Festive. I should not have to hear such things.

I think we all know that when they come downstairs in the morning, all the soddingChristmascards will be lying on the hall floor. It happens every year.

I'm a tadge concerned that a visit to the Evil Vet is imminent. One of my eyes is a bit sticky and She keeps Coming At Me with wet kitchen towel to clean it. I heard some muttering about ohgreat justwhatIneed eyeinfection vetbilljustbeforeChristmas and other things like that. Well, I can tell you now, they'll have to muzzle me. Any Vet comes near my eyes/ears/anal glands, I'll have them. Plus, what annoys me is that Gingercat has a constantly mucky eye. He's had it looked at a few times, but they no longer bother. I would be happy if they didn't bother having my eye looked at, but oh no. As I write, Gingercat is pulling baubles off the Christmas tree and throwing them on the floor. His particular favourite is a red felt robin. He probably thinks it's a real bird; he's quite thick, is Gingercat. Readers, if I was pulling stuff off the tree and kicking it round the floor, what would happen? Yes indeed, I'd be shouted at. But no, Gingercat is "funny" and "sweet" and "let's take a picture." Teacher's pet.

Once the bldyChristmas cards had been put up, She sat down with the phone for a quick chat with Nana aged 86. I chose this moment to notice a tennis ball, pounce on it and take it to her for a game! I don't often have these playful moments, and feel they should be celebrated rather than being frowned at. It's a great game – I let her get close enough to touch the tennis ball in my mouth with her fingers, then growl and run away at the last minute. This is repeated thirty-seven times, and is great fun.

At the moment, He and Young Lad are watching something called River Monsters. It's ridiculous. The same old bit of river and a sedated crocodile filmed over and over again, with atmospheric music and dramatic, pseudo-sombre voice overs. "Beneath the floating papyrus, there is NO sunlight......" " I need to stay alert..." "Then, Something Big Comes Looming out of the Shadows...." Dear God. How can they watch this nonsense? It's worse than Blue "he's in his 90s you know!"

Planet on Sunday nights.

Tomorrow night She is out for her work Christmas Do so it will be a boys' night in. I will let you know then how quickly the cards fell down in the hall. And whether anyone trod on a drawing pin.

CHAPTER TWENTY-SIX

Captain Bird's Eye

December 16th

Hello Friends. I didn't get up to much yesterday while they were all at work, apart from tearing up a fish fingers box and leaving it in the study. Yet again, they had failed to put the recycling outside the back door. There were quite a few breadcrumbs left in the bottom of the box, so I was pleased. After that I went to Ebony's and was As Good As Gold.

Well, incredibly the Christmas cards haven't fallen down in the hall yet! This is a first. There has been the odd drawing pin, however, that has been discovered when stepped on. The Christmas season continues, as they have People Coming to Lunch tomorrow, which for some reason requires a half-dead twig from the garden to be dragged in and put in the hall, to look more 'welcoming'. She then spent, and I measured the time closely, 45 minutes trying to untangle yet another set of lights. This was begun in Good Spirits with a cup of tea and a mini mince pie, but ended up Not in Good Spirits as She had failed to untangle them and ended up throwing them on the twig in a tangled mess. I'm not convinced how welcoming this looks.

A Large Food Shop was needed to be done this morning, which meant "popping into town." Homeless Guy was in his usual spot, and thankfully someone had given him a blanket as it is still cold. And some fags. He'd already got a coffee (someone more generous than her had bought him one from Costalotta) so he had to make do with a chat and a couple of coins today. Then there was a Major Guilt Problem, because round the corner was a Big Issue seller, and She now had no coins left to give them. Tricky. This will play on her mind for a while.

This afternoon I had a great walk, with He, She and Young Lad. Lad had stayed behind as he was still in his night attire, and was supposed to be Doing The Cleaning. Well, Readers, you'll like this. I found a super, new patch of fox poo and had a good roll – I had stayed well back from them, so by the time they looked back and saw me it was far too late and I was plastered. It smelled divine. The funny thing was that Lad had just cleaned the bathroom and scrubbed the bath, so wasn't thrilled when She texted him to say I was covered in fox poo and needed a bath. In fact, he made me go in the spare shower instead, which was a new experience. I didn't like it.

There has been a lot of cooking going on today as there are these People for Lunch tomorrow. This is good news for me, as I will have a lot of attention and pretty AD is coming, so I will probably get my lipstick out. It smells nice in the kitchen, and a new recipe has been tried – some sort of chocolate cheesecake with Baileys or something – and I've heard her complimenting herself on how nice it is. The kitchen is a bombsite, mind you. There will be various bits to lick off the front of the washing machine later. There was a minor panic as She started making shortbread and couldn't find her recipe. Thankfully LovelyDor down the road has the same recipe, and doesn't lose things. She read it out over the phone and calm was restored.

He has been home today so Young Lad and Lad have joined him watching football and rugby on the telly. It's very peaceful. It was quiet here last evening, too, as Lad was in the study on the Xbox all evening, so Young Lad, He and I cuddled up for the evening watching telly. She, if you remember, was out at her Work Christmas Do. Readers, this didn't go well. Blithely, She had offered to drive and pick people up. Blithely they had accepted. They won't be doing that again. One hour and ten minutes to collect three people, and find the venue, which was about eight miles away. Shockingly bad. She really had no idea whatsoever, and tried to blame Satnav. In fact, Satnav was thrown on the floor at one point. And as if that wasn't bad enough, rumour has it She couldn't find her way out of the car park at the end of the evening. So there is some tiredness and bad temper today.

I have a new neighbour. One one side there is a Bouncy Young Labrador, and now the other side have been to collect a Very Young Cockapoo. My family are going round to see it in a minute, and I expect I will be introduced at some stage. I am the old geezer in this part of the street, but this means I have lots of experience and things to teach them. So long as they know their place.

Lad is doing English revision at the moment, and asking questions like, "what's a word for the opposite of elevating love?" Then he needed to think of a word to describe the ugliness of an onion. I fail to see how any of this is going to equip him for anything in life. I thought the

Physics was dull!

Yes, as I suspected, they're all eager to go and see the new puppy. No consideration to how hurtful that is to me. I'm hoping they'll forget to put the bin out – I'll let you know.

CHAPTER TWENTY-SEVEN

Dr Love

December 17th

Evening all, yes, the Hits of The Seventies CD has been on again. She had a long car journey this afternoon so I'll be paying the price on my next walk. It will be a toss- up between power walking to Bat Out of Hell or something by Tina Marie. (Might be tricky marching uphill in welly boots at the right speed for Bat out of Hell though.)

A nice day today; we had People For Lunch. There were loads of good smells from the kitchen, and the odd bit of Tempura Prawn nibbles dropped on the floor. I whined and stamped my feet while they sat around eating the hors'd'oeuvre, but nobody gave me anything. I then stood up at the counter in the kitchen while the carrots were being chopped, but pretty AD told me to get down. She doesn't know that I ALWAYS stand at the counter during Carrot Chopping. I often fart during this, as standing up on two feet stretches out my stomach, and some gas often pops out. Loudly. Anyway, they all sat at the festive table eating and drinking, and chatting away. I sat under the festive table, waiting for someone to drop something. Not much was forthcoming so I had to bark. I was told off.

Even though there were a lot of people, and not many chairs, I refused to give up my chair. People had to perch on the edge while I curled up comfortably. Some of the people were in their Eighties and I was told to get out the chair, but I dug my heels in for as long as possible. You'll be pleased to know that the Chocolate Baileys cheesecake was a triumph (though the portions were quite small if you ask me), but less successful was the cheeseboard. One poor guest nearly ingested the plastic packaging on the brie, that hadn't been removed properly. Shoddy hosting. Lad and Young Lad were forced to be unpaid waiting staff and 'look after' everyone. Mostly this involved refilling wine glasses. Thankfully there was lots of residue on the plates, so loading the dishwasher will be fun.

He took me for a nice walk this morning while She, listen to this, went and played with the puppy next door. Oh yes, She called this "helping out" while the puppy's owners were out for a few hours, but in reality She just wanted to spend time with something small and fluffy that doesn't smell bad. She even took a cup of tea with her. I'm a bit hurt, Readers. She never plays with me while having a cup of tea. I will remember this.

Anyway, after lunch He was left to do the hosting as She had to drive a long, long way to see Nana aged 86, who is in hospital. He, Lad and Young Lad were left with all the washing up to do. And there was a lot of it. Readers, you know I told you about the work Christmas Do the other night where She kept getting lost? Today wasn't a lot better. The main journey was fine, but it took half an hour and asking no less than FOUR people, to find the entrance to the hospital car park, and nearly as long to find the correct ward. I'm very glad we stick to the same route for our walk most days, as Lord knows where we'd end up.

So I have a slightly worrying night tonight, as Pack Leader isn't here and I'm in an entirely Male Environment. I feel anxious without Pack Leader and did my best sad face when I saw her overnight bag going in the car. I know that She will be missing me too, and had to pop into Sparks Mean Marks at the petrol station to buy a can of her friend Gordon to see her through the evening.

Time for a nap; entertaining people for lunch is exhausting.

CHAPTER TWENTY-EIGHT

Red Robin

December 18th

   Gingercat sat by the Christmas tree last night, cleverly pretending that he wasn't interested in it, so that the felt red robin isn't expecting an attack. Quick as a flash, that robin will be off that tree and dashed to the ground. Such is the household in which I live.

   Well Readers, Pack Leader is home. After driving about threebldyhundred miles in 24 hours, She wearily stepped through the front door late this afternoon. I rushed to greet her, with Young Lad, and made a big fuss of her. I never get this treatment. Perhaps this will prick her conscience. I barked and barked, pretending I hadn't been fed to see if I could fool her into giving me a second dinner. It didn't work. However there was some carrot chopping for dinner, so I stood in my usual position at the counter, with the usual consequence. No pretty AD to tell me to get down today. She's back home with Nastygit.

   It's been a quiet day. He took me for a lovely walk; Young Lad was supposed to come too, but couldn't be bothered. Lad was at school. She was driving up and down motorways listening to her Godforsaken 70s CD. I did knock the kitchen bin over this morning, for something to do, but somebody had already emptied it. I then dragged a blue plastic bag into the lounge; they think it was empty, and if that makes them happy, let them think that. Tomorrow She and Lad are at school/work so it will be peaceful again. I need to up the ante a bit.

   I'm not going to write much tonight as She is oh so tired and wants an Early Night. Don't we all? In fact there wasn't going to be any writing at all tonight, but I gave her a stern look and reminded her of all the people for whom this is the highlight of their day.

   Readers, it gets worse. Remember the getting lost to the Works Christmas Do? And the half hour to find the entrance to the hospital car park? Well. Today She smugly entered the hospital car park efficiently, then drove round for a while trying to find a space. She kept going past empty spaces marked "midwives only" or "renal unit. " She actually got quite cross and began muttering about why on earth is there an empty midwives/renal unit bay in the same position on each floor of the multistorey? Readers. It took ages for her to work out that if you go up a ramp, and a little further on, down a ramp, you are in fact on the same floor. Yes, Friends, She had managed to go round level 6A of the car park several times.

CHAPTER TWENTY-NINE

Begging

December 20th

Give us a chip? Go on, just a chip? Look how huge and brown my eyes are. Look how my velvet ears are perched forward on my handsome head. Look how nicely I'm sitting. GIVE ME A RUDDY CHIP! Or a bit of fish, anything!

Readers, tonight they are being extra slovenly and having fish and chips on the sofa. This is because everyone has now broken up from school and She's too bldytired to cook dinner. Again. So they are feasting on the four million calories in fish and chips from up the road, although She shares a small portion with Young Lad as She can't justify the amount of calories, and much Power Walking will be needed tomorrow to burn it off. I have suggested She shares her portion of a portion with me, to reduce the guilt further, but this hasn't been acknowledged.

Yesterday was again fairly quiet for me, as He and Young Lad were here. I did find a green compostable bag of carrot ends and broccoli stems that had been put in the back porch ready to give next door's rabbit, so I pulled that down and waded through it. I had a nice walk with He and Young Lad (yes, Young Lad could be bothered to come for once) and bumped into the Young Labrador from next door. He is Young and Bumptious, and jumped all over me. This is uncomfortable as he is quite large. I patiently waited for him to finish jumping on me, but the final straw was when he started licking my ear. I drew the line at this and put him in his place. I needed a sleep after this.

Things livened up somewhat when She arrived home from work, muttering that things were on a tightbldyschedule as TraditionalbldyChristmasShortbread needed baking, dinner cooking and washing put on, all in the space of one hour before She had to go to a carol service. The good thing about Christmas Shortbread baking, Reader, is that it goes EVERYWHERE. The kitchen is plastered in dough, icing sugar, flour...I have such fun licking it all off the floor, and splodges of it all down the front of the washing machine. I did laugh when I saw the state of her – trousers plastered in flour and dough all under the fingernails. Why the Christmas Apron hanging on the door hadn't been donned, I don't know. Slatternly attitude. But I did enjoy it – this really is an excellent recipe. It didn't need all the huffing and moaning and looking at the clock, and general stress that went with it. An hour is plenty of time to get all those things done (and change flour-encrusted clothes and slap on some make-up) and clean up the filthy kitchen, if you are organised.

So then it was just The Boys home alone again for the evening. I did have some troublesome flatulence, due to the carrots and broccoli stem – well, it wasn't troublesome to me, but everyone else seemed bothered. The room in which I slept stunk like old parsnips this morning.

Today was our Last Day of Peace as She finished work for Christmas tonight. He took me for a lovely walk, though He doesn't know my friends' names, and claims I didn't see anyone I knew. I did. Young Lad did a bit of hoovering, which required a sit-down afterwards and Lad did some revision once he finally got his backside out of bed. I will be very glad when these GCSEs or whatever they are have finished – it's so tedious. Then, Readers, She came home with several bags of presents from her Clients. Young Lad enjoys the yearly ritual of opening these, and I sniffed out all the things that might be edible. I have my eye on some Belgian chocolates. I prefer those to the inferior quality Lidl own brand. Please make a note of this for future reference. At the moment, the numerous boxes of chocolates and biscuits are perched precariously in the kitchen as She's toobldytired to put them away, and I'm bearing this in mind.

Tomorrow I'm hoping to get up to more of my old tricks. He has to go somewhere during the day, and She has to go somewhere else (John Lewis, in case you're wondering, as her mental health needs some soothing). With a bit of luck, they'll forget to put the bin out, and nobody has realised yet that there is one remaining chocolate on the tree, and I can reach it. The possibilities are very exciting, tomorrow. Then there will be a Fast Power Walk for three miles to work off the tiny portion of a portion of fish and chips, and then we've been promised the sofa, a cuddle, and a Christmas film. This is bound to require snacks, so will be lovely.

By the way, someone sent me a Christmas Card! Yes, my very

own! I was very chuffed. I would have been more chuffed if they'd put a biscuit inside the envelope but it's the thought that counts.

I hope Meghan Markle sends me a Christmas Card. With an invitation to live with her.

CHAPTER THIRTY

Lie In

December 21st

Evening all. Well, for the first time in months there was no horrid alarm clock ringing at six o'clock this morning. The Whole Family have now finished for Christmas. Gingercat still yowled at 5am to be let in, and then I needed a comfort break at 6.30, but really, this was a lovely lie- in today. I was happy to stay there until lunchtime, but sadly She got up early as the traffic would be bldymurder as the whole world would be bldyChristmasshopping today.

Just as I predicted yesterday, there was a swift visit to John Lewis and the usual coffee/gazing at a lifestyle just out of reach. Before long, though, She was home and we were out for our walk. Our power walk today was in time to Mariah Carey (shocking) and I'm REALLY glad that was going round her head, not being sung out loud as those high notes would have been embarrassing. I simply could not keep up with the tempo, and lagged a long way behind.

We saw some children at the river, hanging over the bridge, doing Magnet Fishing. This involved dangling a very large magnet into the river and seeing what was attracted to it. I really couldn't see the point, as rusty screws and nails aren't edible (even for me) and it seemed very dull. However, She thought it was charming to see children leading a healthy outdoor lifestyle, and wondered why her own offspring couldn't be more like this. There was a time they played Pooh Sticks on this bridge, but those days are well over. Partly as Pooh Sticks isn't licensed by Microsoft or Sony, and partly because the river is clogged up and sticks get stuck. Such is the way of things.

So, up to Top Field we went, and Readers, I had a bit of a moment. Coming down towards me – yes all right, a long way away but even so – were THREE huge collies. They were black, lively and looked ominous.

Even with a ball in their mouths. I didn't like the way one of them looked at me (well, squinted from a distance), and I froze. Readers, I just couldn't move. She showed no sensitivity to the situation at all, and carried on marching towards them, singing "all I want for Christmas...is youuuuuu" in her head. I didn't know what to do. I faffed around, hopping from one foot to the other for quite a while, and had to wait until She had reached the collies and was stroking them before I felt able to move. Perhaps they weren't such a threat. There was no need to shout "for God's sake, Russell, MAN UP!" down the field at me, though. After that I stayed well back for the rest of the walk, which annoyed her and meant I was grumbled at. Barney the Oh So Adorable Beagle was down there today, and of course there was lots of oohing and aahing about what a lovely Gentle, Sweet Beagle he is. It gets right up my nose. When we got home, Lad failed to notice I was plastered in mud (sadly didn't find any fox poo today), and let me in the lounge. There was some shouting.

Young Lad has done, er, very little today and Lad did some revision, though he had the usual physical impairment in getting outofbldybed. She and Young Lad popped round to "have a cup of tea" with Lovelyneighbourontheright, which actually means going to play with the puppy cockapoo. Again, this is hurtful. He may well be adorable and such fun, but so am I, only they don't notice. Anyway, Lovelyneighbourontheright is very kind and has bought me a dog mince pie for Christmas. There was a discussion about whether I would like it, and She said, "is the Pope Catholic?" and snorted. They have invited us in for a drink on Christmas Eve, but I doubt I'm included in the "us." One Christmas Eve, back in the day when Lad and Young Lad could still be forced to church, I ate a whole bag of frozen oven chips that had been left out of the freezer. They were nice. Cold and hard, but nice.

This afternoon was Christmas Film time, which I liked because there was a range of snacks. Young Lad made quite a mess with some crisps and I had plenty to clear up. There are a few chocolates left at the bottom of the Cadbury's Heroes, as nobody likes the Creme Egg ones – She says why do they put those in and nobodybldylikesthem. I like them. Anyway, apparently this time of year (three days before Christmas) is a bit of a nightmare for Mothers and Women in General. She asked her friend Loadsakids how she was feeling, and they agreed they had both wanted to swear a lot today. Then She asked her friend ChelseaGirl, who also feels less than festive and wants to scream. I can't see what all the fuss is about. I had a wander under the Christmas tree tonight to see if I could knock anything off, and to quality control the Swedish Nordic non-drop claims (still a lie.) Dinner smelled nice tonight – asparagus risotto again, (very limited repertoire in this house) and there were lots of extra vegetables to atone for the Calorific Slovenly Fish and Chips from last night.

Tomorrow will be fun as we are going to Grandma's for lunch. This is great, because Grandma Loves Me and I am always welcome there. I have a sleep in the car for the journey, and usually make some smells from which there is no escape as it's too cold to put the windows down. Grandma will be kind to me, and her cooking smells fabulous. I try hard to get at the plates as they go in the dishwasher but am usually barged out the way.

Well, I'm quite worn out from the trauma of the Three Collies Looking Ominous, and need a sleep now. They will all soon be settling down to watch Chicago PD, which is an improvement on River Monsters. Just.

CHAPTER THIRTY-ONE

New Balls

December 22nd

Evening friends, a busy old day today! While She had an early coffee in Barstucks with Lovelydor down the road, I had a walk with He and Young Lad and met my old chum Kobi, a massive Akita. Back in the early days, Kobi and I used to frolic happily together and do lots of chasing, but for some reason he has taken a dislike to me. I tend to forget this, and think we are still in the halcyon days – I bounce up to him and jump on his back, and wonder why he tries to kill me. Then I remember. Luckily Kobi was on the lead this morning, so his rejection of my friendship was under some sort of control.

Nicedogwalkerlady was there with the Brown Labs and we had a chat. It was somewhat muddy at the river and I was a bit plastered by the time I got home, but again, no fox poo. Good job, really, as we were going to Grandma's for Lunch. There was a frantic twenty minutes or so with a lot of shouting of whatdoyoumean you'renotintheshoweryet? Much stomping around followed, as is always the case when the whole family needs to leave the house. Young Lad was in trouble for wearing a pair of trousers with a hole in the knee (not to lunch at Grandma's!) but an alternative pair was nowhere to be found and time was running out. I suspect he hadn't brushed his teeth properly, either. Never mind, once at Grandma's the smell was wonderful, and my nose guessed (correctly) that it was coq-au-vin. Better still, there were more of those tempura prawn things and mini spring rolls, as 'appetisers'. Yes indeed, they whet my appetite. Bravely, Grandma put them on plates on a low table. I sat very, very close to the low table and stared hard at them. Eventually She took pity on me, and gave me a fragment of battered prawn tail. Once Grandma sat down with her appetisers, I leapt onto her lap and was within a WHISKER, Readers, of snatching it from her mouth. Darn it, I was close! I even put the tip of my nose right against her face in case a tiny bit made its way out of her mouth. It didn't.

After lunch, we opened Christmas presents. There was one for me. They kept telling me to open it, in rather silly voices, but there was no point as I knew that by sitting and staring at it, someone would open it for me. Inside was a new pack of tennis balls! Food would have been better, but even so! What a thoughtful present. I dutifully chased one round the lounge and played with it for a bit. Then I sat down with it and ripped it into pieces. It took three seconds to destroy. Grandma was shocked and hurt – she had obviously thought these were long-lasting tennis balls – and then read the instructions that came with them. I kid you not, Readers, it said "do not give these to your dog to play with unless you are sure they are suitable. Some dogs play with these in a rough way and may cause damage." What the heck? Anyway, I was thoroughly cheesed off as they took my new tennis ball (or what was left of it) away and put it in the bin. I had been enjoying spitting bits of black rubber over Grandma's carpet.

This was funny – She had only been saying, before lunch, that my anal glands weren't too bad at the moment, and they were reminiscing in a sniggery way about all the pre-Christmas trips to the Evil Vet over the years to have them drained. I soon shut her up, Readers, by sitting on Grandma's sofa this afternoon and I have a feeling there was a Slight Leakage. I did look round and try to lick up any residue, but She noticed the smell. However, Readers, She WASN'T honest enough to fess up to Grandma! Who will only find out about the possible leakage by sitting on the sofa, or reading this book.

Unbelievably, nobody had taken any dinner for me to Grandma's and by mid-afternoon I was STARVING. One fragment of prawn in batter tail really isn't enough. I started making this clear by whimpering and whining. She took me out to the kitchen to shut me up, by giving me three leftover new potatoes and some coq-au-vin sauce. Again, Grandma didn't know any of this. I hope she wasn't banking on those leftovers for her tea. I'll make some cracking smells tonight, as I think there were a lot of red onions in the sauce. And that reminds me, her brother, who we'll call Funnygit, sent Young Lad a version of 'Last Christmas' that was all about farting. Funnygit is 53. Worrying, isn't it?

The journey back was boring. I had a sleep in the car, and so did He. Lad and Young Lad argued non-stop about something called Game of Thrones and whether it's a 15 or an 18, and whether it has more violence and sex than The Walking Dead. I think they're both rubbish, to be honest. I'm hoping they'll all be out at some point tomorrow – He and Lad are going to Wet Sham yet again in the afternoon, and I'm praying that She and Young Lad go out and give me five minutes' peace....to have a go at that ruddy chocolate that's still twinkling at the top of the ruddy tree!

CHAPTER THIRTY-TWO

Bad Dog

December 23rd

I have been very, very bad. I'm in a Lot of Trouble. At long last, Readers, I had the house to myself for an hour this afternoon – it's been over a week!! Oh, it was a blast! You'd be amazed what you can fit into an hour. To think She was worried about the three batches of shortbread cooling in the kitchen! I watched her pushing it all to the back of the working surface, and then moving it again, and again.... so worried was She that I would get it. My plan did not involve the shortbread. First, I went and emptied the bin in the bathroom to see if there was anything rank in there I could eat. I threw some stuff round the bathroom floor.

But then, THEN, Readers, it was time to carry out the plan. I spent a very long time trashing the Christmas Tree. I got underneath it and walked round slowly, making sure that it turned round in its stand several times, round and round and round. This ensured that the careful decoration, whereby the best baubles were at the front, was ruined. The best baubles were now crammed up against the wall, and the empty back part of the tree - on which hang the home-made decorations lovingly created from cardboard, glitter and felt by Lad and Young Lad at primary school - faced the room. I managed to drag off six baubles, including a glass one, which smashed into tiny weenie pieces all over the carpet. They'll be treading on it for days! Red robin ended up behind the sofa and lots and lots of the Swedish Nordic non-drop pine needles dropped. They'll be treading on those for days, too!! But, Friends, I hadn't finished there. For good measure, I bit through the electric cord of the tree lights. Yes, they were on at the time, and I've lived tell the tale. So now they have a choice of no lights on the tree, or the multi-coloured set that are all tangled and thrown on the twig in the hall. Tomorrow is Christmas Eve, and I can't imagine anywhere will have any lights left on sale. The fun! Really, it was great. I've been scolded severely and there was loads of moaning about the lights – it was extremely difficult to get them offthesoddingtree because I had managed to tangle them up when I twisted the tree round. She was in a foul mood. I even saw her comfort eating smoked salmon straight from the packet – this is unacceptable, as this Is Meant To Be For Christmas. I bet Gordon will be large tonight. Oh it was ace – such a good afternoon. I haven't had that much fun for ages.

Prior to that, I'd rolled in fox poo in Top Field, and made sure I rubbed it hard into my neck and ears. It reeks. I had a good walk, though I was rather alarmed by two large Alsatians, and had to take a detour of about half a mile to avoid them. Somebody in one of the houses had kindly put out some carrot on the grass – it wasn't the diced sort in vomit – and I ran like the wind to grab several mouthfuls before She caught up with me, screeching. I even chased my ball a couple of times – I was quite energetic today.

She and Lad went into town early today to do The Big Food Shop. Town was likely to be bldyheaving so She made Lad get up at 8.30am – I know! – to make sure of a parking space (he had to be bribed with a hot chocolate at Costalotta). Homeless Guy was outside Sainsbury's and said yes please to her offer of coffee. Hmm, a dilemma. Not wanting to appear tight-fisted to Lad, She had to splash out on a Costalotta coffee for Homeless Guy instead of going to Dreggs for his, and saving the 50p. It would have been too difficult to explain to Lad, and anyway it is Christmas. The Big Food Shop was done, although Lad is rather too old to be swinging round on the trolley and acting like a four year old, but there you go. He was, in fact, Helpful.

When they got home, She took me for a long walk whilst Young Lad unpacked the six huge bags of food and put everything away. He did a reasonable job of this – it was only the Paxo stuffing mix in the freezer, the special cat food that he thought was tuna and put on the Tins shelf, and the pigs in blankets on the pasta shelf that were wrong. He was gently reminded that sausages/meat need to be in the fridge. I wish nobody had noticed – I can reach the pasta shelf.

This afternoon there has been yet more Shortbread baking – dear God. The kitchen is DISGUSTING, Readers, and needs a deep clean. A quick wipe round with some Flash isn't enough after all this baking. And as for the oven....

I really am quite tired tonight, after all the fun. I smell a bit fox pooey, as they were lazy and just tried to scrub it off with a baby wipe due to bldytimeconstrictions. I have been threatened with a bath tomorrow. The scented candles have been lit, which annoys me intensely. I find this rude. Anyway, time for a kip. He and Lad have been at Wet Sham again this afternoon, and I gather they've lost (they usually do) so there will be An Atmosphere later. I'll sleep through it.

CHAPTER THIRTY-THREE

'Twas The Night Before Christmas

December 24th

And I'm asleep on the new fleece She bought the boys for snuggling under whilst watching Christmas films. There are four people, myself and Gingercat on the sofa, and I've got most of the fleece. It's nice.

Well, Christmas Eve is here. There have been tears and despair (a French stick escaped from its packaging in Sainsbury's and rolled across the floor in aisle 12), the queues were awful, and the blender broke just as She was making bread sauce for Christmas lunch tomorrow. It is extremely lumpy bread sauce, and no way can She turn up at someone's house with something so abominable. So Lovelyneighbourontheright has to lend her a blender tomorrow morning, as if there isn't enough to think about on Christmas Day. Selfish.

She and Young Lad drove around this afternoon delivering presents, and popped into LovelyDor's for a cuppa. LovelyDor has lent them some tree lights to replace the ones I chewed through yesterday. They also went to PetsRVetsRToysRus or whatever it's called, but I'm not allowed to know what for. There has been some frantic present wrapping this afternoon, with Christmas songs blaring out to try to create "the mood." It hasn't. And there are still some presents to wrap; jobs are always half done in this house.

Anyway, I had a nice walk with He and Young Lad this morning and saw Nicedogwalkerlady and the Chocolate labs. I rolled in some more fox poo as it's Christmas Eve and they haven't got much to do except bath me. Lad bathed me this afternoon and now I smell lovely for my day with Ebony tomorrow.

Readers, this was funny. They all went next door at teatime to Lovelyneighbourontheright for Drinks and Nibbles. They shut ALL the doors in the house, thinking there was no damage I could do. They were wrong. I chewed through the pockets of her coat, just in case there was a snack in there. I spat the white fluffy lining from the coat all over the stairs. Wicked.

As well as the bread sauce, there has been brandy butter making this afternoon. After She found her ripped coat pockets, She was comfort eating the brandy butter from the fridge (the smoked salmon has gone, the next lot is still in the freezer). There now isn't enough brandy butter for 10 people tomorrow, and She will have to make more in the morning. There has been some suggestion of going to Midnight Mass tonight; I didn't see anyone jumping up and down with excitement. She may well be going on her own, as I imagine they'll still be comfy under my new fleece. Sorry, THEIR new fleece. Lad and Young Lad are sharing a bedroom tonight, which is traditional on Christmas Eve, so I may join them. Two boys and me; that will smell lovely in the morning.

The penny has dropped that there are still jobs to do. I knew that Gordon on ice whilst watching Home Alone was a mistake. Nuts and nibbles need to be dispensed into bowls and placed at (hopefully) low level areas. And there is still wrapping to do. Talking of which, I had a secret present left outside my front door! Turkey twizzlers! So exciting, thank you.

Well, Friends, tomorrow is Christmas Day. I'm going to Ebony's house at lunchtime, about which I'm very excited as they are nice people and care about me. Doubtless my family will deign to come home at some point in the evening, over fed and over watered. I will have to catch up with you all on Boxing Day.

Readers, thank you so much for still reading my book up to this point. I can't work out why you bother, but I'm so pleased you do. It's fun telling you all about my dreary life and the things I have to put up with.

A very happy Christmas to you all.

CHAPTER THIRTY-FOUR

Oh Come All Ye Faithful

December 26th

Happy Boxing Day, everyone! Settle down with a nice Christmas drink, because I have LOTS to tell you! Has it really only been two days since I last wrote? I've fitted such a lot into this time, including knocking the VERY full kitchen bin over on Christmas night. I find it disgusting that nobody found two minutes to empty a large, overflowing bin somewhere during the day. They were asking for trouble, but more of this later.

Well, Readers, against all expectations She managed to drag everyone to Midnight Mass on Christmas Eve. I wouldn't say there was a lot of enthusiasm, and I did hear them moaning about the number of verses in Hark the Herald Angels Sing when they finally returned in the small hours, but at least they went. I want to make it clear that I behaved extremely well while they were at church. This had nothing to do with all the doors being shut and the bins being put out, but more with my respect for their rare church-going activity. Eventually everyone went to bed and I slept in Lad's room with him and Young Lad, for a bit of a laugh.

Christmas Day was ace, absolutely ACE! Gingercat yowled to come in at 5.30am, which didn't please her, and then I needed a comfort break at 6.30. Lad and Young Lad opened their stockings in bed, and there was plenty of chocolate going on in there. I've got my eye on where they put it. Then there was Breakfast and Present Opening under the tree. Readers, you may remember the notebook I mentioned in one of my earlier chapters, where She assiduously (anally) has written down the list of Christmas and Birthday presents every year from birth. Needless to say, this notebook was used efficiently again, but there was a small cry of anguish when it was realised there is only one page left.

Never mind, a trip down memory lane was had as they read out the entries from 2007 (Power Rangers crap) and 2010 (Scalextric). Actually, the Scalextric went straight back to Argos as it didn'tbldywork. I was becoming a little bored by this, so they eventually put on their silly voices and waved a present at me, trying to force it into my face. "Open it!" they kept cajoling, so I ignored them. They got the idea and opened it for me. Inside was a rubber bone (boring) and a pack of low-fat treats from PetsRVetsRToysRUs or whatever it's called. These were nice. But, Friends, unbelievably they had the STUPID idea of stuffing one of the low-fat treats into the blue rubber bone. I have tried and tried, but can't get the bldy thing out. Stupid. Gingercat was given a ball with a bell in it. That won't be irritating, will it?

Then it was Christmas Morning Walk with He and She time. I met lots of friends down at the river, but the best part was bumping into NicetallLadywithTheStaffie on the way back. It turns out that Molly (the Staffie) is sometimes as "badly behaved" as me. Last week She pulled her Pack Leader over, completely over, while they were at a cafe on a pier. Molly was alarmed by the sound of scraping tables and chairs, and tried to escape, pulling her Pack Leader with her. Unfortunately her Pack Leader's fish and chips and cup of coffee also escaped, all over the pier. But it's nice to hear of someone else being told off for a change.

When we returned home, things improved even more as there was More Present Opening on the agenda, along with Christmas Morning Nibbles. Yum. These include smoked salmon on Ritz crackers (cheaper than blinis), hot mini sausage rolls, mozzarella bites, and of course, Tempura Prawns. Again. These seem to be rather a feature this year. Then She faffed around in the kitchen making more brandy butter (see previous chapter) and blending the bread sauce (also see previous chapter.) While the dishwasher was being loaded, I climbed in and grabbed the bowl that the brandy butter had been in, and ran off with it. Sensing pursuit, I ran under the table in the lounge and growled. Unfortunately the coffee cafetiere had been on the top shelf of the dishwasher, and had dripped all over my head and face. I reeked of coffee and have brown streaks everywhere. But the brandy butter was glorious.

Once they had all Dressed Up a Bit (although Lad had his flipfloppy slider things on -how common) they were ready to go off to AD's house for the rest of the day. Readers, this is where my day improved considerably. I went down to Ebony's house and just couldn't wait to get inside, with people that genuinely want to be with me. Ebony was very pleased to see me, and we bounced around very energetically for a while. Then went to sleep. I had a LOVELY, LOVELY day with these wonderful people, who have the right priorities in life. It was simply heavenly. Then Ebony's Pack Leader walked me home in the evening, and I only had 45 minutes with the house to myself before the others got home. I didn't waste this time. Nobody had remembered to put the kitchen bin out, in their rush to leave home without me. Friends, just stop for a moment and think what your own kitchen bin looked like over Christmas. And you probably empty yours. Well, I chucked it all over the kitchen floor, and dragged some upstairs to the landing. There was SO much stuff everywhere! And SO much to eat! Glorious! Of course, I was scolded as soon as they came in.

I slept like a log last night – what with Christmas Day at Ebony's plus emptying the bin. Today has been rather nice – two walks! She took me this morning, as She neededsomebldyexercise and then A Family Walk was insisted on this afternoon. This morning I saw Barney the Oh So Adorable Beagle, and he was extremely white and clean. I wasn't. My friend Pippa was down there and we'd been romping for ages, with her jumping all over my back. So Barney was clean and beautiful and I was covered in mud and stuff. Anyway, I was pleased to hear that Barney also misbehaves by being difficult when it is recycling day and houses have bags of nice-smelling recycling outside them. He also runs off towards the houses in an attempt to go through their bins. See? It isn't just me.

Then another walk this afternoon. This was fun – we bumped into someone called LovelyBird and her three gigantic Italian Spinonis. They are HUGE, Readers. I was a little unsure around them. She stood chatting to LovelyBird and LovelyBird's Friend for ages, so I had to man up a bit and pretend I wasn't scared of the mahoosive Spinonis.

Readers, I nearly laughed myself silly today. One of them was given a Shark Jigsaw for Christmas. He and Young Lad spent most of the morning trying to do it. Then She helped. Then Lad had to help. It's now nearly 9pm and they still haven't managed it!! Four people! And it's only 250 pieces! Oh it does make me chuckle; they're a bit thick. There has been the annual game of Monopoly, and Gingercat and I both walked over the board at various points, knocking everything over. It's a laugh. Gingercat has also knocked loads of things off the tree today.

After Monopoly, it was Family Film time. This involved snuggling under the new fleece on the sofa, and enjoying a film together as a family. They watched Psycho.

There are no words.

CHAPTER THIRTY-FIVE

Filth

December 27th

Evening Friends. At the moment I am staring very hard at something, and stamping my feet. They are having a slovenly meal on the sofa, which in fact is ready meals from SparksmeanMarks as She is bldyfedup with cooking apparently. Not only will I have the ready meal trays to lick, but I am determined, Friends, to get my gnashers round a piece of chocolate Yule Log. I am whinging, stamping, looking sad and trying all my usual tactics. Someone is bound to drop a bit on the carpet soon. I'm patient.

It's appalling about the ready meals, isn't it? Do they know how high in fat and salt these things are? Admittedly Young Lad and She are sharing one, like the fish and chips, but this has backfired because Young Lad is saying he's still hungry, is there any more and why did She have a bit of his? She is muttering that She's been chained to the kitchen for days – we all know that's not true as they weren't even here for Christmas lunch – and if She will choose to make leek and potato soup two days running, what does She expect? Yes, it was warming on a cold day, but quit the moaning about the work involved. Readers, it was a bit on the lumpy side to be honest, anyway. And the trifle wasn't all that, as Lad had eaten the Hartleys jelly pots. Plus, Boxing Day lunch is only putting cold meats on a plate and jacket potatoes in the oven, for God's sake, so the ready meals really aren't justified.

Anyway. A bit of a surprise happened today – snow! We had a lie in (well, after the 5.30am alarm call from Gingercat), and when we all surfaced it was raining. Before long, this turned into the big white stuff and by golly, it threw it down for a couple of hours. I had no choice but to curl up in my chair and sleep. I was eventually dragged out for a walk late afternoon, once it had stopped snowing, but it was chuffing cold, I can tell you. Too cold for all the standing around chatting to people, and certainly too cold to go all the way to Far Field. I managed to annoy her by camouflaging myself in the field and She couldn't find me, several times. It was very funny. There was a covering of snow on the browny greeny muddy field, and being white and brown myself, I blended right in. There was a lot of shrieking of my name and blowing on the whistle, as I couldn't be seen from one end of the field to the other. I laughed. There weren't many friends down there today, but we did bump into the old black labrador with three legs. Apparently he is an "inspiration to us all" (She always says this, unoriginal) because he had a nasty disease in his leg two years ago, so the Evil Vet sawed it off and saved his life. And two years on, the black labrador is still limping happily at the river, and being told he's an inspiration. Yawn. Nobody tells me I'm an inspiration.

It was a funny old morning. Despite the snow, She decided to "pop into town" for half an hour. Lad sat in his onesie doing his revision, whilst He and Young Lad tried to finish the shark jigsaw. They still haven't managed it, and there has been some heated suggestion that it's a dodgy jigsaw without all the right pieces. Apparently there are too many straight edges, whatever that means. It was cheap, to be fair. After that, they started on the Airfix Spitfire plane that was a Christmas present for Young Lad. Young Lad sat and watched for five minutes while He started the project, then went off to do play on the Xbox. Luckily, He has great staying power and carried on for another three hours. Young Lad is now playing with the model Spitfire that he did bugger all to assemble.

I forgot to mention! The heating packed up again yesterday. I know – the unexciting saga of the boiler has been rumbling on for months, but it all ground to a halt on Boxing Day and there was no heating. She said, "bldytypicalonBoxingDay" but phoned British Gas anyway, who said they'd be round today. They were as good as their word and a nice engineer called Lee spent an hour and a half banging around in the airing cupboard (which is filthy, by the way) and the loft (also filthy). Eventually he somehow managed to restore heating via a 20- year-old boiler, which is clearly not going to last till the installation of the new one in four weeks' time. So I expect he will be called out again. She had the decency to apologise to him about the state of the kitchen floor – it was shocking – and blamed me, for walking in and out from the garden on a wet snowy day. What am I supposed to do? Call me old-fashioned but they could always clean it. I've seen advertisements on TV where muddy dogs run in and out of kitchens, and their attractive Pack Leader just laughs and mops it all up with something magical called Flash. Their kitchens are pristine, and do not have mud halfway up the cupboards, and leek and potato soup spattered up the tiles behind the hob.

So the heating is back on, which is a goodbldyjob as it's freezing out. This afternoon was meant to involve Tidying Up, but after our walk She was too tired, and curled up with a cup of tea and a new book. It was remarkably peaceful, Readers. Lad was still revising (Physics again, can't be arsed with English Literature apparently), He was still doing the Airfix, and they had forgotten Young Lad on the Xbox in the study, which pleased him greatly. It was so quiet and relaxing! I dropped off and had a lovely deep sleep.

I am feeling quite smug again today, as I've heard on the grapevine that my dear friend Ebony has been in a spot of bother. She has Stolen, yes Stolen, a large jug of gravy which was Extremely Rich as it was probably made from turkey giblets and the like. Ebony enjoyed slurping down this large jug of delight, but her Pack Leader is cross and worried about what might appear from Ebony's rear end. As a result, Ebony has been told off and made to sit on her special mat. I tell you what amazes me – I get blamed for this! Not for the first time, when my friends have misbehaved, their Pack Leaders have claimed they are copying MY behaviour! Maybe I am inspirational, after all.

I'll tell you another thing that amazed me – how many views my blog got on Christmas Day. What the heck were you all doing? Who had time to faff around reading about a Beagle, when you should have been Very Very Busy?!! I'm really quite astonished that Christmas Day was one of the biggest days for views for a while, and am incredibly pleased that I'm right up there with entertaining relatives and the Queen's Speech.

Readers, I have failed to steal any chocolate log. The rotters have taken it back to the kitchen and Put It Up High. I'll have to make do with the Four Cheese Ravioli ready meal tray.

CHAPTER THIRTY-SIX

Camouflage

December 28th

Ha Ha! I couldn't be seen again today in Far Field, as I'm so good at blending in to a snowy landscape. Oh it was a laugh – I stood still and faffed around for ages while She blew the whistle and screeched like a fishwife. She had to march right back across the field bleating on about the bldydog, until I strolled into a less snowy part to be visible. Serves her right. She got right up my nose on our walk today. It was a beautiful day – crisp, cold and clear – a day made for ambling along, sniffing. Not marching.

First of all I found some more carrot sticks outside a house, and a random cherry tomato, but was moaned at and put on the lead. When we went over the bridge, there was a long delay while She and some strangers ooohed and aaahed about how high the river was. Tiresome. Yes, the river was high, and yes, it was flowing very swiftly (they could even have played Poohsticks for the first time in years) but really? Is it worth a lengthy conversation? I'm sure one isn't meant to talk to strangers, but the Dog Walking Community have their own rather odd rules. If someone has a dog with them they aren't a serial killer, seems to be the logic.

Eventually they ran out of things to say about the high river, and we went to Top Field. This is where She really cheesed me off. Very Clearly, there was something dead and decaying in the middle of the Top Field. I could smell it from miles off. She knew damn well, that once my head went down, my ears flopped forward and I did that slightly hysterical running around in a circle with my nose on the ground, that I was tracking something. But oh, no, I was yanked out of the middle of the field and put on the lead again. Then marched for the rest of the walk in Top Field. I did slip my collar twice and run back to the Bad Stuff but

She caught up with me.

The day was so beautiful that we went into the Far Field as well, which is where I hid myself. Coming back, I ran off into the woods and found some bread, probably left by a fisherman (hate them). I was just tucking into this, when a Huge Bulldog type thing appeared and tried to befriend me – instantly fearing he was after the bread, I went for him. Yes, Beagle takes on Bulldog and wins. I was shouted at and put on the lead yet again. Anyway, we had a walk for an hour and a half today and it was pretty good on the whole.

I suspect her bad mood is down to some Frustrating Things that have happened today. Firstly, the heating has packed up again. Gasman managed to get it going yesterday afternoon, but it's packed up again. The house is FREEZING, Readers. She phoned up and in her best telephone voice told them to bring forward the date of the New Boiler Installation, as ours is Knackered, but they said they can't. So apparently we will have to phone up on a daily basis for an engineer until the end of January. This pleased her greatly. On the bright side, they said they would send another engineer this afternoon. Then She asked her good friend Loadsakids if she wanted to meet for a coffee, but Loadsakids had to drive her husband to a bldytrainstation bldymilesway because there were no trains on our line today. Loadsakids says the train company and British Gas are both bldyuseless.

Then some Tidying Up was done because the house is a ruddy tip, but really this meant moving everything from the lounge to the study and shutting the door. This is not Tidying Up. Lad's revision notes are taking over the house and there seems to be no system involved whatsoever. She tried to Instil Some Semblance of Order into his revision notes, but got no thanks. Whilst hoovering, a tiny weenie airman from the Airfix Spitfire was sucked up, and so was Young Lad's tooth that fell out the other day and is meant to be under his pillow. She has not admitted to this yet. The hoover bag is going to be taken apart in a futile attempt to find both. Good luck with that.

A quick update, Readers – the Christmas cards in the hall have fallen down four times so far. I told you they would. He was meant to put them back up yesterday, but was far too busy putting together the Airfix Spitfire. Young Lad broke the wheel off this within minutes of picking it up. He was cross. She wants to rip the bldydecorations down and put everything away, but it's only December 28th.

Anyway, it was extremely cold here after our walk, what with no heating. I couldn't even use the new fleece to warm up, as it has been washed. Apparently it smells of anal glands. So we put the fire on and extra jumpers, and She said it was just like her own childhood. Lad and Young Lad weren't interested.

Actually, thinking about it, She was a bit crabby with me first thing this morning, saying that I was taking up too much of the John Lewis whiteish duvet, and that She was cold. It's not my fault the boiler is crap.

In fact, it was so cold that when Loadsakids texted to say she was now free for coffee, the chance to sit somewhere with heating was a no-brainer. But despite the lovely chat (moaning about teenagers and dogs, more like) even this proved frustrating as Homeless Guy was outside Sainsbury's and said yes please to a coffee. So She went to the cheaper cafe to get his after seeing Loadsakids, but had spent so long laughing in a deranged manner about Family Life that Homeless Guy had given up and gone for the night. So She was left with a coffee that had a lot of sugar in it. She took it home and pretended it had been bought for He all along. By this stage Gas Man had arrived, and put a new fan into the boiler. He now says we do not need a new boiler, as it has a brand new pump, valve and now a fan. So they can save themselves threebldygrand. There is some suspicion about this, though, and they're not cancelling the new one just yet.

He went into work for a bit today, probably to get warm. He's still wearing his coat now, even though the boiler is fixed. Everyone seems a little wary.

Well, Readers, tonight's excitement is the annual writing on the New Family Organiser Calendar. Don't make me laugh. Piss up and brewery come to mind.

Before I go, I simply must let you know that despite the giblet-rich pint of gravy she stole, my dear friend Ebony's rear end has been ok. I know many of you will have been worrying.

CHAPTER THIRTY-SEVEN

Royalty

December 29th

You see, Friends, if Meghan Markle adopted me to live with her other Beagle, my life would be so different. I would lie on a chaise longue behind the Queen, when she addressed the nation each year, as Meghan and the Queen both love dogs. Instead of this, I'm dumped with the neighbours and told I smell every five minutes. I feel I'm in the wrong life.

It was LASHING down with rain early this morning, so I went out for my early comfort break and then raced back to bed. I decided to stay there for a good couple more hours. The heating is still working – I know! – so it was very pleasant. Young Lad had been promised the cinema today with his friends, about which he was excited. It was just a shame that She hadn't checked how long Star Wars went on for, as She mis-timed the ending by about three hours and had to sit in a crowded car park for an entire afternoon. This was Annoying as there were many other things that needed doing. He gave me a lovely long walk once the sun came out this afternoon, right through Far Field, and because it had been Lashing Down earlier, it was extremely muddy. I was plastered. Due to this, and the fact that we're visiting Nana aged 86 tomorrow, Lad had to give me yet another bath. I am now white and clean, but it's still the cheap shampoo. They haven't learned. Despite having lovely clean fur, I'm giving off some shocking smells tonight which will please Nana aged 86 when we get there. She isn't keen on me as it is.

There was some mild swearing in the kitchen a while ago, as there is a Big Family Lunch with her brother Funnygit and The Cousins this weekend. She has made another Chocolate Baileys cheesecake, as this was a crowd-pleaser the other day, and also decided on a Pecan Pie. She couldn't be bothered to make pastry though, which is good as her pastry is cack, so a ready-made pastry case was needed. Nowhere in town had one, so a trip to SparksmeanMarks was required. Hurrah! They had one left, costing £35 (well, not quite but you get my point.) Back home, the Pecan Pie filling was made and poured into the ready-made all-butter pastry case – only this was broken into eight pieces, so the filling oozed all over the place and some of the pastry was floating on the top of it. Feckity Feckity Feckity, She said, and had to make her own pastry after all. It was cack.

I have been barking in the garden a lot lately. They seem very puzzled, and keep saying, "why does he keep barking?" The only way they can stop me barking is by shouting, "Russell, what's this?!" and I come running in for a small piece of turkey or gammon. And yet they cannot work out why I keep going out in the garden, barking.......

My regular Readers will remember my young friend J, who has been having some Nasty Treatment in the Marsden. Well, J was meant to be in there again, starting his last round of Nasty Treatment, but instead he has been in a local hospital with Bad Flu. She was thinking of going to visit, but it's the same hospital car park that was problematic the other week, and She'll be stuck going round level 6A again for twenty minutes. Might be best to give it a miss. Hope you're better soon, J.

Young Lad was tied to a chair yesterday and made to write Thank You letters until his ears bled. In fact, he only did three. Lad has been excused this torture as He Is Revising, as we all bldy know. He was asked to clear up his bldypigsty of a bedroom today, and insists he has, but it doesn't look any different from before. Or smell any different. "Clear up" is a rather vague instruction, if you ask me, and I think Lad needed better direction.

CHAPTER THIRTY-EIGHT

Cambozola

January 1st

Happy New Year, Friends!! I've been busy. I've had a lovely couple of days away visiting family. First of all, four people plus me plus their bags plus large bags of food were crammed into an ordinary car, and set off for a 100 mile journey. What fun. There was no arguing or fighting whatsoever in the run-up to leaving home. It was seamless. Ha ha.

Lad insisted on bringing his own duvet and pillow, which added to the uncomfortable squash in the car, but meant that he had a nice sleep. Young Lad had been told over and over again not to go on his phone in the car, but ignored advice and then threw up two seconds from our destination. Luckily he got it into the washing detergent plastic tub kept in the car for this purpose. I was shocked, Readers, that She simply emptied this out into the gutter in the road, saying "the rain will wash it away." What an awful attitude. One hundred miles with four people, a dog and a ridiculous amount of stuff in the car is no excuse for that sort of bad mood.

Lad and Young Lad were dumped with Nana aged 86 while He and She took me in the lovely park nearby for a walk and a coffee. This was nice – it's a massive park on the edge of a farm, and has wondrous smells. They didn't let me off through the cow fields this time, though, as I usually find a good, fresh cowpat to roll in. Instead, She insisted on walking up through the woods as it would be "less muddy" – yes of course. It was shocking. But I loved it. Most of the time we were walking, they were wittering on about the Price of the Coffee in the Lovely Manor House that we often go to. It seems that £6.30 for two bldysmalllukewarm coffees is rather a lot, and they are takingthebldybiscuit.

Then we had lunch at Nana aged 86's house. I like Nana aged 86.

She is clever and fun, and is an 'animal lover'. However, Nana aged 86 doesn't like me. I'm not sure why. She says I smell, and frighten her cat. Generally I just sleep quietly on her sofa, though I will admit my anal glands often play up when we visit her. I tried my hardest to ingratiate myself with her, by laying my head on her knee and going to sleep, but she still doesn't like me.

It was fish and chips from down the road for tea, which was excellent – the smell was divine and I did a lot of whining and stamping my feet (She shared a portion of a portion with Young Lad again, of course. Three mouthfuls, in fact). There was nothing on telly, so they played board games all evening. This is quite impressive, bearing in mind Nana is 86 years old, and was more up for it than She was.

New Year's Eve was excellent – we all had a lovely lie in. In fact, She woke up screaming, "for the love of God it's quartertoten!" as there were People Coming For Lunch. Thankfully He took me out for a nice walk, so we could both get away from the general stress of Lunch Preparation. He and I like going for walks at times like this. Anyway, her brother Funnygit, his wife and The Cousins arrived and it was all very jolly. There were drinks and nibbles BUT, and I know this will come as a shock to my Regular Readers – NO TEMPURA PRAWNS!! I know! Asda just didn't have any so they had to make do with mini hash browns and red pepper and feta parcels. I missed the Tempura prawns, to be honest.

Lunch was a veritable feast, but I was still trying to impress Nana aged 86 and slept soundly on the sofa in the other room, rather than scrounging at the table. Eventually I gave up trying to impress her, and scrounged at the table which was more fun. There were meat platters, fish platters, cheese platters, salads and jacket potatoes. It would be hard to tell you what my favourite is, out of all this, as I don't actually taste anything as it flies down my throat. The Chocolate Baileys cheesecake went down a treat again – I know for a fact Funnygit's wife and one of the cousins had two helpings. The pecan pie was not a crowd-pleaser, Readers, and will not be repeated. The Cousins kept calling it Pigeon Pie and sniggering. I would quite like Pigeon Pie, I think. Or pecan pie, come to that.

They had a lot of fun after lunch, crammed into a small room playing board games, and they all screamed with laughter when She moved back on her plastic garden chair, and it broke – violently throwing her to the ground. Funnygit showed some compassion for once in his life, and helped her up, whilst everyone else laughed. Apart from Nana aged 86 who was concerned about her broken chair. I was asleep on the sofa during all this.

The highlight of my New Year's Eve came when they were clearing up the kitchen. He had done about three hundred bowls of washing up over the weekend, due to the lack of a working dishwasher, and Funnygit was carefully wrapping up the left-over cheeses in clingfilm. Well, not that carefully as it turned out. I pretended I wasn't looking, but my reflexes were SUPERB as he dropped a large piece of Cambozola onto the kitchen floor. I had it down in three gulps.

Now, Readers, try to imagine the effect of Blue Brie on my flatulence...and they had 100 miles to drive back with me in the car.... By golly, it was GORGEOUS! Have you tried Cambozola? So creamy, with that slight bite of the blue veins. What a treat. Try some! You may like to eat a small piece, rather than a large wedge of it, like I did.

Well it's nice to be home again, and back to normal. He and Young Lad have been busy today taking down all the decorations and putting them back in the roof for next year. She had a minor nervous breakdown this morning when She "popped into town" and discovered that She has left her purse 100 miles away at Nana aged 86's house. You may be worried, Readers, that She had no money, credit cards, bank cards with her, but it's ok! She had 234 points on her Costalotta app on the phone, which meant She could sob into a small Americano. But Homeless Guy had to go without today, and She explained why. He didn't look convinced.

She took me for a long, fast power walk to de-stress from finding She has left her purse 100 miles away, and it was lovely down there. The river has Burst Its Banks (see previous chapter re: tedious conversation on the bridge about how high the river was), and some of the path is flooded. I got rather wet. We went up through Top Field, but I couldn't find anything decomposing today. I did, however, see a few friends; Barney the Oh So Adorable Beagle was there, and we both ran off to the regular places that have food smells. I also saw someone who looked like Teddy the Australian Labradoodle, but it turned out to be Colin the Cockapoo. I came home very muddy and had to dry off in my bed.

Well, Readers, tomorrow will be interesting. They are Back To Work and School. I will be home alone, although Lad is here for "Study Week". There has been a conversation about this, as it is not "Stay In bed till Lunch" week. Now, whether I can get up to anything naughty before Lad stirs himself out of bed tomorrow, I don't know. I will do my best and let you know.

CHAPTER THIRTY-NINE

Move Over

January 3rd

Evening, Friends. I was the guest at Ebony's house today and to be honest I was disappointed by her hospitality. True friends would give up their bed for their visitor, but no – she insisted on squeezing in too. There simply wasn't enough room for us both to have a comfortable sleep. This was annoying and tiring.

Anyway. The First Day Back at Work was oh-so-strenuous, so I actually behaved really well while they went back to school and work – but don't forget Lad was here all day, on "study leave". My opportunities for raiding the bins and pulling stuff out of cupboards was limited. Lad was rudely awakened with a cup of coffee when they left for work. He soon went back to sleep, but was later rudely awakened again by an alarm clock carefully placed by his bed – this was in case he forgot what "study day" actually meant. He finally got the message at lunchtime. Despite the very inclement weather, and the fact that Lad and I were perfectly happy cuddled up under the new fleece while he "revised", various text messages were sent all day telling him to take me out for a walk. Lad lost the will to live just before they returned from work, and dragged me round the rec. Or that's his story, anyway. The empty crisp packets/selection boxes scattered round the house suggest a different version of events.

Readers, I feel some updates are overdue. The shark jigsaw has still not been finished. I know many of you will have been wondering. It is on the snooker table, to get it out thebldyway but sadly nobody has managed to solve the puzzle. They seem to have lost interest and have no staying power. I feel it is a cop-out to claim it doesn't have the right piece; they are just lazy. They need to learn from Lad, who completed Lego Tower Bridge when he was 10. Go on, Google it. It has 4,295 pieces and costs over £200. Compare this to a shark jigsaw that has 250 pieces and cost six quid. I rest my case – no resilience whatsoever.

Likewise, only one Airfix model has been completed. And Young Lad contributed nothing to this.

Secondly, LovelyDor's Christmas tree lights, that she lent us to replace the ones I ate through, have been mistakenly stashed in the roof with the rest of the decorations. She will have to go up in the roof when she has a bldyspareminute to retrieve them. Thirdly, they had another Nice Family Film afternoon on New Year's Day. This time it was The Birds by Alfred Hitchcock. Their parenting style is odd, if you ask me. And the ending was rubbish.

Remember the nervous breakdown on Monday? Her purse has now been posted Special Delivery, so She might be reunited with her Tesco clubcard and spending ability tomorrow. I will let you know when it is safely back in her handbag, and we can all stop worrying.

While I lie here tonight, they are watching the news. I can't believe my ears. Donald Trump has tweeted that his nuclear weapon button is bigger and more powerful than Kim Jong Un's nuclear button. Have I heard that right? I must be having some sort of nasty dream.

Last night He and Lad went to Wet Sham yet again. I really don't know why they bother, and She felt this was Foolish the night before Lad had a mock exam. Lad said it was only English Language and doesn't count. It was nice though – Young Lad, She and I cuddled up under the fleece on the sofa (yes, I had been there pretty much all day), and watched Eastenders. This was rubbish, but the cuddle on the sofa was nice. Then She made Young Lad go to bed early as he "looked tired", but this was really only so She could put another Nordic Noir Weirdo Crime thing on. It was better than River Monsters but still a bit odd for my liking. The wind was howling outside, thanks to Storm Eleanor building up, which added to the atmosphere of the Nordic Noir Weirdo Crime thing. During the night Storm Eleanor really got going and my sleep was disturbed several times by rattling windows and trees. This was annoying.

So this morning, everyone was up at 6.15 am, or at least, Lad was being encouraged to lower his legs to the floor from his bed and stand upright. This took a further thirty minutes to be successful. I was told to get out the way several times, as She tried to make packed lunches, and I was underherbldyfeet. There were crumbs on the (dirty) floor as usual, and I even found some old cat biscuits under the fridge, which I coaxed out. I can't help it if She chooses this particular time to make the packed lunches. Most working mothers do it the night before, and show some sense of organisation. I was quite annoyed when they all left, as the kitchen bin (full again, disgusting) was put outside the back door, the bathroom bin (also disgusting) was put into the bath where I can't reach it, and all the bedroom doors were shut. Boring, boring. Thankfully Ebony's Pack Leader came to my rescue and took me out for a walk with Ebony, even though Storm Eleanor was still having a go. I tried so hard to keep up with Ebony, and had to bark at her a couple of times to get her to wait for me. As a result I am really, really tired tonight, and can't wait for bedtime.

CHAPTER FORTY

Sixty Minutes

January 4th

 Readers, what can you do in one hour? Sixty minutes? Here's what I managed in that amount of time this morning:

1. Ate a large bulky broccoli stem from the back porch.

2. Pulled my new box of food from out of the cupboard under the stairs (still not tidied out and worse than ever), dragged it into the lounge, ripped through the box, ripped through the packet and ate loads of it.

3. I needed some dessert after that, so went up to Lad's bedroom, found his Christmas stocking, chewed holes in it and found two chocolate coins at the bottom. Ate them.

That's not bad going for sixty minutes, is it? If you did a time and motion study on me, I'd score quite well for efficiency. Of course, this isn't appreciated by my family and I was shouted at for the mess I'd made, and the extra meals I'd eaten. I only had the house to myself for that one hour, while She did the school run, so I made the most of it. She screeched the usual stupid, "WHO did this?" when She saw the mess, so I stayed where I was on Young Lad's bed, and wagged my tail at the thought of what a nice time I'd had.

It was a funny old day after that. She stayed home all day, which was nice once I'd been forgiven and we cuddled up under the fleece. As She was feeling Under The Weather, there was less of the normal charging around with hoovers and cleaning implements. I had a snooze while She attempted to watch another episode of the Scandi Nordi Noir crime thriller thing, but She fell asleep, and by the time She awoke, some of the characters had turned into plants. No, I have no idea why either.

I did look out the window at one point and the elderly lady with the walking frame was at the bus stop. BUT, Readers, she also had a sinister looking umbrella as it was pouring, so I had to bark a bit extra at her to make sure she didn't attack my house. I also barked at the postman when he came to deliver the missing purse – yes,we can all breathe again, and those Tesco clubcard points can now stack up once more.

Despite feeling Under The Weather, we did have a walk as fresh air can be invigorating. There weren't many friends down there today –I saw Lexie and her stick in the distance – because we had missed the popular 10.30am walking slot. While we were out, Storm Eleanor decided to pop back, so the walk was cut short and a return to the fleece on the sofa was in order. The problem with being out in high winds for Beagle, is that our ears blow out like the flaps on a plane and we look ridiculous.

Lad came home at lunchtime after doing another Mock exam. This dreary state of affairs stretches on for another TWO weeks, yet. He claimed he didn't feel well enough for revision so he might go on the Xbox instead, but was told there was no logic in this argument whatsoever. Readers, I actually saw her put the Xbox controller in the oven, so he couldn't find it. Lad dutifully worked all afternoon on Maths, which is Not His Favourite Subject, and there was some tension. Simplifying quadratic algebraic fractions seems to require a lot of Bad Language. And YouTube, to find out how to bldy do it.

Young Lad had a good day at school, largely because there was some 'beef' at lunchtime. This isn't the sort of beef I like, but involves schoolboys fighting. According to Young Lad, this happens every day. He loves watching. Today's beef was particularly good as there was some juicy swearing as well. I wonder whether Young Lad has missed the point of secondary education.

Another update for my regular readers. The hoover bag has been carefully cut open, and the grim insides pulled apart. Success! The small airfix pilot has been found, as has a sock and several drawing pins. Sadly, Readers, Young Lad's tooth was not easy to find. Instead, there was a dried up sweetcorn kernel, so She lied and said that was his tooth, and gave him a quid.

Well, I have made it clear to them today that the cupboard under the stairs is STILL shocking, and they really should have put away the Christmas stockings by now. But will I be thanked for my help? Oh no.

They're all at work and school tomorrow, Readers, and I have a good feeling about it. I'll keep you posted.

CHAPTER FORTY-ONE

Windy

January 5th

    Readers, I hope you're not eating while you read this, but such is the extent of the horrific smells and loud FPPFFF type noises I'm making, that it's only fair to lighten your Friday evening with the details. In all the years they've had me, they can't remember noises like it. As my Regular Readers know, I do make the odd pfft noise when standing up at the kitchen counter begging for carrot ends. But this, tonight, is in a league of its own. They've had to turn the telly up. I feel this is all rather undignified. It's not as though they never have this type of problem – I know for a fact, that when we're out for a walk, there is sometimes a furtive look round in the woods followed by a small emission. I won't tell you which of my family that is, as I don't believe in humiliating them. Wouldn't it be nice if they took the same approach to me? So yes, there it is – I have exceptionally awful wind tonight, which smells like bad eggs and sounds like the air being squashed out of a balloon.

    This is, unfortunately, self-inflicted. Which is why they are cross with me. Everyone thought I'd been so good today! I went for a walk with Ebony and was ANGELIC – it was Ebony who ran off screaming with laughter, all across the fields and round the houses. It was Ebony (this time) who had builders trying to catch her. Ebony's Pack Leader was so annoyed with her, and so pleased with me for being good. I behaved impeccably at their house, and it was only when I was back home alone that things went awry. I managed to open a cupboard in the kitchen – well, I was bored – and had a good look. Readers, there was a box of Winalot dog biscuits right there in front of me, and it said on the pack, "It's A Dog's Life." Yes indeed it is, I thought to myself, and dragged them into the lounge where I tucked in.

    Now these biscuits had been confiscated because they are bad for me on two counts: 1) the colours and additives affect my skin and 2) they're verybldyfattening. Now we can add a third, can't we? As I write this, Young Lad and She have their jumpers pulled over their faces as they can't cope with the odour created by the Winalot biscuits. This will go on all evening; needless to say, the scented bldy candles have all been lit. I must admit, the noises I'm making do actually make me jump occasionally, as they are quite explosive. Anyway, I don't regret eating two thirds of a box of confiscated biscuits – they were nice. I'm just a little tired of hearing, "OHMYGOD RUSSELL!" every two minutes. Or, "Take Cover!"

In other news, there was a treat in store for Lad tonight. She felt he deserved a little reward for revising hard (ish) and managing to fit in some exams around the Xbox. So instead of Tesco Thin Crust Cheese Feast pizza (£2.50 each) She splashed out on Dominohsopricey pizza from up the road. Lad was very pleased as this rarely happens, due to it being overpriced rubbish. Even with the Buy One Get One Free if-you-can- be-bothered to-go-and-collect offer, this is astronomically expensive for a bit of flour and water, with cheese and tomato on. But of course, the Price wasn't mentioned (much) as Lad and Young Lad enjoyed their takeaway treat. It's important to point out that they had crudites of carrots, cucumber, celery and tomatoes though – it wasn't just junk. And She didn't have pizza at all due to the Christmas Calories; instead opting for a healthy piece of lightly dusted plaice from Sparks Mean Marks. This has nothing to do with the fact that the zip on her trousers broke at work as She was leaving tonight, and She had to stagger to the car holding her coat round her in the hope her trousers didn't fall down.

Anyway, I digress. They are all bldy glad it's the bldy weekend, although I've a suspicion that Young Lad has a lot of homework to do, as he's done bugger all during the week. He will be sad about this. Time management is such an important life skill. Lad will have more revision, but will, of course, need a lie in first. He and Young Lad want to watch a football match on TV tonight, so there has been some negotiation going on as She wants to chill out with decent telly. We all know this means the ScandiNordiNoir Weird Crime Thriller thing, where the people are turning into plants. I fail to see the attraction of this nonsense.

I've heard a rumour that She is working virtually full-time next week, Readers. This isn't on, and I am planning how to show my distaste. The good thing is that I'll be spending time with dear, dear Pippa and dear, dear Ebony, if she is off the naughty step by then. I haven't seen the lovely Chuck at the river for ages, so am hoping we'll catch up over the weekend.

I have now been banished from the sofa, Readers – it's Friday night, for Goodness sake! But no, I am to spend the evening in my chair across the room, so they have some hope of breathing. And nobody wants me to sleep near them tonight – how hurtful. Even Gingercat's nostrils are flaring a bit. Let's hope this passes through soon.

Hope this has all cheered your day along. I can assure you wholeheartedly that wherever you are at the moment, Friends, it smells better than here.

CHAPTER FORTY-TWO

Problem Solving

January 6th

Today I became tangled up around a lampost. It's perfectly simple, Readers. Go the way I want to go round the lampost when I'm on the lead, then tangling problems don't arise. I refused to give in and She had to walk round to my side. I met a couple of new friends down at the river today, who joined me in finding a pile of something rank to eat. I had a real spring in my step as well – it must have been those banned Winalot biscuits – and I ran at a cracking pace to chase a moorhen, that only got away by about half a mile. Then I set off across Far Field after a squirrel, but that got away, too. It's frustrating, but these things happen. On the way back, a small white Highland Terrier appeared to be terrified of me and it had to be carried by its Pack Leader to get past me in the alleyway. Pathetic. She of course made insulting comments about Beagles not being scary, just bldy greedy.

You'll be relieved to know that the appalling flatulence seems to have passed through. There was rather a lot to clear up in the garden this morning, and it wasn't pleasant, as He likes to keep telling everyone. He even had to Hose It Down. I've been on Reduced Rations all day to make up for stealing half a box of contraband biscuits yesterday, and I'm starving. The room I slept in last night surprisingly didn't smell like a sulphur factory this morning, but the lounge still did from all the evening's releases. The scented candles are back on tonight.

You'll also be relieved to know that She has found five minutes to watch the final episode of the NordicScandiNoir Weirdo Crime Thriller thing. The main character's daughter died, but as she was half child half pine tree, this wasn't surprising. What drivel. Thank God I haven't got to sit through any more of that. Unless there is a season two.

Lad had a nice lie in after all his hard work with mock exams this week; he finally surfaced at lunchtime and has worked hard all afternoon. Young Lad was forced to hoover upstairs, but this was punctuated by cries of, "it makes my arms hurt" every so often. He received no sympathy. He also had to spend half the afternoon on homework, which, as usual, ended up with She and Young Lad shouting at each other and nearly crying. Gingercat didn't help by sitting on the laptop and patting Young Lad on the face – this did nothing for his concentration.

In a desperate attempt to clean up the filthy kitchen, a lot of bleach was flung around. It is no cleaner, but smells like the local swimming pool. And – yes how could I forget this nugget – my MUZZLE was put on me again and I was held down while ear drops were administered this morning. This is because they are bldyfedup with me violently shaking my head. That bastard muzzle is horrid. I look like Hannibal Lecter in it.

Well, Regular Readers, my young friend J is back in the Marsden having another week of nasty things done to him. The good news is that this time he's in an isolation ward, as he had flu last week – this is excellent, because if his Pack Leader makes a Show Of Herself in the middle of the night, like she did once before, at least it won't be in public. I'm not sure how easy it is to smuggle in miniature bottles of wine to an isolation ward, but I'm sure she's found a way.

On the subject of J's Pack Leader, there is some consternation here today. In a few weeks' time, She is going to ParkyCentres with her old friend KentGirl and about 400 other people, to celebrate KentGirl's birthday. Now... She and J's Pack Leader, who is also going, had envisaged this as a weekend of sitting around in pyjamas chatting and laughing, going for the odd swim and lying in the spa reading a Good Book. Imagine their dismay today when they saw the itinerary. KentGirl has envisaged things rather differently – to include late night bowling, geocaching, short tennis, golf and – rumour has it – line dancing. She and J's Pack Leader are having to rethink their image of this weekend at ParkyCentres. She might even have to practise riding her bike before She goes.

I'm quite exhausted tonight, as after my walk some stale chocolate brioche things were put out on the bird table. This is a pain, because I then have to spend the next two hours running in and out, to check if any starlings have dropped a bit. It's very tiring, and requires a lot of whining by the back door, which gets right up her nose. Can I just say, at this point, that my Regular Readers might remember the afternoon spent whimsically threading monkey nuts onto a bit of cotton and hanging on the bird table? They have not been touched. Total.Waste.Of.Bldy.Time.

I'll tell you something that annoyed me today. When we started off for our walk, we had to stop and chat to neighbours for HOURS. There I am, all raring to roll in fox crap and eat vomit, but no. We have to stand stock still for half an hour talking. First it was Ebony's Pack Leader whom I love dearly, but I wasn't happy when She tried to blame me for Ebony's bad behaviour yesterday. Ebony's Pack Leader is kind and understanding, and it's not my fault if Ebony is jealous of my excellent behaviour and decided to play up. Then it was a neighbour further up the road for another half an hour on the way back. Yawn.

Tomorrow will be lovely as we are going for lunch at Grandma's house again. Grandma loves me and appreciates me for who I am. And cooks excellent food. There will be a Lot of Family there, and I am bound to get some snacks. The car will smell shocking on the way back.

CHAPTER FORTY-THREE

Cold Porridge

January 6th

Today, Readers, they all left early for school and work. She gave me my Kong (a big rubber ball type thing with a hole in it), which had the remains of Lad's porridge stuffed into it. Stone cold porridge. Friends, how would you have felt if someone had served this up to you? I mean, I ate it, obviously, as I don't like waste, but really, cold porridge isn't good enough. I felt I needed to make a point.

And so I did. With bells on. Before I was collected for daycare at dear, dear Pippa's house, I ripped up a box from the back porch and spat it over the lounge floor. Then I went to the study and pulled the art and craft stuff out again, emptying a tray of it over the carpet. Then I went up to Lad's room, and – oh joy!! – found half a large Toblerone that hadn't been put somewhere sensible. I ate it. Nice. Swiss chocolate has a certain style. After that, I spotted a box of David Beckham toiletries, so I ripped that open and chucked the shower gel on the floor. I could happily have gone on with this protest all morning, but I needed a nap on the sofa, and then it was time for Pippa's house. I certainly hope they've learned their lesson, and don't ever think of giving me cold porridge again.

Apart from that little blip on their part, I've had a fantastic day. Not only did I chill out at Pippa's with people that care about me, but I even Went Visiting!! Yes, Pippa's Pack Leader put me in her car, and drove me to visit her Mum in The Countryside. Reader, I had a great time. I went for a long walk in the woods, and then made myself at home in her Mum's best armchair. Golly, it was so comfortable. She'd even put a cushion in exactly the right spot for my head. People who know me seem to understand that I'm just not a floor dog. It really has been an exhausting day, and I'm struggling a little tonight as my eyes keep glazing. These damned third eyelid things keep coming over and I've nearly fallen asleep sitting bolt upright.

However, let's go back a little. We were all very tired last night, and bloated after lunch at Grandma's. She had the bldy school uniforms to iron and a bldy button to sew onto Young Lad's blazer for the fiftieth bldy time so the mood wasn't pleasant. Largely this was due to the bldy time constraints of trying to get the bldy sewing and bldy ironing finished before James Norton phwoar was acting superbly in something called McMafia at 9pm.

Anyway. It had been a marvellous day at Grandma's for lunch – Pork casserole this time, exceptionally tasty from the feedback I heard. I did crack a couple of shocking smells from under the table, but I think I got away with it as it all blended in with the casserole. Before sitting down, there had been nibbles on the low table, which you know I like, and the Tempura Prawns made a welcome return. I had several tail ends.

It was quite a tiring afternoon, as The Derby Chicks were there and they do like taking me in and out of the garden, seven hundred times. This wasn't a bad thing, though, as Grandma had thoughtfully put some bread out for the birds. The birds didn't get it. There was an amusing moment, Readers, when Lad was stroking me under the table, only I was in the kitchen at the time. It turned out he was stroking one of The Derby Chicks, age 9, who was under the table for no apparent reason. I feel Lad is under a lot of stress at the moment, and can't tell the difference between a dog and a child.

Back home in the evening, I curled up on Pack Leader's lap and had a lovely sleep. Until I was pushed off and shouted at, because of the same digestive problem I had the other night. I will be glad when these scented candles have burned down. Lad did some more revision, and was tested on the Nervous System. There was some conversation about homeostasis and reflex arcs which bored me to tears. Young Lad was meant to do some Maths revision, but seemed very happy when he attained 50% and shouted, "that's good, that'll do," and went back to the Xbox. I'm not sure that 50% is the right level of aspiration but I don't think Young Lad cares. There was more 'beef' at his school today, apparently, with a Year 9 calling a Year 7 a ****head, and some physicality. Young Lad loved it.

She and J's Pack Leader are feeling a little better about the upcoming weekend at ParkyCentres, as Kentgirl has now explained that she doesn't expect them to join in all the physical activities. Kentgirl knows that they both have severe limitations in this respect. And hasn't forgotten the image of them on a tennis court thirty years ago.

Well, I thoroughly enjoyed the dishwasher loading tonight – it was lasagne again, and as we know, this makes a shocking mess. There was so much to slurp up off the plates as they went in – She fought me tooth and nail to get me out of the way, but I was determined. Consequently the dishwasher had to be put on an extra hot setting to make sure everything is sterilised. She only cooked lasagne as a guilt thing again, due to working Nearly Full Time this week. The half-hearted attempt at home-cooking makes up for having a filthy house and neglected children and dogs, in her eyes. It doesn't.

Meghan Markle doesn't neglect her Beagle, and won't neglect her children. Mind you, I would imagine her children won't be very like Lad and Young Lad. I can't imagine Meghan Markle's dishwasher has loads of food at the bottom of it, that should have been cleaned out months ago, nor do her kitchen cupboards have paw prints and leek and potato soup (yes, still) on the doors. Life would be so different if I lived with Meghan.

Never mind; another day at Pippa's tomorrow! I'll let you know if I find anything to do before I go in the morning, and whether I am given anything as insulting as cold porridge again.

CHAPTER FORTY-FOUR

Spicy Snack

January 9th

Today was very confusing, Readers. I was meant to be going to dear, dear Pippa's again for daycare, but sadly she wasn't well – or pretended to be ill as she didn't want me there,who knows – so I couldn't go. This caused a flurry of text messages at 7.30am to find someone else to have the bldy dog. Thankfully Lad wasn't going into school until a bit later, and Lovelyneighbourontheright agreed to let me out at lunchtime. However, all this change unsettled me, and I felt the need to raid the food cupboard once Lad had finally gone to school. I knocked the tins onto the floor as they are boring, but behind them found a pack of Chilli Edamame Beans left over from Christmas! I know! A very upmarket snack, and spicy to boot. I cleared up the half packet that was left, and had another look behind the pasta packets. Hidden away I found a pack of dog chews – about eight of them – which was just the thing after the Chilli Edamame Beans. I spat the packaging onto the floor. I must admit I felt a bit puffed up after that so went for a sleep.

Lovelyneighbourontheright came to let me out at lunchtime, but I was finding it difficult to move. The combination of chilli and eight dog chews was a bit bloating. Anyway. Lovelyneighbourontheright cleared up all the tins that I'd knocked onto the (dirty) kitchen floor, and tidied up.

I just want to make a point here – there was a pack of Blueberry Muffins left out on the worktop last night. This morning, the pack had been broken into, and half a muffin eaten. This isn't an issue for Neighbourhood Watch because I know who it was. Gingercat. He does exactly the same to packets of scones. Just rips the packet, and eats the top part of the scone/muffin with his manky fishy cat breath. Does he get shouted at? Moaned at? No. He gets away with bldy murder, that cat. (Be assured, She does throw out the rest of the cat-chewed muffin, and doesn't give it to her offspring. The birds get it, and drop bits for me.

Win win.)

So needless to say I've been told off, once She got in from work and found out about the food cupboard. I heard her muttering that they'll have to get bldychildlocks put on it – you would have thought this might have occurred to them several years ago. She is going to add this to the bldylist of things that need a handyman in for, such as the broken light switch in the downstairs toilet (that happened well before Christmas) and still nobody has bothered to do anything about it.) And an electric towel rail in the new small bathroom as it's bldyfreezing and nobody wants to use the shower at 6am in minus four degrees. And the toilet seat in the downstairs toilet that veers off sharply to the right if you sit down too quickly.

There has been other tension here tonight, Readers. Lad is in even more trouble than me. She received a phone call at work this morning from his school to say he hadn't turned up for his exam. This was concerning, as it either meant he was still asleep in bed, had been involved in an accident, or had got lost via KFC on the way to school. Much frantic phoning around was needed. Finally Lad turned up at school, saying his bus was delayed. There has been a lot of firm discussion of the Need To Let People Know and Bldywellcommunicate and Do You Know How Bldy Worried I was and that sort of thing. Young Lad and I kept out of the way while this discussion took place. In fact, Young Lad has worked quite hard revising for a Maths Test tomorrow. I know! I'm surprised, too. Young Lad is in for a tricky day tomorrow, with PE, after-school Football Club, and Indoor Cricket Training in the evening. This is a lot to ask of someone who rarely leaves the sofa. I feel for him.

Dinner didn't go down well tonight. She attempted cauliflower cheese, mashed potato and baby carrots, but nobody liked it. This is because all the vegetables were old and past their best. She was wittering on about why do cauliflowers sometimes go allbldygreyandwatery and there was a lot for me to clean off the plates as they went into the dishwasher. I didn't mind it being grey and watery. It looked like glue. Poor Lad and Young Lad. But I fear the addition of cauliflower to the chilli edamame beans and dog chews might prove challenging for everyone. The scented candles (hooray, two have burned out!) have been lit in readiness.

Tomorrow will be excellent as I'm going to my dear friend Ebony's house. Here I will be allowed to sit on the sofas, get into her bed and generally make myself at home. I am FED UP with the fact She is working every day, and intend to make my feelings known. But at the moment, those chilli edamame beans are beginning to repeat a little, so I'll settle down for a sleep.

Before I do, a quick shout out to my young friend J in the Marsden, who only has one more night of horrid things being done and then he can go home. J's Pack Leader is looking forward to this immensely, as she has spent six days eating microwave ready meals. I would love to spend six days eating microwave ready meals. And I do hope that dear, dear Pippa feels better soon.

CHAPTER FORTY-FIVE

Bolts

January 11th

A wonderful walk this morning, Reader, simply wonderful. Despite
the grey leaden skies and drizzle, it was three miles of joy. First of all I
bumped into Teddy the Copper Australian Labradoodle and we bounced
around together a little. Teddy more so than me. Teddy was absolutely
filthy, and it makes me wonder what their kitchen floor is like, as ours is
disgustingly dirty, but I imagine Teddy's Pack Leader has higher
standards. Teddy's Pack Leader had a friend with her today –
unfortunately he was of the skin colour that I don't like, plus he had an
American accent, which was all too much. I did a lot of merciless racist
barking at him, and made a complete bldy show of myself,
apparently. She then marched me over the bridge into Top Field. This
wasn't a good decision as it was extremely wet and muddy, but having
stood on the bathroom scales this morning and screamed, there was a
need for a Power Walk up a soggy, uneven hill. I thought this was rude
and antisocial as we could have continued walking with Teddy instead,
but She wouldn't listen. Actually, I'm glad we didn't as She had already
given some of my Training Treats (ha ha) to Teddy and his brother Alfie,
and there weren't many left.

There was some diarrhoea on the bridge, but I didn't get a good
look as She pushed me away sharply. Anyway, once back at the river,
whom did I see but my dear friend Chuck. Yes! I'd only been saying the
other day that I hadn't seen him for ages. We sniffed each others'
backsides happily for ages and Chuck seemed to have an extra spring in
his step. His coat was beautiful, and it glistened even though there wasn't
any sunlight.

Nicedogwalkerlady and her husband were down there too, with
their three hundred dogs. We stopped and had a chat. On the way back, a
squirrel ran alongside me singing, "Come and Have A Go if you Think
You're Hard Enough," but as I was on the lead, I pretended I hadn't

heard to save my dignity. The squirrel laughed and ran up a tree.

It really was a lovely walk. Then She was dreadfully busy here again last night – what with Indoor Cricket Nets for Young Lad etc. Actually, this is cobblers, Readers, as He went to collect Young Lad while She was lying on the sofa with One Of Her Heads. Anyway, when Young Lad came in at 8.30pm, he announced that he had History homework due in today. So some reading and essay writing was in order at getting on for bldy 9pm, on how William the First successfully controlled England. (Castles, Feudal System and the Domesday Book, in case you want to know.) I pricked up my ears at the words Feudal System as that sounded interesting, but it wasn't. I hope She gets a very good mark for Young Lad's homework.

We were all very glad to get to bed last night. I had spent the day at dear, dear Ebony's house, where she quickly removed the comfortable stuffing from her bed so that I couldn't sit on it. This was inhospitable, and meant I only had the bare shell of her bed in which to sleep, while she had the fluffy bit. Yes I do realise it's her bed. Ebony and I had two very long walks and I was shattered last night.

I think the One of Her Heads was partly caused by Lad and Young Lad. Driving to work in the morning, there was a panicky phone call on her mobile from Young Lad. Worried he'd had an accident, She safely pulled over to the side of the road, to find out he'd left his Maths book at home. Later on in the day during an Important Meeting, Lad texted her to say he'd just had the "shittiest Maths exam EVER, not even the NEEKS could do it." This was all calmly and gently discussed in the evening, and the Good Parenting model of reasoning, not shouting, was followed. To the Letter.

Readers, you will be pleased to know that She has booked a Swedish Full Body Massage for herself and J's Pack Leader when they go to ParkyCenters next weekend. The good news is that this clashes with Short Tennis. It does, however, mean they will have to join in Geocaching. She and J's Pack Leader hope that this is a nice walk through the woods, stopping off at Barstucks to sit by the fire. I think we all know that it won't be anything like this. She has been ASTOUNDED that, having booked two bldyexpensive treatments, She and J's Pack Leader are not allowed to use the spa facilities afterwards unless they pay for a spa day as well. This is outrageous and a rip-off apparently. My feeling is that if you will go to Butlins for the Rich, what do you expect?

Lad only has two more days of Mock GCSEs, thank God. It has been trying, to say the least. I'm very glad I don't have to do any of these things.

Do you know where She's going this afternoon, friends? To somewhere called Q & B, to buy bolts for the kitchen cupboards. This is a rather extreme reaction to my behaviour this week, but She is sicktobldydeath of coming home from work and finding the cupboards in chaos. As if they are ever clean and organised! I'll let you into a secret here. Recently, when in someone else's house, She looked in their cupboard under the sink. It was immaculate. If one needed a light bulb, one could see they were clearly in the light bulb box. If one needed a brillo pad, these were carefully in a plastic box with neatly folded cloths. She came home and looked at ours. I rest my case.

I am annoyed about the bolts for the cupboard doors. But don't worry – DIY skills are so poor round here that I doubt they'll be fitted properly. It's just another challenge for me.

Well, my dear friend Pippa is still unwell and I'm quite worried about her. I hope I'm not the cause of her ailment.

Tomorrow night, Readers, She is going out with her friend Madame and others, for a drink and Tapas. I think I would like Tapas, not that anyone offers me any. I make my own Tapas. Surely Tapas just means small portions of anything you can find.

CHAPTER FORTY-SIX

Epic Fail 1

January 13th

Oh Readers, I was crying with laughter, watching her try to fit a bolt onto the food cupboard door. I did tell you it was never going to happen.

For a start, the bolt that was purchased was far too small for the door; I mean, is it not logical to think about the size needed? So I laughed and laughed, as I watched her holding this soppy little bolt in various positions, trying to find a way to fit it. Even more amusingly, She has lost the receipt so has bldywasted threepoundfifty in the process. The only thing that stopped me laughing, was that the Man in Q&B suggested She tries Self-Adhesive Velcro to keep the door out of my grasp. I can't see that working either. And it will look dreadful, but they won't care. The blue paddling pool (see earlier chapter) is still piled on top of the garden table to block off the hole in the fence; such is the squalor in which we live here. She "popped into town" this morning and scoured the shops until the Self Adhesive Velcro was found. I'll let you know how this goes. Personally I think the Man in Q&B knew that the silly little bolt She was holding was never going to work, but a sale is a sale.

A good walk this morning, Readers. Due to the concerns caused by standing on the bathroom scales this week, we had to do a 3.5 mile power walk through Top Field AND Far Field. I slowed things down a lot by stopping to pee on every molehill, and the moles had been very busy last night. I was shouted at several times and told to hurry up. The walk was marched in time to Carly Simon's "You're So Vain" today – no, I've no idea. I imagine there is a lesson in there somewhere.

I was TOTALLY cheesed off in Far Field when a Spaniel's Pack Leader told her that there was a dead bird up ahead, and her dog had tried to roll in it. So of course, I was put on the lead before I could smear blackbird intestine under my neck. This annoyed the heck out of me. The whole point of a walk in the fields and woods is to embrace the smells and textures of nature. That texture and smell would have been very special.

The walk back home was a little stressful as I bounced up to a different spaniel that I didn't know, but I momentarily forgot the words for, "hey, let's play and be friends" and accidentally growled and snapped at him. I was told off. A few hundred yards later, a Pug with a Christmas Jumper on made a beeline for me and didn't look friendly. She said it was karma. Then we suddenly had to increase our pace drastically, as we had been walking fast for an hour and a quarter, and the pelvic floor problem was beginning to rear its head. It's possible that the pint of Diet Coke at the end of the Evening Out Socialising last night contributed to this. Anyway, we made it through the front door JUST in time, and thank the Lord there is a downstairs toilet.

Last night was fairly peaceful here, as Lad was on the Xbox all evening in the other room. There was NOTHING on telly, apparently, so He and Young Lad ended up watching three episodes of Chicago Fire. How much drama involving fires and explosions does anyone need? Drivel. I slept through it. She, of course, was out Selfish Socialising. It was a very nice evening, apparently, with wine and Sharing Platters but I'm not sure She understood the 'sharing' aspect of Sharing Platters. I would struggle with that, too. It was very late by the time She went to bed, and we rewarded this by Gingercat yowling at 5.30am, an alarm clock going off at 6am (necessitating a stagger round the bedrooms without glasses on to work out whose bastard alarm clock it was), and then I needed a comfort break at 7am. I sensed some tetchiness this morning.

Readers, in an attempt to do something about the problems with the bathroom scales, a decision has been made to eat a little more healthily. So Jamie Oliver's Brown Windsor Soup has just been made, for lunch. It involved finding the dregs of some pearl barley at the back of the cupboard, scraping out some very old Marmite, and a dash of also very old Worcester sauce. It has taken an hour to make, and looks like what was on the bridge the other day (you'll have to go back a chapter or two, or use your imagination.) Still, lessons have been learned. Pearl barley doesn't break down in the blender. The whole thing is reminiscent of baby food. I'd eat it though.

Lad has just struggled out of bed for lunch, and has an afternoon of PE revision ahead of him, if he ever getsoffthebldyphone. Young Lad put away three bags of food shopping this morning, and is consequently exhausted. He, too, has homework to do this afternoon. There is a discussion going on about whether this requires one to be out of one's bldy pyjamas and dressed. Young Lad feels not. At the moment, Young Lad and Lad are sitting in their onesies discussing the variety of names for male genitalia. She is trying to get through four loads of bldywashing including the duvet covers and sheets, as apparently Gingercat and I have been on people's beds with muddy paws.

On the subject of Gingercat, I feel he is being very neglected. His fur is becoming somewhat thick and matted – not sleek and shiny like mine – and nobody ever bothers to comb him. I don't feel that "it's a rightbldyfaff" is a very caring attitude. It is on her List of Jobs to do today, but we all know how effective that is.

The allocated food list for the weekend at ParkyCenters has come through. She has been allocated "cakes" and "butter/spreads." This is disappointing, as She wanted to make the Chocolate Baileys Cheesecake for the three thousandth time. Cheesecake is in the Desserts category, though, and someone else has this. So She must stick to Lemon Drizzle and Shortbread. We all know what the kitchen will look like after these have been made – even though it was properly cleaned yesterday (not by her, obviously.)

I had a lovely day at dear, dear Ebony's yesterday, though she did that new thing of dragging the fleecy lining out of her bed so I can't have it. It's rather rude. My dear friend Pippa is picking up a little, and feels a tadge better so I hope I can go and see her next week, as She will be working LOADS again.

I will let you know how the Velcro locking of the cupboards go. Don't hold your breath.

CHAPTER FORTY-SEVEN

Bad Spillage

January 14th

Oh Readers, it was all going so well. In attempt to look like a normal family, a Sunday Lunch was cooked with all the usual components. Just as it was served up, however, the saucepan with the gravy bubbling happily in it was knocked flying. It crashed onto the hard floor, ejecting a large quantity of brown goo all over the place. If you remember, the filthy kitchen was finally cleaned on Friday. Well. Had She stopped what She was doing and cleaned it up straight away it wouldn't have been so bad, but oh no – She was so desperate to eat her Sunday Lunch that the mess was just left for me to lick up. Readers, I did my best! But the combination of glutinous gravy and my saliva was fatal, and it all dried in. It was EVERYWHERE. Over the fridge door, washing machine, up the walls, cupboard doors.........dear God, it looked like a gravy slaughterhouse. But more to the point, the Roasties didn't have anything on them, which was obviously not really up to scratch.

The Velcro Strips have been stuck on the food cupboard door, ready to try out the next time they leave me alone. I can guarantee I will either rip the Velcro Strips straight off or they simply won't be strong enough to hold the cupboard shut. What a ridiculous idea- I'm really looking forward to trying this out.

I was rather put out this morning, actually, as She was looking after the Young Cockapoo puppy next door, and decided to bring him into my house. This got right on my nerves. Not only did the young upstart keep jumping all over me, trying to FORCE me to play, but he even dragged my toys out of my basket and chewed them. Now, I haven't taken any notice of the toys for several years, but that isn't the point. I had to bark a few times at the little sausage, to put him firmly in his place. Then I sat on the sofa and sulked for an hour, giving everyone filthy looks.

It was quite a barky morning. The man over the back was in his garden, which upsets me. And there was someone else with him, climbing up a tree to saw bits off! This really irritated me and I had to let rip. Then the nice neighbours on the left got into their car to go out, so I had to bay loudly at them as well, from the safety of the sofa. I wish people wouldn't do these intimidating things.

It is Sunday today, which is always a Spiritual Day here. He shows his devotion to the Sunday Torygraph, especially the Sports Section, while Lad meditates in bed, and Young Lad reveres the Xbox. She, of course, "popped into town" and reflected heavily in Costalotta. Homeless Guy was outside Sainsbury's, and was pleased with his Greggs coffee (still 50p cheaper than Costalotta) and a raspberry doughnut.

However, the day had not started in a Spiritually Pleasant way for me. Yesterday the White John Lewis duvet cover was put back on the bed. There is a manky old sheet put on top of this so I don't spoil it. We had a little stand off this morning, as I wanted to get onto the nice white John Lewis pillows, and She said I had to sit on the manky sheet. She dragged me, bodily, off the nice white John Lewis part, and dumped me on the manky sheet. I waited till She left the room and went back to where I started. She came back in and dragged me off again. I waited till She left....anyway, you get the idea. This charade went on for about twenty minutes, by which time I was bored and went downstairs to look for food. Those of you thinking, oh how disgusting that a dog gets on a bed -jog on. I am not, and never have been, a floor dog. And the time they tried to crate train me! Ha ha! Lasted half an hour.

Quite incredibly, a family dog walk was achieved this afternoon! Lad and Young Lad, despite being in their pyjamas, were told that No was not being taken for an answer, and they had to put on old clothes and wellies. It was splendid – we went over the bridge, up through Far Field and into the woods to the Pheasant Field. It was a long, muddy and gorgeous-smelling walk. Several times, I thought I saw some prey and took off at a cracking pace, so that Lad had to run after me. I didn't catch anything. There were hundreds of other Families down there, out for a Sunday walk. He always says hello to everyone we pass, which is very polite, but gets on Lad's nerves, who prefers to put his hood up, head down, and make no eye contact with anyone. Young Lad didn't stop talking for the entire three miles, and it was complete claptrap. But I did have a lovely time, and am exhausted now.

Other than that, it has been an afternoon of homework and bldylaundry yet again. I think we are up to six loads this weekend. Friends, things are rather behind schedule tonight as none of the bldyschoolshirts have been ironed and there is still a damp load of stuff in the tumble dryer. She needs to get a move on as James Norton (that fine young actor whose acting talents are the main attraction) is on the telly at 9pm in McMafia, and there are still lots of jobs to do. It bothers me that nobody has hoovered the lounge this weekend – standards are slipping even further. Lad hoovered upstairs yesterday but seemed to feel the bottom of the stairs was some sort of geographical border so put the hoover away. Lad has also ordered a pair of Designer Jeans tonight, which will make a pleasant change from the Designer Tracksuits, but there was lots of old fuddy duddy comments about "how much?!!!" and "they've got rips in them, how much?!!!" Lad says they are out of touch. I could have ripped some for him for a fraction of the price.

Well, Young Lad is now on his fifth episode of Chicago Fire of the weekend, which is helping me to sleep deeply. Don't worry, he has done some homework too – this morning he had to write six important facts about the life of Muhammad. He was told to try again, this time finding some interesting facts about Muhammad.

I will let you know how I get on with the Velcro. I think we all know how I will get on with it.

CHAPTER FORTY-EIGHT

Popcorn

January 16th

Evening all. It says on the packet, "Proper Corn", and I can vouch for this. It's great! Just the right balance of sweet and salty, and low calorie as well. So they shouldn't be moaning at me just because they found this ripped-up empty packet on the study floor, when they came home tonight. They should be grateful I helped myself to a healthy snack, rather than half a large Toblerone (see previous chapter).

Anyway, I feel this indiscretion was justified today, because of what was put in my Kong this morning. Friends, you will not believe it. Do you remember the cold porridge from last week? This was worse. As She and Young Lad left home, they threw me my Kong, which was filled with.........leftover Jamie Oliver Brown Windsor Soup. Yep. Congealed into a thick paste (that's the pearl barley for you), bright orange (that's the carrots for you), and it was the texture of sick with Worcestershire sauce in it. Utterly gross. I ate it, of course, but really. If anyone dares have a go at me about flatulence tonight... well, I will have something to say on the matter. After eating this cack out of the Kong, I had a quick look round and found an ice cream tub, which I took into the lounge. Unfortunately it was empty. That's when I found the popcorn, which left a nicer taste than the Brown Windsor Soup had done.

Last night was bldy busy as usual. Young Lad had some English Homework to do which took Rather A Long Time, With A Lot of Help. Plus nobody had ironed the bldyschoolshirts at the weekend, so they had to be done. Plus Young Lad had spilled something all over his blazer, so yet another bldyload of washing had to go on. After all that She was too work-shy to get the laptop out; there's a new Jo Nesbo book next to the bed, and it seems this was more important than writing my book.. Poor, I know.

We had, in fact, a relatively pleasant day. I was heavily asleep in the morning, and didn't really fancy a walk in heavy grey drizzle, but I was given no choice. It was no surprise to find very few friends down at the river, as their Pack Leaders had more sense. That said, I did bump into dear, dear Ebony on the way down and stopped for a chat. But Ebony was on her way home in the heavy grey drizzle, whereas we idiots were on our way out. We went over the bridge into Top Field – I have to say, I haven't seen the Bastard Swans or their offspring for quite a while now. Long may it last. Hate them. There was no poo or intestines to roll in over in Top Field, which was a shame, so I had to make do with being caked in mud. Needless to say I was shoved unceremoniously into my bed in the kitchen when we got home, and told to STAY THERE. I did, for five minutes, then walked across the light-coloured lounge carpet to my chair.

Dinner was curry, rice and popadoms last night. This is one of my favourites, as the rice goes everywhere and the popadoms break into tiny weeny bits that fall on the floor for me. In an attempt to eat more healthily, the jar of Sharwoods sauce was eschewed in favour of Making Your Own From Scratch. That way there would be no sugar, additives, loads of salt etc. Readers, we all know that it was fairly tasteless. The "onions lightly sauteed with garam masala" is no match for mass-produced salt and fat-laden curry sauce. Anyway, everyone ate it because they were very hungry. I had a good time with the dishwasher-loading, as the plates were plastered. Then He was given a very out-of-date microwave steamed syrup pudding for dessert, while the others had just-in-date yogurt.

During Coronation Street last night, I fell asleep very, very heavily. I'm sure I wasn't alone in this. Apparently I was snoring violently and had to be pushed occasionally. What annoyed me most was that when I woke up later on, I was rather bleary eyed and disorientated and they all laughed at me. I don't see what was so funny. Yes my eyes were a little unfocused and my head wobbled a bit, and I clearly didn't know what day of the week it was, but it would be nice if I was greeted with gentle, reassuring voices rather than snorts of laughter.

Today was rather lovely, because after the Brown Windsor Soup and Popcorn incidents, it was time to go to dear, dear Pippa's house. Pippa is feeling better and I cheered her up no end today. I have this effect on my friends. Except when I sleep in their beds and get right up their noses. So I've had a super day at Pippa's, and they very kindly brought me home this afternoon as Lad was home early from school.

Yes, this is the moment we've been waiting for. The Last Mock Exam. Dear Lord, it feels like this has been going on for months. Today was the last one, which was PE. You would think this was quite easy really – how hard can Physical Education be? Running, sniffing, picking up sticks, chasing squirrels, paddling in the river.... apparently it's a WELL difficult subject at GCSE level. Regardless, thank the Lord they've finished. Of course, this means Lad wants to go to another Party at the weekend, quite a long way away. I'm sure he and the other Lads will sit around with a can of sugar-free Lilt, sensibly discussing their mock exams and the Future, while the female versions of the Lads are all drunk and throwing up in the garden.

I had to snap at Lad tonight. He was about to shut the dishwasher door, but I hadn't quite finished trying to get the smears of Macaroni Cheese off the plates. Lad tried to be assertive by pulling me off and shouting, "No," so I had to snarl and curl my lip, to show how much I respected his authority. The dishwasher has gone on the extra hot setting again.

As I write, Young Lad and He are cuddled up watching Eastenders, which is very depressing. I find it hard to smile at the best of times, but listening to this grim crap makes me even more dispirited. I'll have a sleep, I think.

Tomorrow will be nice, as I'm going to dear Ebony's house. I haven't tried to open the Velcro-locked food cupboard yet (I was too busy with the Brown Windsor puree), but I might do that before I go in the morning. I'll let you know. I'll also be thinking of my Young Friend J who has to go back to the Marsden tomorrow, to get some test results. This will tell him whether all the horrid things his Evil Vets did to him, have been worth it.

CHAPTER FORTY-NINE

Epic Fai1 2

January 17th

Ha ha ha ha ha! OMG, I cannot stop laughing! Readers, you knew it and I knew it. The soppy Velcro Strips were never going to keep the food cupboard shut. All I had to do was simply open the cupboard with more force than usual, which ripped the Velcro strips apart. I know! I didn't even need to chew them off! Oh dear, dear, dear...what on earth made them think that some annoying nylon with a schwip noise would be a match for me?

Let's give you a little tour of the cupboard. On the floor (slovenly) her slippers. Plus some Christmas Dog Treats I found. Bottom shelf – my big plastic box of food. As usual, they hadn't put the lid on properly. Also on the bottom shelf, Spot-On flea treatment, and worming stuff. I left these alone. Next shelf up; pasta and rice. It's a mess, frankly. Third shelf; tins. Boring. But I didn't knock them all on the floor today. One day I will find a way to get into the Ambrosia custard and Heinz spaghetti hoops. Oh, what a start to the day – it was sublime.

Before long, Ebony's Pack Leader came to collect me for a fun day at her house. I had a smashing time, and was As Good As Gold. There was an error of judgement, however, when I was put into the car with Ebony to go somewhere different for our walk today. I had a small problem with excessively smelly flatulence, due to the stuff I'd eaten from the food cupboard. Ebony and her Pack Leader regretted choosing a different location today, as they were trapped in the car with my foul smells. Had they stuck to the river, we would have been out in the fresh air. I don't think it was kind or necessary to tell me that they couldn't wait to get out of the car, though. I tried to have a good Clear Out while I was out for our walk, but it hasn't improved the wind issue tonight. One word: Eggs.

She said that She had to explain to Colleague today, what a Kong is. For the uninitiated like him, it's a rubber ball thing that you stick nice treats in, to stop dogs becoming bored. Though in my case, it is filled with cold porridge, Jamie Oliver Brown Windsor soup gloop, or out-of-date houmous. These are hardly treats. Today was a tadge better as a few bits of Gingercats's breakfast had been left, so that was shoved into the Kong. Anyway, Colleague has learned something.

It's Wednesday today, which is never a good day in terms of giving me any attention, or on the culinary front. Due to the bldyshortwindow between getting home from work and getting out to Indoor Cricket Nets, it is fish fingers and potato waffles. Dreadful processed rubbish.

What other updates are due? Ah yes, the Shark Jigsaw is still on the snooker table, still unfinished. Nobody has attempted it since Christmas as they are happy to write it off as 'faulty'. Young Lad has still not finished his Thank You Letters, and LovelyDor down the road could be waiting for hers till Easter. Young Lad will be exhausted tonight, as not only has he walked to and from school today (over a mile each way) plus had Cricket Training, but he also had to walk all the way home yesterday which is a forty minute walk. Poor Young Lad didn't even have the strength to stick his English homework into his book, so She had to do it as they were bldyleavinghome this morning. Time. Management. Again. And although He took down the Christmas decorations and put them away this year, He has failed to notice that the lights are still up round the window and door. I imagine they will be too bone idle to remove them now, and keep them up until next year. Shoddy.

Am I building a picture of where I live? The blue paddling pool standing up against the fence to block the hole? The Velcro on the kitchen doors? The dreadful cupboard under the stairs? The Christmas lights left up and dangling? Classy.

Oooh golly, that was a shocker that just popped out. Even though I say so myself.

Lad is on the Xbox as a treat. This is Not Normally Allowed on School Nights, but it is a reward for receiving some decent marks in his English and PE Mock exams. Maths was a different matter, however, and there will be a conversation later. This might possibly involve the words Tutor whether you bldy like it or not. Gingercat and I will keep our heads down during this.

He has just come in the door from work, and I feel a little sorry for him. In an attempt to be an Organised Working Mother, there was a pathetic bid to put the oven timer on today, to cook jacket potatoes. The idea was to set the clock, and the smell of jacket potatoes would fill the house tonight as everyone arrived home. However, it was 7.15am when this was attempted, and way before the first coffee of the day, so there was no real clue as to how to set the oven timer. The result is flaccid, black potatoes. But, as we've now run out of fish fingers and potato waffles, He is going to be served up these potatoes, microwaved, with baked beans and cheese. Luckily He will eat absolutely anything (including a dog treat once, I kid you not).

I've just heard the weather forecast. It's going to be very windy out tonight, as well as in. Batten down the hatches, everyone – especially if you're anywhere near me.

CHAPTER FIFTY

Gale Force

January 18th

What a night! Well, Readers, they said it would be windy but by golly, that was violent. Both the wind inside the house, and out. I was rudely awoken from my sleep at 4am by the howling gale, and the rattling windows. I decided to go out in the garden for a comfort break, and took my time absorbing the atmosphere of a hurricane. It was quite magical, spoilt only by the screeching at me to hurryup and bldywellgetbackin. No sooner had we settled back to sleep than Gingercat started yowling from the kitchen to be let in. This went down like a lead balloon. Gingercat and I were exhausted by the time everyone left for school and work, and needed another sleep.

It was quite funny, Friends, because as they were all getting ready this morning, the lights kept flickering and a Power Cut loomed. There was some shouting of hurryup and getin thebldyshower and use thebldyhairdryer before the power goes off. They seemed to be dashing around a lot (well, not Lad, obviously) and there was some frantic wondering of where the bldytorch is. If they tidied out the disgraceful cupboard under the stairs, they might find the bldytorch.

Readers, I have some Wonderful News. My young friend J saw the Evil Vets at the Marsden Hospital yesterday, and they told him the horrible things they've done to him for three months have been worth it, and the Nasty Thing he's got is now much, much smaller. He will still have many happy visits to the Marsden and enjoy the Therapy Clowns, as some Zapping now has to take place – I don't think this is the technical term, and it sounds much like squeezing anal glands. But it is very good news, and J's Pack Leader can relax and celebrate at ParkyCentres this weekend. If she can stay awake long enough. She and J's Pack Leader are sharing a room, as they are well known for being complete lightweights and going to bed early.

I've had a lovely day at dear, dear Pippa's house. We had a smashing walk this afternoon, but mis-timed this to coincide with a downpour on the way back. We were soaked. Thankfully Pippa's Pack Leader is kind and caring, and rubbed me down with a towel. Not once did she moan Ihaven'tgotbldytimeforthis. When She came to collect me tonight, there was a discussion about how much I had smelled today. It was a little undignified to hear them laughing about the moment I let one go, then stood up and looked round at my bottom to see who had done it. It's very childish, to be frank. Anyway, dear Pippa seems a lot happier this week and I feel sure it's my presence that has caused this.

Young Lad is exhausted again, having had to walk all the way home from school for the second time this week. In actual fact, he had a lift with a friend's Grandad, but has only just owned up to this. So all sympathy for him has disappeared fairly promptly and he's being told to turn off Chicago Fire and finish the thank you letters. He appears to have gone deaf. Lad is in the other room on the Xbox, but has been told firmly that next week we go back to normal rules. He is looking forward to the Party tomorrow night where they will be able to relax. He and She are glad they haven't got girl versions of Lad, as they will all be In A Bad Way at this party.

With a bit of luck, I may get some attention tomorrow as She may not be working. This is excellent news, as I can do something naughty while She "pops into town" after the school drop off, and then we'll have a long walk. Later in the afternoon, Grandma is coming to stay while She goes to ParkyCentres. I'm pleased about this, as Grandma loves me unconditionally. There was a big food shop tonight, in theory to stock up here for the weekend. There seems to be a separate bag being organised, with her friend Gordon in it, some lemons and lots of snacks. I haven't worked out what this is for yet, but I like the look of the snacks. Good quality.

After tea tonight, He started bagging up the recycling, ready for the dustmen tomorrow. I tried to help by snatching a plastic tray that had contained lightly dusted plaice fillets, and running off with it. This is all part of Organising the Recycling and I didn't take kindly to being chased. Growling and snarling was needed.

CHAPTER FIFTY-ONE

Crackers

January 22nd

Evening, Friends! I've got so much to tell you, I just don't know where to start. I suggest you make yourselves a nice drink and curl up with me for the evening; I'll try to finish before Silent Witness. I've had a cracking day being an absolute pain in the backside – this is payback for Going Away for the Weekend, followed by a Monday at Work! What the heck. This cavalier attitude towards me is obviously going to be met with some disappointment on my part, which I needed to express today.

So I pulled open the food cupboard as soon as She and Young Lad had left for school/work and actually managed to fully rip off the ruddy Velcro this time. I knocked the flea spray onto the floor, and also my ear-cleaning lotion. I hate both of them. Then I pulled out a pet hairbrush. Moving up a shelf, I found the tin foil and dragged that into the study for something to do. There was a box of Ritz crackers at the back of this shelf – actually they were Sainsbury's own Ritz-type crackers, as they're too tight to pay for the Brand Name ones – so I pulled those down and was pleased to find they were open. Stale, but open. I finished them off, and put the box in the study next to the foil. Still bored, I went back and pulled off a strip of the cheap laminate stuff that covers the cupboard door. This is more fitting for the general slum-like appearance of this home.

And all this before Pippa's Pack Leader came to collect me for daycare this morning. I was quite tired from my efforts.

Anyway, Readers, let's go back a little. As you know, She spent the weekend at ParkyCenters with friends, and although we had an extra long walk on Friday before She left home, and a cuddle over lunch, I was pretty hacked off when I saw her putting the overnight bag in the car. So as soon as She had left on Friday afternoon, driving in blissful ignorance, I found her handbag and went through the contents. I distributed these evenly across the floor in the study and lounge – it looked quite pretty. As usual, there were a couple of old Tictacs and half a Polo stuck to the lining at the bottom of the bag, so I ate them even though they were covered in fluff. They were quite tricky to pull off the inside of the handbag, so I had to do a lot of chewing through the lining and in fact ripped holes into it. In case you're worrying, this is a Tesco handbag, not a Radley one.

Then I dragged my box of dog food out of the "Velcro-secured" food cupboard and helped myself to a large mid-afternoon snack. We all paid for this later with some unfortunate flatulence. Grandma arrived later in the afternoon, and from then on I behaved impeccably. Though I did still smell quite ripe, and she found it hard getting into bed as I beat her to it, and she isn't used to elbowing me out of the way and shouting, "Move!" like other people do. The weekend went quite smoothly after that, as I had plenty of attention and long walks. Lad was away at a party, so Young Lad, He and Grandma had some peace.

Look, this book is meant to be about me, so if you're not interested in how She got on at ParkyCenters, skip the next bit. I would do the same.

Considering there was a Satnav in the car, She found it remarkably stressful finding ParkyCenters as She had not chosen the "quickest route" setting on Satnav, and discovered many, many pretty villages and B roads on the way there. (But then don't you remember the Works Christmas Party, Readers? Her colleagues haven't forgotten. And will never ask for a lift again).

In fact, this theme continued when She eventually found ParkyCenters but couldn't negotiate her way out of the car park to the Lodge. It took several attempts and actually exiting ParkyCenters twice to come back in, before it was managed. This was very entertaining for the bored people manning the Arrivals Check in who had to keep waving her through. In fairness, it is a bldyridiculous car park and the signs are bldyuseless.

Before night fell, though, the good old friend Gordon was unpacked and placed lovingly on the counter, ready for the evening. Kentgirl, whose birthday was being celebrated, and the 300 friends arrived and a pleasant evening of food, wine and laughter was had. Until Kentgirl reminded everyone about ten pin bowling having been booked for 10pm. I quite sympathise with them-wild horses wouldn't drag me out for organised fun at that time of night.

Oh dear, Readers, the theme of being geographically impaired carried on into the next day! Having said a firm, "NO!" to the offer of

10am clay pigeon shooting (even I'm struggling to see the point of that, and I'm a hunting dog) She, J's Pack Leader and another, er, similar friend we'll call Wancy set off nice and early to join the others for Geocaching. In the pouringbldyrain. Now, Wancy and J's Pack Leader aren't known for their sense of direction any more than She is. It took them 40 minutes to simply find the meeting point. They were all to blame, but had a lovely chat on the way round. The plan then was an hour of romping through the forest following clues and using some satnav type thing to show them the way. Yes. You're thinking the same as me. Track record with satnavs isn't good. And indeed it wasn't, as this bldything "didn't work properly", but I suspect this is a euphemism for "sod this for a game of soldiers, let's go for coffee". What a poor attitude – no resilience whatsoever. And yes it was pouring with rain, but so what?

There was another example of this lethargic spirit in the afternoon, when Short Tennis was bypassed in favour of the spa, with J's Pack Leader. All this nonsense about "J's Pack Leader has had a Tough Time and needs to Relax" is a load of cobblers, Reader. They just couldn't be bothered to run round a sports hall. I'm not sure they ought to be invited on one of these weekends again. Even Wancy managed some energetic swimming. Well, swimming.

Oh dear God, the number of times I've heard about the lovelylittle muntjac deer that visited them outside their Lodge in the snow.....what do they expect? They were in a forest, for the love of God, and had thrown loads of bread out! I'd have given Bambi and the squirrels something to think about, if I'd been there.

Anyway, Reader, She finally deigned to come home late Sunday afternoon. Good of her. The others all went home too, as luckily Wancy's car keys that had been "lost" the moment they arrived, and had necessitated two days of emptying bags, turning furniture upside down and general hysteria, turned out to be in Wancy's hoodie pocket.

I gave her a HUGE welcome, Readers, and did lots of sliding along the hall floor. I had even, and this is touching, managed to time a bad onset of anal gland blockage with her return and stunk the house out. This wasn't appreciated, of course. We did have a nice cuddle during that very fine actor James Norton's appearance in McMafia, and all was well with the world. However, at 4.30 this morning my bottom was really playing up and I had to whine and grizzle to be let out in the garden. This went down well.

Apparently one of the nice friends at ParkyCenters also has a Beagle, and they spent much time comparing us. We both have anal gland issues and stink, but my behaviour is worse. Allegedly.

Lad had been in charge of cleaning yesterday, and had made a reasonable job of the hoovering, kitchen and bathroom. Young Lad and He were in charge of laundry and school uniforms. This went well, to an extent, though there has been some discussion about what sort of things you can and can't put in a tumble dryer. The proof is in the pudding.

I have been scolded for my exploits with the tin foil, flea spray and Ritzish crackers today, but am now forgiven and am cuddled up, making shocking smells. Pippa's house was fun today, but I'm exhausted now. In theory I might get a decent walk in the morning, but I'll try to get up to something during the school drop. I'll let you know what I think of.

CHAPTER FIFTY-TWO

Spag Bol

January 23rd
Spag bol
Excellent. Tonight it was spaghetti bolognaise for dinner, which is always messy and leaves oily tomatoey residue on the plates. I planted my feet firmly on the dishwasher door while they were loading it, and refused to budge; this meant I managed to clear most of it off the plates before I was shoved away. It was fairly tasty, though a dash of Worcestershire sauce would have given it a little more bite in my opinion.

Readers, imagine my delight when I realised a chocolate cake was being knocked up as well! This was a Guilt Cake, to make up for being away for the weekend. You would think that something with less fat and sugar would be more appropriate if you love your offspring and want them to live long, healthy lives, but there you go. Anyway, there was cake mixture all over the place as usual, which was a treat. I helped to clean up. The kitchen floor has even been washed tonight – wonders will never cease.

Lad was at home in bed today, due to a Bad Headache. Readers, you know that these usually coincide with Double Games, and yes, it was Double Games today. He slept until 3.30pm, so wasn't much company for me. I did try to cheer him up by running round the lounge with a cat food packet when he fed Gingercat, and I'm sure the ensuing chase made his head feel better. His Art teacher has kindly emailed him a list of things he should be Getting On With, which made him smile. I think.

Oh Readers, it was a wonderful morning at the river today. First I bumped into dear Mr Squibb, who was on his way home for a bath and blow-dry. I get a rough towel if I'm lucky. Then, who did I see but dear Teddy! That cheeky young Australian copper labradoodle – we romped around for a bit but then I bored somewhat, so ran off to look for some food. I'll tell you what REALLY annoyed me, though. Teddy's Pack

Leader asked her how the weekend at ParkyCenters went – and then, what do you know, they're comparing notes on the spa! Not content with that, Teddy's Pack Leader even told her you can go for the day! DON'T GIVE HER IDEAS! I was annoyed by this. Thankfully my dear friend Chuck was a little further on, and his grey marbled coat was magnificent again today. The white bits were like the driven snow. He really is the most spectacular creature.

So I left Teddy and the irritating spa discussion, plus his Pack Leader's friend who is the Wrong Skin Colour for me, and American, and I ran off with Chuck for a while. The river was very, very high today and one part of the field was flooded so we had to wade through it. I was soaked and a tadge muddy. Further on, in Far Field, I needed a comfort break, and thought it would be funny to wait till She was a long way ahead, then drop it in some very long grass. It took her AGES to find it!! It was hilarious. But ten out of ten for determination, and putting one of those little black bags to use. What a shame She had to carry it for half a mile to find a bin.

Bizarrely, our 'power walk' today was to the tune from the Benny Hill show, going round her head. Most of you will have no idea about this, and are better off for that. I think it's because there was an article in the Torygraph about the increased popularity of milk bottle deliveries and this subconsciously sparked memories of Benny Hill.

Back home from our walk, I was really, really muddy. I was still annoyed about the spa day discussion, so I shook myself violently from side to side in the kitchen, and plastered both the floor and her Work Shoes in mud spatters. Serves her right. I was then shut in my bed in the kitchen to 'dry off'; She had a cup of tea and did lots of important emailing and telephoning, whilst simultaneously watching Big Little Lies. I could hear some of this through the wall, Reader, and I don't think it was appropriate at all. I hope She was concentrating on those emails – Lord knows what might have been written. Then I was left in peace with Gingercat while She went to work, and it was bliss. All the bins had been put out of my reach, which was a bit dull, so I had to content myself with making horrid smells in the lounge.

In other news, Young Lad has finally finished his Thank You Letters, as He and Grandma pinned him to the table at the weekend until they were done. LovelyDor down the road might even get hers soon. I had hoped that Grandma might finish the shark jigsaw when she was here at the weekend, but she was rather busy with the Daily Mail and Young Lad's Thank You Letters.

It's been quite a peaceful evening here so far tonight, as He is reading the paper, Young Lad is watching Chicago Fire having been told to turn off "Craziest Police Pursuits", and Lad is walking around with the new red fleece draped over him, sighing. I'm hoping that they don't push the chocolate cake right to the back of the working surface tomorrow when they go to work, as I have my eye on it. Nothing will equal the 10 square inch, three layer chocolate birthday cake that I ate in its entirety on Lad's birthday last year, but this small, feeble version would do. Unfortunately, Ebony's Pack Leader has a nasty habit of moving everything off the working surface when she pops in to see me, and I'm chez Ebony tomorrow. Humph.

Friends, I can't imagine I'll have much attention tomorrow night, what with it being Wednesday and all. Young Lad has indoor cricket in the evening, if you remember (do keep up with our schedule), and it's All A Bit Of A BldyRush. There are only so many bldyhoursinthebldyday.

I bet Meghan Markle's Beagle shakes mud over her work shoes, and doesn't get shouted at. I still want to live with them.

CHAPTER FIFTY-THREE

Torn

January 25th

I was a bit naffed off this morning, Readers, so I tore a nice strip of cheap laminate off the food cupboard door. What had upset me? Well, as they left the house in the usual stressy shouty way at 7.40am, I was thrown HALF a carrot to keep me occupied. HALF. This is pretty poor. Yesterday morning I at least had my Kong with some left over cold fish pie stuffed in it. Consistency of glue, but the smoked haddock still tasted nice. But today? Half a manky carrot. I showed my disappointment while She had "popped into town" after the school drop by tearing some more laminate off and chucking one of her work shoes on the floor. I was shouted at, of course, and the usual silly, "WHO did this/Did YOU do this?" routine went on for a while. Tiresome.

It was a glorious morning at the river, though – absolutely beautiful. A day that made me glad to be alive. I really wanted a slow, leisurely stroll for a couple of hours – after yesterday's double walk with Ebony I was quite content with gentle trotting speed today. But oh no, it was the usual hard-paced stomping through thick mud. Today it was to the tune of Elvis Costello's "Pump It Up." An improvement on the Benny Hill theme, but still rather dated. Every so often a shrill, "For God's Sake Hurry UP!!" pierced the otherwise tranquil setting, and it got on my nerves, frankly. We'd seen Ebony on the way down there, so of course there was the usual discussion of which of us was the worst behaved, blah blah blah.... Ebony and I were bored by this. Dear, dear Teddy was down there again, really rather frisky today, but I didn't want to chase around playing. Can't see the point. Luckily a young cockapoo came along and jumped all over Teddy. It was all a bit infantile for me.

Let's go back a day, Readers. It was busy here last night, as I had warned you. This was ostensibly because Young Lad was at cricket so it was too bldybusy, but it turned out to be because She had to bring a lot of work home with her. He went to collect Young Lad from cricket due to this Heavy Workload. I tried to help by sitting very firmly next to her on the sofa, but I had an itchy paw and evidently it's verybldyannoying when you're trying to work and something keeps scratching and jiggling around next to you. I was sent to my chair in the end.

I'd had a LOVELY day, Friends, with dear Ebony. We had not one, but TWO smashing walks! Because Ebony's Pack Leader is kind and caring. The first walk was uneventful, but the second one was a little problematic. Ebony ran off across the fields and wouldn't come back. This was unacceptable behaviour. Then I picked up a wonderful scent – I suspect it was muntjac – so I couldn't help taking off at full speed with my nose on the ground. I had problems with my ears and couldn't hear Ebony's Pack Leader calling me. Ebony and I then both refused to come back to her Pack Leader, which was rather fraught for her. However, I eventually gave up on hunting the muntjac as I heard the desperate scream, "sausage", and decided that was a better bet. All's well that ends well. When we got home, we had to be hosed down, and then made to sit in the kennel outside to dry off.

There has been a fair amount of culinary effort here this week, to make amends for being away at the weekend, as this meant Lad and Young Lad ate pizza and fish and chips. Monday's fish pie took bldyages to make and stunk the house out, but was at least nutritious. Tuesday's spag bol was served with lots of green vegetables. Last night was a bit of a shocker – fish fingers and chips, as sobldybusy – but tonight we were back to form with homemade soup, jacket potatoes and so on. The kitchen is filthy again. I had hoped, as She wasn't working today, that maybe the Christmas lights that are still sellotaped up round the window, might get taken down and put away. But no. Neither has anyone noticed the lone artificial poinsettia that is still rammed into a picture frame in the lounge. The NordicNonDrop Christmas Tree is slung out on the back patio, still waiting for someone to saw it into pieces and take it to the tip. I cock my leg on it most mornings. But on the bright side, LovelyDor down the road has finally received her Thank You letter. Before February.

There was a meeting at Lad's school today to discuss ways in which to help him with his Many Medical Issues and, I would think, how to get him out of bed a bit quicker. Rocket and backside come to mind. Anyway, as Lad's school is not a million miles from a branch of John Lewis, a decision was made to kill two birds with one stone, and sit in its hallowed halls for half an hour with a coffee and scone – thanks to the twice-yearly voucher for a free coffee and cake. Never knowingly over-generous. There was some loving hand-sweeping over 220 thread count Egyptian cotton duvet covers, and a browse round the sale rail at the Mint Velvet concession. As usual, the shop was exited without a Single Bldy Purchase due to the bldyprice. Keep dreaming.

It seems my anal glands are a little on the strong side tonight, and I'm being moaned at a lot. He is the only person in this house who still loves me when my anal glands are playing up – I'm not sure he notices. Even Gingercat keeps his distance. It could be a result of the fish pie, as my glands smell like an oilier version of it. Meghan Markle's Beagle undoubtedly has problems with his anal glands, too, but I would think he gets more sympathy. Anyway, if Meghan made a fish pie I doubt it would be with smoked haddock from Lidl. Is there a Lidl in Kensington High Street? Now there's a thought. Meghan would love me unconditionally.

Young Lad has a wobbly tooth that is very painful – he's making a right ruddy fuss about it, if you ask me. I've just emitted something that might take his mind off his wobbly tooth for a while.

They're all out at work/school tomorrow. I'm planning a biggie.

CHAPTER FIFTY-FOUR

It Wasn't Me

January 26th

It definitely wasn't me that threw a pack of spaghetti around the lounge this morning. I was sound asleep with a red fleece on my head, so couldn't have been involved with opening the food cupboard door, helping myself to my food, and dragging an open packet of spaghetti around the lounge. There was some suggestion today that Ebony's Pack Leader comes in and trashes the house, then pretends it's me, but I feel this is Terrible Slur on her remarkably good nature. Oh all right, it was me.

It was a right laugh. I managed to cause chaos in the 40 minutes between them all leaving home and Ebony's Pack Leader coming to collect me. And don't forget I had a Kong to clear out as well – tuna mayonnaise today. An improvement on the half carrot from yesterday. So yet again, Readers, I feel my time management and efficiency is something to be proud of – that's not bad going for 40 minutes. Oh yes, and by the way, the food cupboard had the stool AND a vegetable rack wedged in front of it, in a vain attempt to keep me out. Can you imagine how nice this looks? Elegant. So I had to drag those out the way as well. There was some swearing about all this and more muttering about bldylocks on the bldydoor but I can't see them ever having the DIY skills to do anything about it. The Velcro!! Oh it still makes me laugh so much.

Anyway, after Ebony's Pack Leader had tidied away the three hundred pieces of spaghetti draped across the kitchen and lounge floor, it was time to go to Ebony's house. I'm sure this pleased Ebony a lot, but I still don't feel it's necessary for her to drag the nice comfortable bedding out of her bed the minute she sees me and sit on it. She's a dear friend, but very territorial like that. We had a lovely walk – a beautiful day again today – and were much better behaved by not running off and ignoring commands.

I arrived home just at the same time as He and Young Lad did, and we had a pleasantly quiet hour and a half until Lad and She got home. Lad was in a mood because he'd been in trouble at school for getting behind with some work. He now has a lot to catch up on over the weekend, and is showing great commitment to this by going straight on the Xbox. Young Lad, on the other hand, had a commendation card for Progress. This was a surprise to everyone, as he does bugger all, and he had no idea whatsoever what it was for. But there you go, it's nice to have some positives, even if nobody knows why. She was rather late home due to bldyFridaynighttraffic and so some pizzas were slung in the oven. To be fair, an attempt at nutrition was made with the usual dull carrot, cucumber and pepper sticks – this is the sort of food you give two-year-olds. But they all ate it hungrily in front of the telly (no sitting at the table on Friday Nights), watching Family Guy, which isn't very suitable. I whined and stamped my feet as usual on a Friday night, until someone gave in and let me have a crust of pizza and a carrot stick.

Unbelievably, I've just heard her say is it really a week since ParkyCenters/Where's the week gone/I had such fun/wish I was back there. What a nice attitude towards her offspring and me. There is, of course, always the option of taking US to ParkyCenters, as I know for a fact that dogs are allowed, but that won't happen as She's too tight and it's too expensive. So I'll have to make do with the river as usual. Day after day.

It will just be He and me out for a walk tomorrow, as Lad, Young Lad and She are going to an Important Place in London to help out with Doctors exams. This is to help trainee Evil Vet type people qualify to become proper Evil Vet type people. They have helped out with these exams before. Lad knows more than the trainee doctors and can point out where they've gone wrong. Young Lad talks complete crap and they are unable to come to a diagnosis, but it's important to learn how to deal with kids that talk complete crap if you are going to be a doctor. Readers, the thing that's bothering me is that they are getting up ridiculously early for this. It's Saturday for the love of God! I will be very, very annoyed if they wake me up, and so will He. We are planning a long lie in tomorrow. I don't want to hear the ruddy hairdryer at 6am, nor the twenty minutes of shouting at Lad to bldywell get up we're going to miss the train. I will be displeased if I'm disturbed at that hour. On the plus side, He and I will have a very peaceful day with nobody here to annoy us.

Well, due to the very early start and long day in London tomorrow, bed-time will be nice and early tonight. It can never be too early for me. I imagine Gordon will be out on the working surface tomorrow evening, as a whole day stuck in a train carriage or hospital with Lad and Young Lad will require a heart to heart with Gordon to get over it. Lad and Young Lad are given a £20 Amazon voucher each for helping out with these exams. She gets diddly squat. And for the second weekend running, Homeless Guy outside Sainsbury's will not get his Greggs coffee.

CHAPTER FIFTY-FIVE

Foxy

January 28th

Evening, Friends – well, I had a lovely walk today and managed to find a nice pile of fox poo in Far Field. Oh, I rolled and rolled – rubbing it hard into the area under my ears and all over my collar. It was fabulous! And the amusing thing was that I waited until She was miles ahead nearly at the telegraph pole, so by the time the penny dropped that I was rolling in poo, it was far too late. I giggled at the hysterical running and shouting that went on. I can't help it if we're always on a tightbldyschedule – one of these days I might actually go for a long, unhurried walk without time constrictions. Anyway, I was put on the lead and marched smartly back through Far Field and along the river. Some very nicely dressed ladies stopped to talk to me – I've no idea what they were doing down there, as they didn't have a dog and were wearing pastels, – so I went all wriggly and lovable, but it was spoilt by the sharp, "he's just rolled in fox poo". This wasn't strictly necessary. Lad has been told he needs to bath me this afternoon, but I'm not convinced he'll get round to it.

So, Readers, I did warn you that it would be bldytiring being in London all day with Lad and Young Lad, but you will be impressed to know they made it onto the 7am train. This is no mean feat on a Saturday morning. I was woken by the hairdryer, as I had feared, but used the opportunity for a comfort break in the garden, then went back to sleep. Lad and Young Lad did very well, helping out with Doctor's exams. Although when Young Lad was asked if there were any other people close to him with medical conditions, I'm not sure they were looking for the answer, "oh yeah, the bloke up the road had a heart attack." Never mind.

Lad was of such interest to the Doctors that he was asked to stay behind for ages afterwards, so that a few more could stare at him and shine lights in his eye. They would have had to muzzle me if they'd tried such a thing. Lad was very patient. They both seemed underwhelmed with their Love2shop £10 e-voucher (it seems I was wrong about the £20 Amazon voucher) but money wasn't the point of the day.

In the meantime, He and I had an absolutely brilliant day. It was so peaceful, Readers! We had a good lie-in, then later in the morning went for a lovely walk. I was extremely well-behaved all day. He sprang into action, taking down the Christmas lights at long last- these lights are now on the dining room table, where they will stay for a few weeks. He also did the washing, and we both needed a sit down in front of the football after our busy morning. When She, Lad and Young Lad returned from London, everyone was too tired to cook properly yet again, so it was Harry Ramsdens and oven chips, with green vegetables of course; to show that their health is not completely neglected. I can't tell you how peaceful it was, just He and I all day. Nobody to nag us or shout at us.

Then, all change this morning. Admittedly everyone had a bit of a lie-in, after the early start yesterday, and then She "popped into town". Homeless Guy was back outside Sainsbury's – worryingly, his spot had been taken recently by a couple of other people, who are rolled up in sleeping bags sound asleep, with a pot out for money. This seems unfair on Homeless Guy, who has been in that spot for a long time and become something of a regular fixture. Plus he smiles and says hello, and tells you his medical problems and is very polite. So it was a relief to see him back there today, and She bought him a raspberry bun to go with his Dreggs coffee, to celebrate.

Then, oh Readers, then my Sunday morning deteriorated. Recently it has been deemed helpful to look after LovelyNeighbourOnTheRight's cockapoo puppy on a Sunday morning while they are out. (This didn't happen last week as She was too selfish and went to ParkyCenters.) But today we were back in this new routine. I don't like it. Cockapoo now comes round to our house, and bounces all over the ruddy place. Round the rooms and particularly, round me. It wants me to play, and I've made it clear on many occasions, that I don't do this.

Well, this morning the flipping thing just would not take NO for an answer. It jumped at me, over me, beside me, on me. It was like being attacked by a black mop. The final straw came when I got into my bed, thoroughly disgruntled, and IT GOT INTO MY BED WITH ME!!! I know! That's MY BED!! I was not having that. Absolutely no way – who the hell did he think he was? So I growled and barked and did a minor snapping thing, until it got out. How dare it get in my bed?!!

Pardon? Did you say something, Reader? "Isn't that what you do at Ebony and Pippa's houses and it really upsets them?" Completely different. No comparison at all. I'm a guest there, and they should celebrate my companionship, not moan that I'm in their bed. I'm not sure what "hypocritical" means, so it's no good saying it to me. I was livid. Eventually LovelyNeighbourOnTheRight's cockapoo was taken back home.

This afternoon Lad has worked hard on his Art. He has used some photos he found on her phone – one of the Bastard Swans at the river, and one of the "oh so gorgeous, just look at him!" muntjac from ParkyCenters last week. Lad is doing some drawing focusing on texture. The fox poo would have been far more interesting than the Bastard Swan or Bambi. Young Lad hoovered the ground floor but said the hoover was too heavy to carry upstairs. Young Lad also dusted the windowsills, but mostly this involved sitting on his bedroom windowsill playing with Airfix planes. Not the ones he got for Christmas(they're still in the boxes) but some old ones that Lad put together years ago. After doing the hoovering Young Lad said he was worn out and went for a sit down. In the meantime, He cut the grass and sawed up the Christmas Tree, taking it to the tip.

She has had a long drive this evening, as Nana aged 86 is having a hip operation tomorrow morning, so is in hospital. As usual, the hospital car park proved challenging for her, as did finding her way back to the main road afterwards. I'm afraid the Best of the Seventies CD was on in the car, so you know what to expect. (By the way, today's walk was in time to Take That's "These Days" – how very middle-aged). So we have been left home alone for the night, but hopefully Pack Leader will be back tomorrow night. I do hope Nana aged 86 gets on ok with her operation, even though she can't stand the sight of me.

Oh my word look at the time! McMafia has started!

CHAPTER FIFTY-SIX

Uncomfortable

January 30th

I had trouble today getting comfortable at Pippa's house. I had one heck of a job scrunching up the sofa cushions, to get them how I like them. Even then, I was on a bit of a slope, and so it wasn't ideal. I just had to make do. Sigh.

Now, Pippa's house has recently had a lot of work done to it, and is Impeccably Decorated and Clean. So it was better that I balanced precariously on top of the sofa, rather than shedding hairs on the new flooring. I am thoughtful, like that. I'm sure Pippa's Pack Leader didn't think I was out of order, treating her soft furnishings like this. Anyway, I had a lovely day at Pippa's, with people who are prepared to spend time with me.

The day had started really well, Readers! Lad left his toast on his bedside table while he was in the shower, so I tidied that up for him. I left the satsuma though, as I'm not a fan of citrus fruit. Then, as soon as they all left for work/school, I prowled around and found a Tupperware box that had contained Tomato Pasta for Lad's lunch yesterday. Instead of taking it out of his bag and washing it out, the box had been dumped on the kitchen work surface, and I could reach it. This was a right result. It was a bit tricky to get the lid off – those Tupperware lids are bastards at times – so I just chewed through the bottom of it. Once I'd cleared out most of the tomato sauce, I chucked it on the lounge floor. Lad won't be able to use that pot for his Tomato Pasta lunch again.

So all in all, a cracking start to the day. Toast and pasta sauce, plus the Guilt Chew they gave me as they left the house. Yesterday was fun, as well, as I went to Ebony's house for daycare, with the other people who Give A Damn About Me. Last night She was oh so tired yet again after a bldynice twoandahalfbldyhour drive back from seeing Nana aged 86, who had her Big Operation. It seems the traffic was a little vexing, so by the time She was home, had eaten, given some attention to all of us, it was time for bed. Incidentally, Nana aged 86 was doing well, and since returning to the ward from theatre hadn't paused for breath in three hours. I am very pleased that she is okay, dodgy heart and all, even though she still can't stand the sight of me. I don't hold grudges. Anyway, being there for Nana aged 86's operation meant She could spend time with her brother Funnygit, in the hospital coffee shop. This is always a Pleasure, and how they laughed as they bickered over whether to walk up the stairs to the ward or get the lift. (Funnygit insisted on the lift. There are only two floors, and I feel this is a poor show.) Thankfully, He, Lad and Young Lad all managed to survive while She was away, and they managed the staple fish fingers and chips, which is the default meal when Pack Leader is not here. Some vegetables wouldn't have gone amiss, though.

Young Lad has had to walk all the way home from school by himself the last two days. This is known as being a Latchkey Kid. It is a very long walk and one would feel sorry for him if he hadn't let slip that a friend's Mum also felt sorry for him and gave him a lift. Young Lad enjoys being the first one home in the afternoon. It enables him to sit on his backside in front of the Xbox with nobody nagging him. He has been told he needs to draw the curtains, put on the lights/heating, feed Gingercat and me, and change out of his school uniform BEFORE he goes on the Xbox, but this is a lot of instructions to process, and it's not surprising that he doesn't remember any of them. Apart from feeding Gingercat and I, as we don't let him forget.

Anyway, I've digressed. Yesterday at Ebony's house was fun, although I was not happy to see Ebony's Pack Leader Male waving a copy of the Screwfix catalogue at me. He is a lovely man but Is On A Mission to keep me out of our food cupboard. He thinks he has found the answer in the Screwfix catalogue and is coming round to Sort It very soon. I thought he was my friend.

What I do need to mention, Readers, is that I inadvertently told you Ebony and I were both well-behaved on our walk on Friday. This is incorrect. I was well-behaved. Ebony was appalling. She ran off with a fisherman's rod bag and had to be chased all over the shop. Then she ran back and took his other bag! I know! Honestly, Ebony was screaming with laughter the whole time, whilst her Pack Leader was Beside Herself. The fisherman was Not A Happy Man, but if you will go fishing in a popular dog-walking area, what do you expect? My behaviour was exemplary.

Then yesterday, Ebony ran off and didn't listen to her Pack Leader, whilst I stood still and paid very close attention to her. And what do you know? We bumped into dear Pippa down at the river! My two very best friends in the whole world - we played and played, until Ebony discovered a foxhole and put her head down it. It was a lovely day, Readers, lovely.

Well it's very peaceful here tonight. He has gone to watch Wet Sham yet again – you would think the attraction would have worn off a long time ago. Young Lad is seemingly unencumbered by homework ("It doesn't need to be in till Thursday") so is watching yet another episode of Chicago Fire. It's an improvement on River Monsters or World's Craziest Weather. Just. Lad is busy on his phone. It's very peaceful, but it won't last. She has just had a long chat to Nana aged 86 on the phone, and Nana aged 86 is Worn Out from a day of X-rays, physiotherapy and other tests. She still managed to talk without pausing for 23 minutes (this was being Kept An Eye On, as it was on mobiles.) I, Readers, am exhausted from a day at Pippa's today, and Ebony's yesterday. Oh what a surprise! I'm farmed out for daycare again tomorrow as they're all at work or school yet again.

Why did they get me? Why can't I live with Meghan Markle? I know for a fact she doesn't go to work every day. Or ever, really.

CHAPTER FIFTY-SEVEN

Hot Chocolate

February 1st

Yesterday morning, Readers, my head was covered in the cold dregs of Lad's hot chocolate. I had simply put my head into the dishwasher as it was being loaded – a perfectly reasonable thing to do – when someone placed a mug upside down on the top rack, and cold hot chocolate dregs spattered all over my white head. This was at the last minute, as they were rushing out the house, so there was nosoddingtime to clean me up. I had to go to Ebony's house with brown stains all over me – it was humiliating. This is clearly Neglect. Thankfully, Ebony's Pack Leader is kind and cleaned me up, so that I didn't have to go out for my walk looking ridiculous. I had a lovely day with Ebony, as usual.

It was fraught here again last night. Yes, it was Wednesday which is always a latehomefromwork night, and yes, Young Lad had cricket, and yes, there was some desperate chasing up of Lad's prescription before the pharmacy bldyshut, but really there was no need for all the stressy shouting. Thankfully He collected Young Lad from cricket, to save more dashing round and moaning.

This morning there was an Early Morning Crisis. Young Lad couldn't find his school tie. He had it last night, at cricket practice but it has since disappeared. This caused a lot of panic as Young Lad was worried he would get a Detention. I think this is a bit like being told "In Your Bed."

Anyway, Readers, the question you and I are asking ourselves, is why has he only got one tie? Anyone with a modicum of sense would always have bought a spare. In fact, this has been on the "to-do" list for several months, but has never made it off the "to-do" list. Poor Young Lad. This is another example of Neglect. A letter was hastily scribbled to explain why Young Lad didn't have a tie, and to ask if the school could lend him one. All this hassle by 7.15am. It was exhausting.

In fact, once She had left to do the school drop and "pop into town", I had a little sleep, then was so bored that I had to go into the cupboard under the stairs – yes, you know quite well that it still hasn't been tidied out – and drag my new pack of food out. I did the usual – ripped it open and helped myself. I also threw some hoover bags round the lounge for something to do. Then She came back and I had to sit through the usual absurd "WHO did this?" routine. Change the record. Now, Readers, I did tuck into my food quite heavily once I'd ripped it open, and haven't even needed dinner tonight. I am making a lot of bad smells, though.

It was a beautiful morning, Friends, absolutely glorious. It was stunning down by the river, and the Bastard Swans still haven't made an appearance. I had such a lovely time – first of all, I spotted his grey marbled coat shining ahead of me; yes, it was my dear friend Chuck. He was in stunning condition, glossy and smooth. We sniffed each others' backsides happily for a while, and then I was shouted at to hurry up.

Over the bridge we went, into Top Field today, which was very muddy. There were lots of new smells and I took my time investigating every one of them. I was a very long way behind her when I stopped for a comfort break – and again, dropped it in some long grass so that it was a challenge to find. The mood was not good. Irritably, She put me back on the lead for the last part of Top Field as I was Too Bldy Slow.

Suddenly, a vision leapt in front of me, and it was Chuck again! He had run away from his Pack Leader to come and find me. I was allowed off the lead, and we romped away for a little while – Chuck's Pack Leader used a different word from romp, but I didn't understand it and I think it was a bit rude. Later on I saw NicedogwalkerLady and the three hundred brown labradors. They stopped for a chat, and NiceDogWalkerLady's husband said something about humans being stupid and dogs being clever. He's absolutely right.

Pardon Me. That was rather a loud one. This doesn't bode well for this evening.

Once home, there was furious cleaning to be done. This bored me, so I stayed in my bed in the kitchen to have a kip. Eventually I was allowed to get into my chair which had a clean sheet on. It wasn't clean for long.

Do you know what happened next, Readers? I can barely find the words. In came Ebony's Pack Leader Male, whom I love dearly. Instead of the Screwfix catalogue he had a package, and a drill. Readers, he fixed a special lock to the Food Cupboard. They think this will keep me out of the Food Cupboard, but I like a challenge. I'm really very upset at this betrayal by someone that I thought cared about me, and intend showing them what I think of the Screwfix lock tomorrow morning, when they've all gone to work. Watch this space. I refused to talk to Ebony's Pack Leader Male, while he was here, and gave him my disappointed look. I don't like to use the word Judas, but I will.

So the house is relatively clean for once, but not if you look in any corners. It's been raining this afternoon and I've been in and out to the garden a lot, so the kitchen floor looks exactly the same as it did before She did the cleaning. But on the plus side, the Christmas Lights have been moved from the dining room table to Lad's bedroom ready to go in the roof. This will happen by Easter at a push.

Lad has yet another House Party to go to this weekend. There will be the usual lecture about behaviour and safety and don'tmakeabldy show of yourself. You'll be pleased to know, Readers, that Nana aged 86 is recovering well from her operation, even though she was high on drugs yesterday. Today she was quite abrupt with a poor Doctor who tried to send her home, so she is staying in hospital for another night or two.

There has been a little problem. When She went down to look after Nana aged 86's cat last weekend, She very sensibly went round Nana aged 86's house, unplugging anything electrical to minimise fire risk. Unfortunately this included the freezer. Apparently the kitchen is now swimming in defrosted salmon in watercress sauce, and other such ready meals. Nana aged 86 laughed about this. I suspect she is still high on drugs. At least I can't be blamed for this disaster, which makes a refreshing change. Though I would have cleaned up the kitchen for her.

Talking of which, dinner tonight was bangers and mash with gravy. This is excellent on the dishwasher loading front, as the plates are a mess. While they were all eating at the dinner table (yes, I know! Civilised!), I inadvertently let out a very, very loud noise from under the table. They all looked at each other in disbelief. It could be an interesting evening.

CHAPTER FIFTY-EIGHT

Screwed by Screwfix

February 3rd

Unbelievable. This old-fashioned, low-tech bit of metal has so far kept me out of the food cupboard. It has succeeded where the Velcro strips failed so spectacularly. (Seriously, Velcro?! What were they thinking?!) Ebony's Pack Leader male, who will from now on be known as Judas, is probably very pleased with himself. But Readers, don't worry – I haven't given up on this. For all you know, I might not have even TRIED to get into the food cupboard yesterday. Perhaps I was too busy and had other things to do! Yes, in fact that's what happened. I didn't even try. Watch this space on Monday when they're all at work/school – don't doubt my resilience, Friends.

I had been impeccably behaved at home, yesterday, when Pippa's Pack Leader came to collect me for daycare. These are rare occurrences, and I get no credit for them of course. Plus, despite having been warned to the contrary, Pippa's Pack Leader said that I smelled absolutely fine all day at their house. That's because I had spent the ENTIRE evening and night before releasing strong and loud gas into the atmosphere at home, which was the result of raiding my new sack of food and rather overdoing it. It was a good job nobody bothered to light the scented candles, because I worry what might have happened when that match was struck. They were too lazy to get off the sofa and hunt for the matches in the disgusting cupboard under the stairs, so they just sat there with their jumpers pulled over their noses shouting, "Oh RUSSELL!" every two minutes. Anyway, by the next morning I had released all the gas from my stomach so didn't stink out Pippa's house the way I had stunk out my own.

I had a lovely day with Pippa. We had a splendid walk down at the river in the afternoon, and I was really quite energetic, running and trying hard to keep up with her. It was all that carbohydrate. He came to collect me once he'd picked Young Lad up from school and we all had a very peaceful hour until Lad and She got home. Being Friday, of course, it was Slovenly Pizza night, which is one of my favourite evenings as my whole family are squeezed on the sofa together, eating Tesco Margherita Stonebaked and Tear and Share garlic bread. I would personally prefer stuffed crust, as there's a bit more to it, but nobody consults me.

I love Friday nights though. I sit and stare at all four of them in turn, making my eyes go all big and extra brown, and lifting my soft ears slightly to look beguiling. If that doesn't work, I whine and bark. Usually someone caves in and gives me a bit of crust and some carrot sticks. It's a lovely weekly ritual we have. Then Lad goes off to the Xbox for the evening, and Young Lad will settle down in front of Chicago Fire. Season 5 seems to be going on forever. I was so tired from my lovely walk with Pippa that I lay upside down in my chair, with paws waving in the air as I slept.

There was one unpleasant moment during the evening, though. I was fast asleep in my chair, when Gingercat came over and decided to sharpen his claws on the arm of the chair. This makes a hideous scratchy noise and doesn't do a lot for the fabric. Readers, it frightened the life out of me. I opened my eyes, looked down and saw Gingercat with his sharp claws, and just for a moment, had no idea who he was! I leapt out of the chair with a whimper and ran in terror to my Family on the Sofa, where I jumped up onto His lap and shook. They, of course, were all laughing hysterically that I had been spooked by a cat with whom I've lived for three years, and showed no concern for my traumatised state at all. It was very scary. Yes, I'm bigger than Gingercat and would clearly win in a fight, but I was VERY disorientated! It took me ages to calm down.

Eventually Chicago Fire finished, and it was time for drinks. There was a bit of a debate, as She had forgotten to buy a bottle of red wine on the way home, so He had to pop up the road to get one. Needless to say, the stock of her friend Gordon in the cupboard was fine – look after number onewhy don't you. There was lots of sighing about, "thank God it's Friday," and He fell asleep before the end of Eastenders. Bedtime was nice and early, I'm pleased to say, except for Lad who managed to keep going until midnight. I was annoyed to be woken when he tried to put Gingercat out at that hour. Gingercat wasn't having any of it and it was rather noisy.

Today, Readers, even though it's the weekend, I have been left alone rather a lot again. This is because Nana aged 86 is coming out of hospital, and so She has to drive a bldylongway to stay with her overnight. I saw her put the overnight bag in the car – I don't like that bag. First of all of course, She 'popped into town' and even bought Homeless Guy outside Sainsbury's a Costalotta coffee. This was due to being on yet another tightbdlyschedule and not having time to queue up in Dreggs. So he had a better quality coffee, but no raspberry bun this time. Young Lad has also been neglected today – dumped with a friend for the day, regardless of how convenient this might or might not be for people. A list of homework has been written out for him, and there is some hope that he might get Maths and French done at his friend's house today, but I would think this unlikely. Lad needed a long lie in this morning, after his late night, and only surfaced in time to go out and meet his friends in a town far away, for yet another House Party tonight. He did manage to send repeated text messages asking if She could transfer some money to his bank account URGENTLY, otherwise he wouldn't be able to buy a healthy, nutritious lunch at KFC. It didn't seem to occur to him that She wouldn't be able to do this while driving on the M25 in the pouring rain.

So Young Lad was dumped with a friend, Lad went out, and He has gone to work. I, Readers, have been rescued from the boredom of all this by Ebony's Pack Leader yet again. She took us for a lovely walk over in the fields, but it had been raining hard, so Ebony and I were rather muddy. When we got home, we were put in the back garden and the Tap was Turned On. This means I'm going to be hosed down and I don't like it. I took on a very cowed and defeated kind of pose in the hope that she would feel sorry for me. It didn't work.

It will be a quiet evening, tonight, with only He and Young Lad here. We will have a lovely time.

CHAPTER FIFTY-NINE

Invincible

February 5th

You knew it. I knew it. And I suspect, in his heart, 'Judas' knew it. I was not going to be kept out of that food cupboard for long. What happened this morning during the school drop off was simply a case of getting my claws in exactly the right spot under the door rim, and using just the right amount of force to yank it clear of that ruddy Screwfix catch. Once in, I knocked the top off my box of food and helped myself to a couple of meals – it was snowing slightly outside, and I was cold! My stomach is rather distended again now, and we all know what that means for a bit later. Anyway, I am VERY pleased with myself and it is one-nil to the Beagle. I needed a sleep after this, so wasn't pleased to be told we were going for a long walk. In fact, I rebelled and refused to get out of my chair, so had to be attached to the lead in the lounge, and dragged bodily from where I was.

That said, it was a pretty good walk today. Firstly I bolted off to the area where some residents throw out food for the birds, or me, and was delighted to find they'd chucked a load of cornflakes on the grass. This was a nice dessert after my extra two meals that I'd just eaten. She was really cross with me and had to march back from half a mile away, to put me on the lead and drag me off. Near the river we bumped into NicedogwalkerLady and her husband, and the three hundred brown labradors. We had a chat, and there was a comment made that it's important for me to misbehave at home, otherwise my book would be boring. This statement has the wisdom of Solomon behind it – how very true.

We went off over the bridge into Far Field, where I rolled in some fox poo and was shouted at. There was some fast marching round the field, this time to Pink's "All About Us." At least this is more contemporary than the usual songs in her head. It was rather aggressive fast walking today – possibly to compensate for sitting in the car on the bldymotorway for half the weekend – and I am quite sure Pink hasn't ever sung "All About Us" at that speed, unless she's taken something. In fact we walked three miles in under fifty minutes, which included stopping for chats with people, so you can see how rushed this was. On the bridge coming back from Far Field, we bumped into dear, dear Chuck who looked as handsome as ever. How he keeps the white parts of his magnificent coat so pristine, out in the woods, I do not know. She had a long chat with Chuck's Pack Leader while he was waiting for someone called Sausage Sue and her many dogs to catch him up.

Further on I could see the Inspirational three-legged dog, but thankfully he was a long way away so we didn't have to stop and tell him, yet again, how inspirational he is. So tedious. On the way back there was a very large white Samoi, which looked a little threatening so I had to do a very wide detour of it. "For God's sake, Russell," and "pathetic" weren't the words of comfort I needed.

I'm trying to have a sleep now that we're home, but oh no, there's frantic hoovering going on and tidying up (that won't extend as far as the cupboard under the stairs, Regular Readers, I can guarantee). So Gingercat and I are trying to sleep against the backdrop of the hoover AND the washing machine. It's awful.

He took me for a lovely walk yesterday afternoon – it was quite late on in the day, and I didn't see many of my friends, but I behaved well for him, as I usually do. Young Lad was supposedly doing his homework – I'm not sure that three sentences will be enough – and Lad had eventually returned from the house party the night before. Apparently this was, "yeah, good" and required not going to sleep until some ridiculous hour. As normal, the female versions of Lad were all in a bad way and being sick in the garden at the house party. People are very strange in what they class as a good time. She eventually rocked home at tea-time, having been looking after Nana aged 86 as she came out of hospital. It had been a Difficult Journey Home, as they had shut thebldymotorway for bldyroadworks so there was a 50 minute bldydiversion through the bldycountryside with three thousand other motorists. Even I thought She looked a little tired, and gave her an extra warm welcome. By the time She had arrived home, knocked up a vegetable curry out of concern for the crap convenience food everyone had eaten in her absence, told Young Lad his homework wasn't good enough, and acquainted herself with Gordon, it was time for McMafia. I still fail to see the attraction of this – half the time it's in Russian with subtitles, and bores me to tears. But I think we probably do all know what the attraction of it is, don't we.

Oooof, that's the first of many making its way out. Readers, you are lucky to not be in the same room as me.

Well, I've heard some muttering about rearranging the kitchen cupboards, as I can clearly breach any kind of lock or catch that Screwfix and 'Judas' care to try. I had better go and keep an eye on where She's putting things. Though I won't worry too much, as I expect He, Lad and Young Lad will soon put things back in their normal place. The cupboards are extra full, due to this morning's Large Food shop. This was done at Tesco, to avoid having to buy Homeless Guy outside Sainsbury's a coffee today. Nice attitude. I sincerely hope something decent to put in my Kong was purchased, as this morning it was two small spoons of cold, going-off custard. I kid you not.

Two biblical references in one chapter! And a cupboard breached. Don't ever underestimate me, dear Friends.

CHAPTER SIXTY

PG Tips

February 6th

I was SO annoyed this morning, Readers. When they all went off to work and school, I went straight to the Food Cupboard- as we all know I can get in there, Screwfix catch or no Screwfix catch. Normally my big box of food is on the bottom shelf, and I like to help myself to an extra breakfast or three. However, what did I find? They've MOVED my food box out of the cupboard! What the actual heck? Not just put it on a higher shelf, Readers, but removed it from the cupboard altogether. I was LIVID.

In sheer and utter frustration, I dragged out a box of PG Tips and took them into the lounge, where I chucked them round the floor. I chewed holes in the box, too. Next I had a look in the back porch and found a Shreddies box that had been put out for recycling (actually it was Tesco's own version as they're at least a pound cheaper. Tightwads.) So, still feeling aggrieved, I threw that round the lounge as well. How dare they move my food! It's now On Top Of The Fridge, for the love of God. How am I meant to get up there? Don't worry, I'm thinking about it.

So that was not a good start to the day. When She came in from the school run, I sensed displeasure about the tea bags all over the carpet, but it serves them right. Under the table was an empty Penne Pasta packet, too, which it took her a while to find. Dried pasta doesn't taste of much, but the crunchiness is good for my teeth. After a while, we decided to kiss and make up, and go for a lovely walk. This didn't start well, either, as at the bottom of our road was a HUGE group of schoolchildren, walking menacingly in twos. The line of them went back as far as the eye could see, and I was terrified by their alarming chatter, and disturbing Hi-Vis jackets. Readers, this was very frightening, and I had to hide behind her legs.

Once we'd bypassed this threat, though, it was yet another stunning day – bitterly cold, it must be said, but blue skies and sunshine all the way. Firstly we bumped into dear Ebony and her Pack Leader, coming home from their walk. Needless to say there was the usual discussion about our respective behaviour, and how bad/good Ebony and I are in different situations. Ebony and I were very bored by this. Moving on down the path, I decided on a whim to take on two German Shepherds. I haven't done this for a while, and had forgotten what an error of judgement it is. Luckily I was on the lead, so could be yanked out of the way. Then, by the river, who should we see but Barney the Oh So Adorable Beagle? Barney and I were quite playful for three and a half seconds, before both finding an interesting scent and going off with our noses on the ground. She walked with Barney's Pack Leader for a long way, discussing the Evils and Merits of Beagles. Barney also gets into the food cupboards at home, and they have had to put child locks on. Notice they didn't try strips of Velcro!!! Still laughing about that one. Then, Readers, I heard She and Barney's Pack Leader oohing and aahing over something by the river. "Oooh look, it's an Egret, you don't often see those, isn't it lovely, so pure white, what a beautiful creature, I wonder if it's nesting," yada yada yada. It's a white bird. Innit. Strewth.

Once they could tear themselves away from an unexciting white bird, we caught up with NiceDogWalkerLady and her husband and the three hundred brown labradors. Plus, to my delight, dear dear Chuck! Still gleaming in the sunshine. Today, though, instead of a lengthy sniff of Chuck's rear end, I stood on my own by the gate into Far Field, looking scared. Readers, large numbers overwhelm me, and there were just too many dogs congregated in one place. It was intimidating. I hope Chuck understands my rejection of his rear end today. I hadn't completely recovered from the Fluorescent Yellow Snake of Horrid Schoolchildren.

Back home it was fairly peaceful for a while, until the Hoover was plugged in again. I have to confess this was a little self-inflicted, as I had spat bits of cardboard from the PG Tips box everywhere. Eventually, She went off to work, and I had a lovely time going through the Food Cupboard once more. They might have moved my food box out, but I can still get hold of the tin foil and chuck it around, plus I knocked a couple of tins down and took a can of sardines into the lounge. I haven't yet worked out how to get into tins, but it won't take me long. When Young Lad came in from school, he had to clear up the tin foil and the cans. This was exhausting for him, and more to the point, delayed his session on the Xbox. Even by my own standards, I have been a bit of a monkey today, but I feel there has been a point to be made.

Lad has had a long day at school and is supposedly doing his Chemistry homework now. Last night we had Quiet Time after tea, so everyone could get on with their work. Young Lad was encouraged to add to the three sentences he wrote at the weekend, though this was thwarted by Gingercat lying on top of his page as he was trying to write. Then Gingercat headbutted Young Lad, and Young Lad's pen. Not known for his concentration, Young Lad found it hard to get on with his English under these circumstances. Lad had a Maths Past Paper which was BLDY IMPOSSIBLE and required a lot of shouting of what the actual hell, and inappropriate things like that. One question was very vexing: "if $P - n + 1$, explain why DBA is a straight line." What a load of cobblers.

He was in late tonight, after a Long Day at Work. Thankfully, dinner was lasagne so it just needed heating up for him, and also the plates were shocking in the dishwasher, which gave me something to do. Don't worry, it's on extra hot wash again for sterilising purposes. She has had an exasperating day at work, as Colleagues 1 and 2 were Whatsapped last night asking if they could bring in their passports to countersign Young Lad's passport – this needs to go in the post pretty pronto. Colleague 1 and C

olleague 2 both said yes of course they would, and Colleague 1 and 2 both then forgot. Although it turns out that Colleague 2 did actually have his passport with him, but forgot that he had it with him. She has been sighing a lot tonight.

It is VERY cold tonight and I've heard some mention of the word snow. I'm at Ebony's house tomorrow, so I don't want snow to interrupt our smashing walk together. I think I might start talking to 'Judas' again – he's had his punishment, and anyway, the silly catch didn't work.

What a busy day I've had! And another one tomorrow as it's Wednesday and everything is on that bldytightschedule as usual.

CHAPTER SIXTY-ONE

Look Who's Back

February 8th

Oh I had a traumatic time at the river today, Friends. It really was a shocker. Not only were the Bastard Swans back – and of course, we couldn't just do a wide detour away from them, we had to go and lean over the ruddy railings to talk to them, as if the Bastard Swans cared – but nearly ALL my phobias were tested in one walk!

Dear Teddy was down there, which was fine, but his Pack Leader will insist on bringing her friend with her, the one with the skin colour I don't like and an American accent. So I had to steer clear of them. Then, up in Top Field, were the three collies that I've seen before, who terrify me! I had to whimper a lot, and stand with my front paw in the air, unsure what to do. I just didn't know how to get past them. One of them had a tennis ball in his mouth, and looked VERY threatening. In the end I managed a half mile detour through some long grass so that I didn't have to walk past them.

As if this wasn't enough, down by the river where the path narrows, came another huge group of schoolchildren! At least this lot didn't have Hi-Vis jackets on, but even so, the nasty mumbling chatter and long, long line of them was frightening. I had to be put on the lead and stand behind her until they'd all gone past. It still wasn't over. We went into Far Field, and I spotted a man in a Dark Blue Coat with a Bobble Hat further over in the field, and felt sure he was up to no good. So I had to bark and bray in my best Beagle voice, to show him who he was up against.

By golly, it was exhausting. Apart from all the scares, it was a lovely walk, as the day was crisp and frosty, with beautiful sunshine. I needed a comfort break at one point, and made sure I found some very long grass in which to deposit it, to heighten the challenge of finding it for the little black bag. I also walked around a bit whilst in the middle of the comfort break, as I know this winds her up even more. We walked for over three miles, covering Top Field and Far Field, and saw virtually everyone – Chuck, Teddy, Nicedogwalkerlady and the three hundred brown labradors. Everyone was out enjoying the sunshine. Even her pelvic floor held up, for once, and we managed the walk back up the hill without the sudden dash. Since I've been back, I've had to have a kip, as all the adrenalin rushing through my body dealing with all my fears has quite worn me out.

Last night Young Lad was at cricket practice, everyone was late home from work and there was such a bldy lot to do. Needless to say, dinner was the usual rushed Wednesday night convenience affair, this time of egg and chips. Not a lot on the plates for me, as they went in the dishwasher. How selfish of them. I was shouted at after tea for grabbing a mixing bowl out of the dishwasher and running off with it; well, there was some cake mixture on it, which I love. I once ran off with the beaters from the food mixer, when they had cake mixture on, and then buried them in the garden when I'd finished with them. This story didn't end well, as they couldn't find the beaters in the garden, until they ran over them with the lawnmower. It was bitterly cold last night, and I did feel a bit sorry for Gingercat being shut in the kitchen as usual – this seems unkind, and just because he walks round the house yowling at 3am and pats everyone on the face, I don't feel he should be ostracised like this.

I had a good root around in the hideous cupboard under the stairs while She was out for an hour this morning. Things became somewhat tricky as the ironing board had been slung in rather precariously and it fell on top of me. This caused the hoover and various other things to topple over. It really is disgusting – apparently this cupboard is to be cleared out next week, but I'll believe it when I see it. There had been Panic Ironing at 6.30am when it was realised that neither Lad nor Young Lad had a clean, ironed school shirt. How many times do I have to say it? Time. Management. In most working parents' households, five clean, ironed school shirts are hung up in wardrobes on a Sunday night for a calm, organised week. But not in this house, oh no. Since we've been back from our walk, bldy paperwork and bldy emails have been attended to, and the large stack of paperwork in the study has been redistributed into several smaller piles.

Yesterday I had a lovely time at dear, dear Ebony's house. We had a smashing walk together, and I decided to forgive her Pack Leader Male (I'll no longer call him Judas) for fixing the inefficient lock to the Food Cupboard. He really is rather nice, and I do love him after all.

Well, Readers, I felt a little frisky after dinner tonight and have been running round the lounge with a tennis ball, growling a lot. Lad has been chasing me, and trying to get the ball away. Lad is meant to be doing his homework. One could suggest that this is an avoidance tactic. Anyway, nobody can get the ball away from me and I am growling and barking very ferociously. Oh look. Young Lad has joined in. Young Lad is also meant to be doing his homework. Lad and Young Lad are now both lying on the carpet with me, and no homework is being done. They will be shouted at soon to bldywellgetonwithit and stopfaffingaround. Oh look. Now He has joined us on the carpet. We really are having a splendid time, He, Lad, Young Lad and I – all chasing around after a tennis ball and rolling on the carpet. Notice the one person who isn't joining in. Typical.

Dinner tonight was disappointing from the messy plates point of view – Harry Ramsdens, creamed potatoes and veg. No gravy or sloppy liquid. It would be nice if this were considered of a day, when dreaming up the haute cuisine menu.

I'm at dear Pippa's house tomorrow, so will have a lovely day.

CHAPTER SIXTY-TWO

Margherita

February 9th

I am In Disgrace, Readers. I was sent to my bed, and the kitchen door was shut on me. All I did was wander into the study, and happen to notice that Lad had put down his plate with a slice of pizza on it, on the table. Whilst his back was turned, I felt I ought to tidy up a bit so snatched the pizza like greased lightning, and dashed off with it. Lad was very, very annoyed and raised his voice – he virtually never gets cross with me. He shouted, "RUSSELL! NAUGHTY!!" so I growled at him, to show how much I respect his authority. Then he sent me to my bed, but I had eaten the pizza by this time and it was jolly nice. I would do the same again.

Anyway, it wasn't long before someone opened the kitchen door and forgot I was In Disgrace, so now I'm back on the sofa cuddled up on the fleece. Look, my Regular Readers know quite well that Friday night is slovenly pizza night, and I think it would be nice to include me in this sometimes.

I'm pretty exhausted tonight, actually, and struggling to keep my eyes open. I've had a lovely day at Pippa's house, and we had a fabulous walk this afternoon. The Bastard Swans weren't there, but Pippa's Pack Leader made a point of going and leaning over the railing to have a look. She pays close attention to my blog. I blotted my copybook rather, though, by finding a wonderful pile of fox poo and having a good old roll. Oh, it felt so nice! All down my back, such a special smell. There were attractive streaks of fox cack all along my back, where I rolled over and over. Such long streaks! And a goodly lot round my collar. It was heavenly. Unfortunately Pippa's Pack Leader didn't agree, and when we got home, I had to be washed thoroughly. Again. Well, it gave her something to do. And she uses a lovely hypo-allergenic shampoo, not the Value Range that we have at home. Pippa didn't roll in any fox poo, and was generally better behaved.

I needed a sleep back at Pippa's house, and before I knew it, She had turned up to collect me. By this time I was starving and wanted to get home for dinner, but oh no, She and Pippa's Pack Leader had to stand there chatting for fifteen minutes...... I was so bored. I tried barking and whining but they did the "ignore him" thing, so in the end I sat down and waited. And waited. It was rather selfish of them.

There was yet another Panic this morning, as Young Lad and She were driving to school/work. Young Lad had painstakingly written a piece of homework last night about the changes in England after William the Conqueror took control. He had thought of one thing. Thankfully, Lad has also covered this period of History and could think of a few more. Once they reached the other side of town this morning, though, Young Lad realised he'd left his History book on the snooker table at home. This is when the Panic ensued. He would be in a Lot Of Trouble. Eventually an agreement was reached – She would text Lovelyneighbourontheright and ask them to pop in and search for the History book, as they surely wouldn't have much else to do at 8am, like get two children ready for school. Then they could deliver the book to her at work, and She would drive down to Young Lad's school with it at lunchtime. Young Lad seemed happy with this arrangement – but I feel Young Lad hasn't learned a lesson from this. Readers, this is Shoddy Parenting and involves relying heavily on the goodwill of neighbours. Yet Again.

Lad has had a long day and says he has a bad headache, but will doubtless manage several hours on the Xbox tonight, as he is such a Trooper. Young Lad is now watching Chicago Fire – yep, still Season 5 – which at the moment is focusing on a chef who has had an accident with a knife and cut his hand off. Readers, I'm thinking the same thing: A) what garbage and B) what's it got to do with the fire brigade? He is reading the paper, and She has been trying to find out what's happened to Nana aged 86. The last She heard (yesterday) Nana aged 86 had gone to hospital as she thought she'd broken her leg. The one that had a new hip only ten days ago. Only Nana aged 86 could manage such a thing. It turns out it isn't broken, but it is a Medical Mystery like so many things about Nana aged 86, and she's still in hospital while they try to work out what's happened. Nana aged 86's medical notes make War and Peace look like a comic, and a special trolley has to be used to wheel them around. I do hope she gets home soon, even though she dislikes me.

I needed a comfort break at 5.30 this morning – it can't be helped! She was so grumpy about it, moaning that it wasn't bldyworth going back to bldysleep as the bldyalarm would be going off in 20 minutes. Most people would have simply got up and seized the day, maybe taking the opportunity to clear out the cupboard under the stairs, but oh no. Back to bed we went, with much huffing and puffing when the alarm went off twenty minutes later. So I wasn't popular. Again. Maybe because of this, my Kong filling this morning was, wait for it, cold baked beans. No word of a lie. Just look at the recent track record – cold porridge, cold fish pie, cold Brown Windsor soup gloup, and now cold baked beans. I mean, I ate it of course, but really.

Well, Friends, thankfully we all have a bit of a lie-in tomorrow! Nobody has to get up early. Gingercat will probably start yowling at 5am, then I'll need a comfort break at 6am, but it's a lie-in of sorts. I'm looking forward to it. Nobody is at school or work for the whole weekend. Marvellous – I'll get some walks and attention. Young Lad wants to meet up with a friend and "hang out" tomorrow, and She has texted her good friend Loadsakids, whom She hasn't seen for ages, to see if she fancies meeting for coffee. Loadsakids has said she was thinking about a trip to Ikea, so She said you need your bldyheadreadwoman, and Loadsakids might change her mind.

Lad will spend the entire morning in bed, and will moan when told to get up at lunchtime. There was a suggestion that Lad might like to go to the cinema to see "Journey's End", which he is studying for GCSE. Lad pulled a very strange face, and said, "are you mad?" when this was suggested. That's a no, then. Never mind, He and Young Lad might go to watch the film about Winston Churchill. This sounds dull beyond belief.

Oh, just a quick update. You'll be glad to know that Young Lad's Passport has now been countersigned. Colleagues 1 and 2 may have been a bit slack earlier in the week, but were virtually fighting over the chance to redeem themselves. Young Lad will now be able to travel, if She remembers to put it in the bldypost.

Golly, I'm exhausted.

CHAPTER SIXTY-THREE

Exhaustion

February 11th

Readers, if you force me out for TWO long walks in one day, I fall asleep sitting bolt upright. This is what happened today, as unprecedented levels of exhaustion hit me – partly due to too many walks, plus, it being Sunday, we 'look after' Lovelyneighbourontheright's Cockapoo puppy. Well. The young whippersnapper came round this morning and got on my nerves, frankly – he does not stop bouncing around and jumping on my head, and it drives me INSANE. Everywhere I went, he followed – he even re-distributed the recycling I had carefully placed round the garden! SO annoying. I have special places for the things out of the recycling sacks – certain things go under certain bushes, and I wasn't happy that he changed my system. The Harry Ramsden Cod in Batter box does NOT go under the rose bush! Grrrr. After an hour and a half of me snapping and barking at the youngster, he was taken back home. Even Gingercat arched his back and hissed at Lovelyneighbourontheright's Cockapoo, but the darned pup still seemed to enjoy himself!

Then we went for a three-mile walk, which was lovely, but just about finished me off. As we were going down the alleyway to the river, She suddenly stopped because her foot was uncomfortable in her wellington boot. When investigated, it transpired there was a drill bit in her boot. I know. It gets better. Up in the fields, when I was rolling in poo, She tried to pull the whistle out of her coat pocket, and instead pulled out a different drill bit. It beggars belief. Thankfully I was saved the embarrassment of her actually blowing the Drill Bit, but even so.
How many other Pack Leaders are wandering around with random items of hardware in their pockets and boots? None.

Never mind, it was a stunning day down at the river – cold, mark you, but a beautiful blue sky and bright sunshine. There were many dogs and children down there, all having a lovely time. It was a slight mistake to vary our route, and go down along the river bank, as this was extremely muddy and potential falling face first scenarios were a real risk. Legs and wellington boots were completely caked in mud, and there was some sliding backwards up the hilly part. Good job there was nobody else around to see, as they had all sensibly stuck to the path. As we should have done. We went over the bridge into Top Field, but some people were riding BMX bikes in there today – ruddy noisy things. I hate them. I barked menacingly at one man in a helmet and muddy overalls, who was sitting astride his BMX by the gate. He knew I meant business.

Once home, I was more than ready for a kip, but no; some dried up French bread was put out on the bird table, which meant I had to run in and out for another hour to snatch up everything the birds dropped. It being a lovely day, some gardening was done – the first of the year! Apparently the Ruddy Buddleia needed to be chopped right down – this is one of the Most Hated Jobs of All Time and has to be done twice a year. With a lot of moaning and groaning, She climbed up a ladder and hacked the poor ten-foot bush to death, and then paid Lad to chop it all up and cram it in the green bin. There was no way it was all going to fit, so both Lad and Young Lad were forced to climb into the green bin on top of all the branches, and jump up and down. This is not the way they wanted to spend their Sunday afternoon, and it seems cruel. At any rate, the garden looks a little better for having some light in it now, but I wasn't thrilled that Lad had to clear up all my recycling collage as part of his payment.

Yesterday, Readers, was the main cause of my tiredness today. He had a day off from work, and decided to take me for a lovely long walk in the morning while She was out. He and I have lovely walks together – He doesn't shout at me or tell me to hurry up all the time. Though I did run off to the houses (to look through the bins) at one point, so He had to put me on the lead after that. Then, in the afternoon, She decided to take me for a long walk as well!! This is for the Exercise Quotient, and my regular Readers will know that we Can't Afford Gym Membership And A Dog, as we like to remind me once a week, so I had to go for another power walk, even longer than the morning's! I could barely move when I got home – yes, most dogs thrive on this kind of lifestyle and enjoy the exercise, but I am not most dogs, as you should know by now. I was shattered, and slept heavily through Chicago Fire and CSI Los Angeles all evening.

Well,Loadsakids took the advice of "you'rebldymadwoman," when considering a trip to Ikea, and changed her mind, so they met up for coffee after all. There was the usual comparison and sniggering about teenagers and dogs and a lovely time was had by them both. The staff at Costalotta were rather surprised to see her splash out on a latte instead of the cheapest coffee on the menu, but sometimes caution has to be thrown to the wind. In the afternoon, much cleaning and tidying up was done in an attempt to get on top of things. It won't last. And no, it didn't extend to the cupboard under the stairs.

Lad had a slight lie-in this morning and was finally ejected from his bed at 1pm just in time for lunch. This was a shoddy affair, really, considering it is Sunday – whilst most families sat down at a table to a lovely roast today, Lad and Young Lad had fish finger sandwiches in front of Come Dine With Me. The irony was not lost on them. This was because He wasn't here today, and She couldn't be bothered to cook a roast for the three of them. They had 'proper dinner' tonight. Well, if that's a proper dinner..........

Talking of which, I'm a little anxious that my food is about to run out. The next delivery isn't due until later this week, and if you remember, I've helped myself on a couple of occasions recently, so the carefully calculated how much left/delivery date is a bit skewed. The answer, it seems, is to reduce my portions until the new box arrives. Yet another example of neglect, Readers.

Tomorrow will be peaceful, Friends, as Lad and She are up in London all day at An Important Place, and they will be gone from early morning until the evening. Young Lad, He and I have the place to ourselves all day. Marvellous. There will be huffing and sighing tomorrow night as She will be tired after coping with the Central Line in the rush hour. Twice.

Well, there are in fact nearly two hours to go before the Finale of McMafia (thank God that's finishing at last) and pyjamas are already donned so that we can get ready for it. I will happily sleep through the ludicrous Russian dialogue for an hour.

CHAPTER SIXTY-FOUR

Delivery

February 13th

Well, Readers, that was a jolly close shave! My food tub was down to barely HALF a scoop of food – yes, HALF! She had planned to pad it out with a bit of cat food tonight; I ask you. Thankfully, just in the nick of time, there was a ring on the doorbell and my new food arrived. Never before have supplies run this low.

You may think it's my fault for having troughed through the food when I wasn't meant to but no. This is down to Poor Organisation. It's all very well feeling smug because you've organised the coloured pencils box and hoovered under Lad's Bed (more later on that one), but really, these weren't priorities. All that time cutting down the Ruddy Buddleia could have been spent ensuring I wasn't going to starve. Anyway, emergency over. A full tub sits on top of the fridge.

So there was 'exhausted lying on the sofa' last night as I had warned you, as She and Lad were at the Important Place in London all day, and yes indeed, the Circle Line was a Shocker. I've had to listen to tales of being stuck under people's armpits for an alarming amount of time while the train in front was "being held", and wondering what would happen if one had a panic attack in these circumstances. I doubt anyone would notice.

By the time Lad and She arrived home, they were very weary and only had the strength to shove a SparksMeansMarks ready meal Macaroni Cheese, and Four Cheese Ravioli in the oven. This was excellent news for me, as I get to clean out the plastic trays. I do love that Four Cheese Ravioli, I must say – it's Lad's all time favourite, too. Then everyone slumped on the sofa, apart from Lad who managed to rally enough energy to spend the evening on the Xbox. Well done, Lad. While they were up at the Important Place in London, one of the questions for Lad was what he does in his spare time when he isn't at school. This wasn't difficult to answer and didn't take long.

At any rate, He, Young Lad and I had a lovely day, as I had predicted. We did some more Clearing Up in the garden, as in addition to cutting down the Ruddy Buddleia, the Poxy Philadelphus had been chopped to bits as well, and that was lying all over the patio. So He collected it all up and tried to squash it into the plastic sacks that Young Lad was holding open. This was tiring for Young Lad, and he had to sit down afterwards. Then we went for a smashing walk down by the river, and I behaved very well, as I always do when He takes me out. Young Lad had to come out for this walk too, which made it quite a strenuous morning for him. I was pleased to find that they went out in the afternoon – they went to the cinema to watch 'Darkest Hour' about someone called Churchill. Uninspiring if you ask me. I'm sure people of Young Lad's age are meant to like things like Avengers. I had a good look around while they were out, but the toerags had shut all the doors and put the bin out. Bah.

This morning I was dragged out for a walk by 10.00am, as the forecast said Heavy Rain on the way. Readers, it was a stressful hour for me. It all started well; the Bastard Swans were in the river by the bridge but I kept my distance. Then we saw Barney the Oh So Adorable Beagle, who stopped to lean on her legs and generally be very appealing. Bleugh. There was the usual chortling by both our Pack Leaders about how naughty/food-obsessed/chunky we both are. The rudeness of this.

No Friends, the main problem was on the way back. Returning through Far Field, a big German Shepherd came bounding up to me; I've met this devil before, and he doesn't like me. The feeling is mutual. I had done nothing, Readers, to upset him but he was soon leaping on top of me, snarling. I snarled back but he was lot bigger, so I ran off with my tail between my legs. A bit further on, a cockapoo came springing up to me, and there were shouts of,"Go on Russell, PLAY!!" But I didn't want to. Back down by the river, not only was there NiceDogWalkerLady and the three hundred brown labradors, but the huge golden retriever known as Chloe. Now, I went bounding up to her, because just for a moment I thought it was my dear friend Pippa, but sadly I was mistaken. Chloe doesn't like me either. She took over from where the German Shepherd had left off, jumping on my back and snarling. This really was the limit. I had just recovered from that, and then Colin the Bouncy Labrador from next door came along the path – he too jumped all over me! At least this was friendly jumping, rather than trying to rip out my vital organs. It was an exhausting walk, Readers – I was glad to get home.

Lad needed a bit of a lie-in after his exhausting day yesterday, so was taken a mug or tea and a warmed croissant at 12.00. I never get this sort of treatment. Then some time was spent tidying up and cleaning Young Lad and Lad's bedrooms. As an annual treat, the beds were pulled out to be hoovered behind. Readers, I cannot begin to describe the scene under Lad's bed. Really, it was appalling. I don't want to go into detail about what was under there. Young Lad's floor under the bed was marginally better, though some missing pieces of Playmobil from three years ago were found, and a piece of wood from the Pirate Island they sold four years ago. I suspect the new owners of the Pirate Island have always wondered why it didn't stand up straight. After all this, a Quiet Afternoon was needed, so Young Lad spent twenty minutes on some homework ("that'll do"), She did some work on the computer, and Lad had a go at some GCSE Maths again. This never ends well. Eventually it was suggested he did some Art instead, as this might be therapeutic. It wasn't.

Oh and I've just remembered – Young Lad's attempt at homework was hindered by Gingercat walking all over the laptop and pressing random keys again. Does he get shouted at? No.

Golly, you should see the kitchen tonight. It's Shrove Tuesday, so a big stack of pancakes was made, and needless to say the 'flipping' was fairly haphazard so there is batter on the front of the cupboard doors. In an attempt to make up for the salt and fat-laden ready meals they had last night, homemade Leek and Potato soup was made as well. Hmm; flipping, batter, soup and blending all in one go. There was plenty for me to clean up, that's all I'll say. I was dragged out for a second walk, late this afternoon, round the rec – (She's been on the bathroom scales again) – but the wind chill was minus four so it was one of the fastest three quarters of a mile ever walked, and we went home to the warm.

All in all, an exhausting day, Friends, but very pleasing on the Food Delivery Front. That had been a worry.

CHAPTER SIXTY-FIVE

Thieving

February 15th

Oh Readers, what an excellent day on the Nicking Food front! It really has been spectacular. It started when Lad took his eyes off his toasted teacake at lunchtime – luckily I'd kept my eye on it! That disappeared quickly, barely touched the sides. It was a day out of date, but still edible.

Then we went for a lovely walk at the river – it was a stunningly beautiful day, and a tadge warmer than of late, so Mothers and Children were out in abundance. As they are wont to do, many of them had taken a picnic with them, which always spices up my walk rather. There was one large family sitting on the logs by the river – well, Readers, how does One Mother think she can control four small children and a dog? Really, I think she'd overestimated her capabilities. The baby had dropped their sandwich on the ground, and quicker than you can say Bldy Beagle, I was in there and snatched it. Oh, how She shouted at me and chased me around, all the while apologising to the Woman Who Had Too Many Children and A Dog. It was nice. I would have preferred wholemeal bread, but beggars can't be choosers.

And it doesn't stop there! When I came in from the garden after I'd had my tea, Gingercat was eating his dinner – in one graceful leap, I dived and grabbed his bowl of food in my mouth and ran off with it. Oh, and I've just stolen a breadstick from under Young Lad's leg on the sofa (slovenly). See? A top day!

Yesterday was like Piccadilly Bldy Circus in our house. She met LovelyDor from down the road for an Early Coffee at Barstucks, which was about the most peaceful part of the day. Then I was raced round the Rec for a pathetic 15 minute 'walk' while Young Lad was in the shower. I was left at home with Lad (he was having a lie in, of course) while Young Lad and She picked up two of his friends and went somewhere for them to 'hang out'. Hanging Out means JD Sports, Macdonalds, and the Pound Shop. Classy. They came home two hours later, with Young Lad's extra friends and played rugby in the lounge (forbidden) while She took me out for a proper walk.

Then Lad had a dentist appointment in town, even though he "really could not be arsed" to go, and one of Young Lad's mates was taken home en route. How many people were left in the house with me? Are you keeping up? That's right, two. On the way back from the dentist, Lad asked if they could pick up one of his friends and bring him home as well. Well yes of course! Why the heck not?! Then He came home from work. A HUGE dinner was cooked in an attempt to impress all these friends (it didn't), and then She had to drive everyone home again. Readers, you think you're tired trying to follow this? I was exhausted. What a ridiculous carry on.

The best part about the day – and coincidentally, it was Valentine's Day – was that down by the river, I saw a Golden Retriever in the distance. Now, I'd learned my lesson the other day when I went bouncing up and it turned out to be Chloe Who Hates Me, so I was a little more guarded this time. But I was right – it was dear, dear Pippa! Oh how we bounded along the river together, jumping over each other, snapping, yelping, romping. I ADORE Pippa, just like my other BFF Ebony. Pippa is very strong, and frequently knocks me over completely, but I laugh as I'm rolling around on the ground having been punched in the head. It was sheer heaven. I was very irritated when I was put back on the lead and dragged off.

There have been less people here today, but still a lot of going in and out. Young Lad went into town to meet another friend to 'hang out', which today involved Dreggs the Baker, and the Milkshake Shop. Lad needed a long lie in, and surfaced at lunch time. I suspect he is going to struggle to return to the 6am alarm next week when they're back at school. She went for a longbldyoverdue appointment to get the bldy grey covered up in her hair. I am really quite flabbergasted, Friends, to learn about who some of you are. It turns out that her Lovely Hairdresser is an avid reader, and even binged on the box set early editions of my blog. Plus Young Lad's best friend from nursery (when he was four), apparently used to download my blog onto her phone. This is concerning, due to her tender age and the inappropriate language. Note to self. It really is amazing.

Dammit, recycling day tomorrow. This means our five sacks of the stuff have been tied up and put out the front for the dustmen. No more Captain Birds Eye boxes for me to throw round the back garden. On the plus side, when I go for my walk tomorrow I have a good nose in everyone's sacks down the road. So does She. I think She makes snobby judgements about what they've been eating, drinking and reading.

Readers, I noticed in the paper that Meghan Markel is touring through the streets of Windsor after her wedding to Harry. Will she have her Beagle in the carriage with her? Should I go up and stand with the crowds, do you think? This might be my best chance of escape! I'm excited – need to get planning! I'll be sad to leave Gingercat, Pippa and Ebony, but not the rest of my family. Young Lad is watching Chicago Fire YET AGAIN, and it is STILL season five. He is reading the paper again, and Lad is on the Xbox again. It all becomes very samey, Readers. Meghan's household would not be like this. Nor would she serve up her family the sort of nonsense dinner my lot have had tonight. Left-over cauliflower cheese (heave), vegetables, sausages. What sort of mixture is that? Plus the sausages were weird because Tesco had wrongly packaged one lot of their 'Finest Free Range They Had a Good Life Really, Right Up To the Abattoir' pork sausages. They clearly had something else in them, such as caramelised onion (who the heck ever came up with that idea?) Meh. Pretentious nonsense.

Well, tomorrow is hopefully A Quiet Day – nothing actually planned! I am really, really hoping that this might mean Clearing Out The Cupboard Under The Stairs at long last. Wouldn't that be something! But I wouldn't hold your breath. I bet something else more important crops up.

CHAPTER SIXTY-SIX

Macaroni Please

February 17th

Yesterday, Readers, I was very bored so I looked through the cupboard that used to have my food in it. Of course, my food is now on top of the fridge, so in frustration I took a packet of macaroni off the shelves and chucked it on the lounge floor. They are jolly lucky that I didn't split the packet open. I did think about it. I had been left for over an hour, while Lad was driven somewhere to 'hang out' with his friends, and Young Lad had to go back to JD Sports to change his purchase for something that actually fits. Young Lad has now learned that it's important to try clothes on before buying, and that a haphazard "it'll do" approach doesn't work with everything in life. Oh, and a new rucksack had to be bought for Lad, as I've ripped up his old one, looking for snacks.

Apart from this period of being left, the day was pretty good. I had two lovely walks, and yet again the sun was shining. Nicedogwalkerlady was down by the river, but seemed to have mislaid some of the three hundred brown labradors, as there were only a small group with her. That's a little careless. I rolled in some cack in Far Field, but it was dry cack so didn't leave much of a mark and certainly didn't necessitate all the moaning at me. When we got home, the sun was so warm that I sat in the garden to bask in it. Gingercat spoiled the moment by jumping on the fence above me, and frightening the life out of me, but up till that point it was a serene few minutes.

The evening started well, although we deviated from Pizza last night, which was a mistake. Lad was still hanging out, so it was decided a healthier option was needed, Friday night or no Friday night. Why paella was chosen, I've no idea. Vegetables and rice, innit. She once made it several years ago, and nobody liked it then. Nothing has changed. Young Lad ended up with a small pizza from the freezer after all, and Lad made himself fish fingers and chips when he got home. There was paella left in the saucepan for him but he gagged. After an evening in front of the telly, it was time for bed and I was very glad about that, having had two walks.

Today we all had a bit of a lie-in, as He wasn't at work. The normal routine of 'popping into town' was adhered to, but there is some concern about Homeless Guy outside Sainsbury's. He hasn't been on his corner for quite some time now, as he has been ousted by some other people with sleeping bags. It goes to show that, as if he doesn't have enough to deal with of a day, even his favourite spot isn't secure. It makes you think, Reader, about how hard some people's lives are. This was pondered about over a small Americano, which I for one find quite ironic.

Then it was time for my morning walk, which was splendid today. We bumped into Barney the Oh So Adorable Beagle, and needless to say he was as enchanting as ever. Hmm. Once safely over the bridge and away from rival beagles, we went through Top Field, and, Readers, today we went into Top, Top Field!! We don't often go up there – and sometimes there is a good old rabbit carcass for me to roll in. There wasn't, but I did find a massive pile of Something and rolled over and over, waving my paws in the air. She was well ahead, and by the time She saw me and started frantically blowing the whistle, it was far too late. I was completely plastered. Anyway, it was good for her Exercise Quotient to have to run uphill in wellington boots to drag me out of it. I had to do the walk of shame all the way home, on the lead, with any passing dogs being warned not to come near me, "he stinks." Even my friend Lexie kept her distance. Once home, I was dumped in the bath and shampooed from head to tail.

Lad needed another long lie-in today, and was taken a toasted muffin with Nutella and a cup of tea just before lunch. I'm sure you're thinking the same thing, that he is thoroughly over-indulged. Oh to get such treatment. To be fair, Lad has cut the grass this afternoon, and "done the edging". What a waste of time. The grass soon grows back and covers up his nice straight lines. Lad is supposed to be doing any outstanding homework at the moment, in a futile attempt to ensure he's on top of things before returning to school on Monday. He is actually looking at designer belts on his phone. I'm not sure which subject this is for.

He and Young Lad went to the tip earlier, to dispose of many bags of cut down Ruddy Buddleia and lots of wine bottles. Then, because it's such a beautiful day, I was taken out for a second walk! He and She took me back to the river – Young Lad had been told he HAD to come, but just in nick of time, two of his friends rang the doorbell and said did he want to hang out again. (Dreggs. Ham salad baguette and a Coke.) What a lovely second walk I had – I met le petit chien Jade, whose Pack Leader comes from Paris. I do sometimes wonder what would make someone leave Paris to live here.....but anyway. Lexie was down there for her second walk of the day, too, and this time she was allowed to get close as I'd had a bath. And then, Readers, guess who caught me unawares from behind?! Yes, it was dear, dear Pippa. We bounded around again and she knocked me flying as usual, but I loved it. The only time I was a teeny weeny bit cross was when she took my stick away from me. It was an extra special stick that I'd found, but Pippa ran off with it. I know one must share with one's friends, though. Grrr.

Part of the reason I had a second walk today was for someone to 'de-stress' from doing Young Lad's English homework with him. This needs the bldypatience of a bldysaint and makes one's blood pressure rise somewhat. Young Lad still needs to write up her his notes in best, but this has been saved for tomorrow, as there is only so much one can bldytake. As a result, I am exhausted from all my walking today – nigh on four miles – and will be snoring heavily this evening.

Dinner could be interesting tonight – Lad and Young Lad have been asking for a while for a Chinese meal, and as takeaway is out of the question due to Price, Calories and TooManyAdditives, home-made Chinese is being attempted. Luckily Ken Hom's recipe for crispy prawns and egg-fried rice is fairly straightforward, though I think we all know the most popular part of the meal will be the Prawn Crackers (I can't see it being the sweet and sour vegetables). I'll let you know, Readers.

There was a lot of moaning last night – this was due to driving halfway around the county to take/collect Lad from hanging out. This is what passes for your bldysociallife if you have bldyteenagers, apparently. And then they don't eat your paella.

CHAPTER SIXTY-SEVEN

Five Miles

February 18th

Ridiculous. It's hardly my fault if the bathroom scales are still saying unpleasant things, yet it's me that has been dragged out for FIVE, yes FIVE miles of marching through countryside today! Okay, we did it in two separate walks, but really it's too much. I am absolutely shattered tonight, and haven't even had the strength to beg for the empty yogurt pots. I am getting thinner by the day (at least one of us is) and will soon be wasting away. It doesn't occur to anyone to increase my food rations, with all this exercise. Negligent, again.

If that wasn't bad enough, it's Sunday. Readers, you know that this means we have Lovelyneighbourontheright's young cockapoo for the morning, and how much I enjoy it. Well, today the youngster did the normal bouncing and jumping at me, landing on my head several times, and I had to put him in his place with some growling and a few gentle-ish snaps. In the end we rubbed along okay together as we spent the morning in the garden, so he could be distracted with tennis balls to stop him jumping on my head. So I didn't get a wink of sleep all morning.

Plus, She and Young Lad were gardening again which involved a lot more hacking down of poor bushes and Young Lad was then forced to pick up all the pieces and shove them into recycling bags. Surely he won't be made to pick up the Bastard Prickly Rose Bush bits, I thought to myself, and indeed, a rare moment of kindness was seen as She donned rubber gloves to do this. During all this, Lad was having another lie-in, but don't worry, Readers, he had to Clean OutThe Car and Do The Ironing this afternoon. I wouldn't want you to think that Lad and Young Lad were being allowed to relax on their last day of half term. Oh no.

The garden does look tidier, but I'm a bit cheesed off as I put all the recycling boxes and tubs under those bushes, and now it's all been cleared up. My hiding places have been ruined. There was a lot of moaning about the number of Gingercat's food bowls that were found under the bushes – they know quite well that this is where I run to when I've grabbed his food and legged it to the garden. It's not my fault there were seven bowls buried in the foliage – they should try tidying up more often! There was also a small Bob The Builder, Scooby Doo and seventy four tennis balls under the bushes. And a lot of ripped up Harry Ramsden's and Capn Birds Eye boxes. Add to the list several Nerf Gun bullets, a shuttlecock (I have NEVER seen anyone play badminton and I've lived here three years) and a lot of broken 99p solar lights. Why they buy 99p solar lights each summer, I do not know – they stick them in the flower beds, Lad and Young Lad come out to play football, the lights get broken. Every single year. But nobody learns.

Well, my morning walk today was fine – happy and uneventful. There were lots of people and their dogs out, as it was such a beautiful day again. I was well-behaved and life was good. However, my second longer walk this afternoon was More Traumatic. Look, it's Sunday afternoon and there is a housing estate the other side of the path – obviously, the smell of Roast Dinners comes wafting down and I can't help myself. THREE TIMES I got wind of a great smell, and took off at terrific speed, following my nose – I'm a dog,for the love of God! But oh no, we had frantic running and shouting, blowing the whistle like a demented netball referee. Well, I took no notice. What a carry-on.

Anyway, I added a good half mile to our walk by these detours. I get no thanks, of course. Wellington boots are very difficult to run in uphill, chasing me, I do appreciate that, but it's not my problem. So I was put on the lead for the rest of the walk, because I couldn't be trusted. We went up into Top Field, but not Top, Top Field due to the stuff that I rolled in yesterday.

This afternoon there has been frantic tidying up as it is the end of Half Term. Lad and Young Lad's piles of school books and random bits of paper – isthishomework/no/areyousure/no/couldyoutrybldylookingat it – and some attempt at order has been made, by putting a Manchester City mug of sharpened pencils and new Biros on the snooker table. By Tuesday I can guarantee that nobody will be able to find a pencil or working Biro. Even the kitchen floor has been cleaned, Readers, but not the disgusting cupboard under the stairs. I know I teased you with that possibility, but it never happened. Lad and Young Lad have packed their bags ready for school tomorrow, in the vain hope that nobody is running around at 7am screaming where'smybldybuspass and things like that.

Tomorrow it will be lovely and peaceful here for Gingercat and I, once they've all gone. I intend having a good look round, and feel it's time to get up to something as I haven't done anything major for ages. If I have the strength.

Well, Readers, Young Lad is about to have some banana tea loaf (now doesn't that sound exciting), so I might just open one eye to have a look.

CHAPTER SIXTY-EIGHT

Potato Peelings

February 20th

Today, Readers, I have chucked a bag of potato peelings over the floor, and knocked the recycling all round the back porch. They should have put it outside in the bags. I've also dragged the bag with carrot ends and a broccoli stalk into the lounge, and eaten them. These were on the shelf in the back porch, ready to give Lovelyneighbourontheright's rabbit. The rabbit will have to do without. I had shocking wind to begin with, way before I did all this, so it's only going to get worse.

I was bored this afternoon, while they were all at work/school and needed something to do. Now, Lad has left a rucksack in his bedroom (the one I chewed through), and I know damned well that there is a Blueberry Cereal Bar in it, somewhat squashed at the bottom. I had planned to deal with that this afternoon. But Lad's bedroom door was shut, which scuppered my plans and annoyed me. I was also tempted to walk mud all over the John Lewis White Duvet Cover, as I was exceptionally muddy from my walk earlier, but oh no. That bedroom door was shut, too. So I had no option but to chuck the peelings around and leave rubbish in the lounge.

Yesterday I had to be dragged from my chair in the morning, as I REALLY didn't want to go for a walk after that ridiculous five mile business the day before. It was drizzling and grey, and nobody in their right mind would swap a comfortable armchair for three miles of grey drizzle. As it was, I bumped into her friend from work, Madame, who was out running in the grey drizzle. Clearly she is not in her right mind, either.

So we plodded on through the rain, and just to spice things up a bit, I ran off towards the houses again. It was a carefully timed, unexpected burst of speed from me, and She was miles ahead before She noticed I had disappeared. So running across the bumpy field in Wellington

Boots, shouting, was the order of the day, yet again. It does make me laugh. We went over the bridge into Top Field, and marched round it fast. Well, I didn't. I took my time and dawdled, as there were some particularly ripe smells. Eventually I was put back on the lead and told to bldyhurryup. I was FILTHY and wet from yesterday's walk, and was sent to my bed in the kitchen to dry off. Until I sneaked out when the door was opened and legged it to my armchair.

It was felt that a hearty, nutritious meal was needed for Young Lad, Lad and He when they returned home at the end of the day, so the entire saucepan collection was used to make lasagne. This is always a good choice for me, as I give the filthy plates a pre-rinse in the dishwasher. Then the kitchen had to be cleaned up from the multi-saucepan lasagne making. It was a quiet evening, although Lad and She started watching a new comedy series on Sky Atlantic that was bldyhilarious but Highly Inappropriate and I was shocked that Lad was allowed to watch it. The sniggering got on my nerves in the end.

Today it has been lashing down with rain all day. Was I allowed to spend the morning, dry and warm in my armchair? Of course not.

Imagine how much I enjoyed my walk in the sodding rain. I was drenched when we got home, and had to sit in my bed again. I suppose I should be grateful that the walk was cut short by half a mile, but really. There were very few dogs down there today, as most Pack Leaders weren't as deranged as the few that were out. I did bump into dear Ebony on the way, but lucky Ebony was coming back from her walk, and would have been dry and warm a lot sooner than me. Nicedogwalkerlady was, of course, down there but really, that was about it. It's all very well saying, "it's only a bit of rain," and "it'll do us good," but it's very easy to say that when you are wearing a thick coat, bobble hat and have an umbrella. So think on. Mind you, I did see one poor dog with a ridiculous purple coat on. If anyone tried to put a purple coat on me, I'd have their hand off.

Golly, we were soaked through. Our march was in time to "Miss You Nights" by Cliff Richard. This is what happens if you listen to Radio 2 whilst making fish pie for dinner. Though it was an acid house version, judging by the tempo at which we marched.

Young Lad had to walk all the way home from school tonight. Oh, hang on, luckily he was given a lift by a friend's grandparent. Young Lad also had to walk to school yesterday morning and this morning, both in the rain. Oh, hang on, he was given a lift by a friend's Dad. Young Lad hasn't in fact walked anywhere this week, and this suits him just fine. He is rather perturbed as there is a chance Football Training is on at school tomorrow, followed by Indoor Cricket nets. This will be exhausting, and I can only hope he is given plenty of lifts by friends' relatives.

Lad is supposed to be doing his English homework, but is looking up designer belts on his phone again. This has nothing to do with Romeo and Juliet, as far as I can see. "Romeo, Romeo, shall I buy Versace or Gucci?" does not ring any bells. It worries me.

He has just come in from a very long day at work. Thankfully they have left him some fish pie, and there will be one more plate for me to pre-wash in the dishwasher. There is some healthy banana tea bread for afterwards, as there is some concern about how much Sugar and Rubbish Lad and Young Lad ate over half term. Young Lad says he'd rather have a bag of crisps than the banana tea bread. I think he's missed the point, but I can see what he's saying.

Well, Readers, it's Wednesday tomorrow. As you know, this is a day that I am left all day and my family show no care for me whatsoever. Thankfully, I'm off to dear Ebony's house for the day, but I'm hoping to get to that Blueberry Cereal Bar beforehand. I know exactly where it is.

CHAPTER SIXTY-NINE

Eggy

February 22nd

I've had a problem for a couple of days, Readers. Although the flatulence I produce is often pretty awful, it has gone up a notch or two recently. I've obviously eaten something that really doesn't agree with me, but have no idea what it was. I'm not feeling quite myself, Friends, and have taken to curling up for a kip in the washing basket, on top of the clean clothes. I've got a bit of a belly ache and I've been threatened with the Evil Vet if things don't improve. I'm eating okay, obviously, as nothing stops me eating, ever. It's just coming out the other end in loud, sulphuric emissions.

I feel better for sharing that with you. It doesn't help, to be honest, being dragged out on these silly extra-long walks. Nearly four miles this morning, Readers, just in the one walk. I know She was hoping I'd have a good empty out in one of the fields, and relieve the problem, but I decided not to. There were so many friends out this morning! Teddy the Australian Labradoodle was barely recognisable; he'd had a Severe Haircut. I felt worried for him, as it was very cold. There was a new chap down there, called Monty – a very lively Cockapoo type thing (there seem to be an awful lot of them lately). Plus the lovely Chuck, glistening in the sun as ever, and the German Shepherd that hates me.

Over the bridge we went, and up through Top Field. Then, to my surprise, we carried on to Top, Top Field! I didn't think we'd be going back there for a while, as I rolled in fox poo last time. She seems to have forgotten. It was hideously muddy, and really a complete mistake to go up there. We seem to make a lot of these mistakes. I was covered in mud, right the way up my belly. Even Wellington boots struggled to cope with the liquid cack everywhere, and there was some amusing sliding around. I'd love it if the sliding around turned into arse over whatsit one day. So off we went, marching around Top, Top Field as fast as it was possible to march in several inches of mud. As we'd stopped to chat to several Pack Leaders early on, we were behind schedule on the Minutes per Mile Pace of Walking, so had to really step it up. There was a dead rabbit in the field, with its back leg chewed off, but I wasn't allowed to go near it. Spoilsport.

I was shattered by the time we got home. On the way back we bumped into Chuck and his Pack Leader again, because they walk at a sensible pace and don't stomp fast. With them was Sausage Sue and her many dogs, and they were discussing something called a Dorgie. Sausage Sue thought this is a cross between a Dachsund and a Corgi, but Chuck's Pack Leader thought it was an activity involving several dogs. I didn't really understand.

I was flat out, asleep and farting, within minutes of getting home. I was left in peace and quiet when She went to collect Lad from school – he has to stay longer on Thursdays now, due to Extra Maths Tuition, which he enjoys a lot. I think that's what he said. Rather than face an hour's bus journey on top of this, pity has been taken on him, and he was met with a Dreggs sausage roll and a bottle of water as a reward for his hard work.

Of course, this meant Young Lad had to walk all the way home from school, and this time there were no lifts from friends' grandparents and the like. Poor Young Lad. As if he wasn't exhausted enough, from the efforts of Wednesday. Not only was football training on after school, followed by indoor cricket nets till 8pm, but Young Lad even went to basketball club in his lunch hour!! Never before has such enthusiasm for physical exertion been seen. I can't see it lasting. Readers, I'm not sure he grasped the idea of basketball, as he didn't take his trainers, so had to do it in his socks. For Health and Safety Reasons, the teacher said, "no running if you have socks on," so Young Lad had to play basketball slowly in his socks. Hmmm.

I'd had a lovely day at dear, dear Ebony's house. We had such fun and I do love her Pack Leader and Pack Leader Male. Unfortunately, my stomach was problematic even there, and I stunk the house out. They were very polite about it.

Readers, are you sitting down? The Disgusting Cupboard Under The Stairs has been cleared out!!! I know!! It took over two hours, and a lot of swearing. A big pile of stuff, including a picnic hamper that has been used once in eighteen years, has been thrown in the back of the car, ready for the charity shop. The three hundred carrier bags have been sent to recycling, and a large rug that is FILTHY is also in the boot of the car while some thought goes into what to do with it. I made it filthy with my muddy feet. The upshot is that the cupboard is now easy to get into; one can actually see the floorboards, and the hoover and ironing board are no longer fighting with the Karcher steam cleaner. On the shelves, there are pots labelled, "nails and screws," "candles", "screwdrivers," and the such like. I have never seen such terrific organisation in this house. It will last all of five minutes. I've been in the cupboard a few times for a good look round, but of course anything of interest has been removed. But I have to say, ten out of ten for effort. If things carry on at this rate, we might even find the oven gets cleaned one day.

Tomorrow I'm at dear Pippa's house for daycare. Hopefully her Pack Leader is reading this tonight, so she is prepared for the awful smell. I'm hoping Lad will put the laptop away soon, as he needs to choose which subjects to do for A Level by tomorrow, and has only started considering this tonight. I have no idea what Philosophy is but it sounds dull, and I don't really want to have to listen to tedious discussions of Nietzsche and the like for two whole years. I do wonder about people at times.

Ooof there goes another one. If this hasn't stopped by tomorrow night, it will be the Evil Vet for me, and we all know that means I have to be muzzled for them to get near me. Life is hard, Readers, at times.

CHAPTER SEVENTY

Windchill

February 24th

By golly it's cold out there tonight, Readers! I've just come back from the river, and it was bearable walking in one direction, but as soon as we turned round into the wind, my ears flapped out wildly and it dropped to minus five. I've had no choice but to climb straight into my chair for a kip. I'll be here for the evening now.

That was my second long walk of the day. Yes, we're still on this ridiculous Exercise Quotient mission, so I've had to trot five miles again today. This morning was glorious, Friends – yet again, blue skies and bright sunshine. There were so many dogs down there, I didn't know where to start. It has to be said I was particularly pleased to see dear Oscar, whom I haven't seen for quite while now – Oscar is a Border Terrier who never fails to jump up and make her jeans very muddy. This makes me laugh. She really likes Oscar but he'd just eaten something hideous today, so we kept well away from his mouth. It was rather boring, though, having to stand around while She and Oscar's Pack Leaders chatted. They even said I should have an Instagram account, whatever that is, but we all know this is well beyond her technical knowledge.

Nicedogwalkerlady and the three hundred brown labradors were there, and who do you think they had with them? None other than Barney The Oh so Adorable Beagle, the one who is cuter, whiter and better behaved than me. Needless to say he leant against her legs and did that silly appealing thing with his eyes as usual. It annoys the heck out of me. We left them all to it, and went over the bridge into Top Field, where we marched around to the rhythm of, "I saw the sign" by Ace of Base. Another dated, forgettable song that most of you will indeed have forgotten, but not us.

Readers, the Bastard Swans were back on the river this morning.

Do you know what they did to my dear friend Pippa? She merely looked at them over the gate, and they HISSED at her. Vicious oiks. I hate them. There were seven Bastard Swans down there earlier in the year, but I've only seen two recently. Good riddance. Poor Pippa. I had a lovely day at her house yesterday – my bad flatulence was still pretty awful at times, but again, everyone at Pippa's house was polite about it unlike my own family who shout, "OH FOR GOD's SAKE RUSSELL", every time something pops out. I never get treated like this at Pippa or Ebony's houses.

Anyway, you'll be glad to know that things are slightly better in that department today, so I haven't been dragged to the Evil Vet. But I'm digressing – on the way back from our stomp around the fields this morning, we bumped into The Friendly Electrician and his wife, who were walking at a normal pace with their well-behaved dog, not striding frantically along to an early 90s melody. Thankfully we slowed down to chat to The Friendly Electrician and his wife, but the conversation was, as usual, about bldy teenagers. It's always that or bldy dogs. Boring as.

This afternoon was astonishingly peaceful as He was at work and so it was deemed to be a Quiet Homework afternoon. (This was after Lad finally got out of bed at lunchtime, as he needed another lie-in.) Young Lad had to learn some Italian music terms such as CRESCENDO! and DIMINUENDO! Readers, I'm sorry to tell you that Young Lad had a test last week on these words at school, and scored an abysmal 0 out of 10. This smacks of a lack of effort if you ask me. So I had to listen to some silly, over-theatrical expressions of words like "fortISSIMO!!" for about half an hour this afternoon. Drivel. Young Lad will be re-tested on these ten words next week, and we're hoping for a score of maybe four. That might be optimistic, actually. But I have to say, it was a peaceful few hours this afternoon while everyone cracked on with their work, and Gingercat and I both had a lovely doze, until I was dragged out for another walk.

I felt sorry for poor He last night, who had to go back to work for A Dinner, and Dress Up Smartly. I'm sure He would rather have slobbed out on the sofa in pyjamas with a pizza like everyone else. Lad spent the evening letting off steam on the Xbox, and so myself, Young Lad and She had the sofa and TV to ourselves. It was lovely, even though Young Lad has now found Season 6 of Chicago Fire. Just how many more burning warehouses will I have to hear about? Honestly.

I was also annoyed that they lit some scented candles again during the evening – it's just so rude. Her friend Gordon made an appearance; the tell-tale clink of ice and fizzing sound as the lemon slice drops in is a dead give-away. I'm not convinced this is part of the Healthy Eating mission. Neither is the Young's Cod in Batter and Aunt Bessie's chips that have just been served up. (What's happened to old Harry Ramsden's, I hear you ask? Too bldy expensive apparently! Re-branded and twice the price.)

Well, Friends, I hope you're all tucked up in the warm for the evening. It's brass monkeys out there tonight and I will be having a VERY quick comfort break in the garden at 10pm. And no, I don't want to go for another soddingfivemiles of walks tomorrow, but will I be consulted? Of course not.

CHAPTER SEVENTY-ONE

Visiting

February 26th

Today was a little different from the normal humdrum, Readers, as I went out visiting. It all started the same way, with alarm clocks at 6am and lots of shouting of hurryup and getintheshower /where'smytie/I/don'tknow/lookforit!!! for about forty minutes, which bored me so I had a sleep. It was so cold out, that when She 'popped into town' after the school run, I didn't even move from the fleece on the sofa to empty the recycling bag everywhere. I was quite tired after another ridiculous amount of walking yesterday – two walks, total just over four miles. Unnecessary.

Once back from town (apparently Costalotta need to turn their heating up as it was brass monkeys in there too), we went for my walk nice and early. It was BITING, Readers, BITING. Lots of friends were out, including poor Teddy the Australian Labradoodle with his rather harsh haircut; it makes you wince looking at him in this weather. Chuck was on fine form, his coat shining more than ever, but it was so cold that neither of us hung around to sniff backsides today. Brrr.

Still, intrepid souls that we are, we marched briskly around Top Field to the rhythm of Donna Summer, "On the Radio" – no, I've no idea either. I took a comfort break in the middle of the field while She had stomped back down to the beginning, so yet again there was moaning and groaning as She had to stomp all the way back up to look for it. I also tried to roll in some cack, but was shouted at and grabbed frantically as, "we're going visiting in a bit!!" On the way back home, we bumped into Nicedogwalkerlady and her husband, and the three hundred brown labradors. They looked cold, too.

Enough of this. The excitement of the day was being put in the car to go and visit her friend (let's call her Sicknote) who was off sick. Now, Readers, it is down to Sicknote that I have ended up living here with my family – it is all her fault. I was perfectly happy where I lived before, grabbing loads of snacks and not being marched out on four mile walks in the cold, but did anyone ask me? No, of course not. But I'm not one to hold a grudge, so agreed to go and visit Sicknote and her brown labrador (yes, another one) called Charlie. Well, it seems I stunk the car out on the way there, so despite it being minus four, She rolled the window down.

As soon as we arrived, I jumped up at the kitchen counter to see if there was anything to eat – apparently this is rude. Then I tried to go upstairs for a look round, as I imagine they have high standards of bedding there, and fancied a kip, but this is Also Rude, and I was dragged back down. This annoyed me so much, Readers, that I had no choice but to climb into a chair and go to sleep. I felt sorry for Charlie the Brown Labrador, as She had sat down in his chair – now who's rude? Initially I sat on her lap, but was very squashed and She refused to get off the chair for me, so I had to make do with another one. Poor Charlie had to sit on the floor. Anyway, She and Sicknote talked incessantly for the best part of two hours, which bored Charlie and I to tears. Then I refused to get off the chair when it was time to go home, as I was perfectly comfortable there. I was moaned at in the car for being an "unsociable git" – Readers, did I get any credit for not farting at Sicknote's and stinking the house out? No, of course not. Sicknote did say I'm very handsome, and clearly appreciates me a lot more than my own family do. It was nice going to visit, and if I'd been allowed to look around upstairs, I wouldn't have been so grumpy. But there you go.

Lad has been at home today with another of his 'headaches'. What's that you're saying? Was Games on the timetable today? Well, blow me down, it was! He was given lots and lots of sympathy at home in the form of a Chemistry GCSE past paper and the Wifi being switched off. Amazingly, Lad has rallied and managed to do all his homework plus the Chemistry Past Paper, without leaving his pyjamas. I'm helping him, by lying on his lap while he tries to draw a graph on top of me.

Young Lad has had a busy day at school, playing Futsall in PE (no idea) and going to Handball Club at lunchtime. We are all rather worried about Young Lad's sudden burst of physical effort in the last week or so – it is not in his nature. Plus he looks like a walking X-ray at the best of times, and all this exercise could make him disappear completely. This would be a shame, as I often sleep on Young Lad's bed with him. There isn't much room for him, but that's okay as he's so slim. Of course, any caring family would buy a double bed for the two of us, not expect me to be squashed up like that all night.

Well, my Regular Readers might remember my young friend J who was having Nasty Things done to him in the Marsden when I started my blog, back in the day. J is doing really well, and his Evil Vets/ doctors are pleased with him. He still has to have some Nasty Things done to him, but hopefully not for much longer. One would like to think that the positive vibes from my musings and all you Readers have helped him and his Pack Leader on their journey, but that is New Age Cobblers, it seems.

Readers, thanks to Oscar the Border Terrier's Pack Leaders, I now have an Instagram account. Yep, really, thanks for that. She has no idea what to do with it, but has managed thus far to post a couple of pictures of me with inane comments. What's the point? None at all. Just more time-wasting when cupboards/the oven/the fridge could be being cleaned out.

It's meant to snow tomorrow, Friends, so I hope you are tucked up in the warm.

CHAPTER SEVENTY-TWO

Bins Down

February 27th

An excellent day, Readers, from the Bad Behaviour point of view. While they were all on their way to work/school this morning, I had a look in the food cupboard, and decided to have a rearrange. I thought the bag of Spiralli pasta and a tin of tomato soup would look much nicer on the lounge carpet, so I dragged them in there and dumped them on the floor. There was also a pack of Basmati rice that had some left in the bottom, so I dragged that in the lounge, too, and ate the rice. It was a bit crunchy. I was moaned at, of course, when She got in, but I'd had a lovely time.

Then, later in the day when there was nobody here, I knocked the kitchen bin over and went through it. There wasn't a lot – for once it had been emptied and cleaned out today, but I did find a big pile of mashed potato that had been sitting in the fridge for a week and was no longer fit for human consumption. Luckily it was fit for Beagle consumption. Fired up by my efforts, I wandered up to the bathroom and yes! They'd forgotten to put the bathroom bin in the bath, so I tipped that over and went through it too. I won't tell you what I ate.

So all in all, an excellent day. I had a good walk this morning, though it was rather cold at minus three. Lots of my friends were out – the usual crew of Chuck and Teddy, plus Rocco the three-legged Oh So Inspirational Labrador. As usual there was ooing and aahing about how Inspirational he is, as he rolled around on his back waving his three paws. Dear me.

It was bitingly cold down by the river, and we stomped along even more quickly than usual. Over in Far Field I found some fox poo and rolled in it, so was put back on the lead and my fun was over. I was jolly glad to get home, I can tell you, as two and a half miles in that temperature was more than enough. Even the Bastard Swans looked cold. It was the sort of day one wanted to be left alone to sleep on the red fleece, or empty bins. But no! This afternoon I was dragged out for a second time, over the Rec.

Admittedly it was a short walk, or would have been, if I hadn't been accosted by a small mongrel of some sort that was hell bent on chasing me. Kayleigh (really?) was a rescue dog from Cyprus, according to her Pack Leader. He had no control over her whatsoever, and it was too funny watching She and Kayleigh's Pack Leader trying to catch a very small but extremely fast dog. They were rubbish! Kayleigh kept darting between their legs or hands, laughing her head off, and I was very amused watching their inept attempts at authority. It went on for hours. Best laugh I've had for ages!

In between the two walks, I've needed to sleep on the fleece as it is very tiring walking through the fields in sub-zero temperatures. I felt very sorry for He today, as He works outside and had to go into work even earlier than usual, due to the adverse weather conditions. It can't have been nice working outdoors today – an hour was enough for me. So He needed a hot bath when He got home, and luckily there was a very warming shepherd's pie for tea; we even put the fire on! Lad was extremely cold from the long journey home from school, and Young Lad was tired from Basketball club at lunchtime plus PE.

Readers, there was some disappointment for Young Lad today. He had been so looking forward to his first ever Food Technology lesson – I think I would enjoy this subject – and poor Young Lad had eagerly packed his new tupperware box with ingredients for Fruit Salad this morning. Imagine his sadness when he found out his Food Technology Teacher was off sick, and there was a Cover Teacher. The Cover Teacher said they couldn't make fruit salad, they would just have to sit and eat the fruit. Now, call me old-fashioned but I wouldn't have thought the method for making fruit salad was too complicated for a non-Food Technology teacher to manage – it's only a bit of chopping, after all. But for various reasons this was not allowed, so Young Lad had to eat a punnet of raspberries, a massive bunch of grapes, an apple and an orange without chopping or mixing. On the plus side, his bowels will be in good shape for a bit.

I've had a few views on my Instagram account! Not many, in all honesty, but I don't know what She expected. Amazingly there have been no silly photos and comments of me uploaded today, as there has been Too Much To Do.

Although they should probably be doing homework, everyone is on the sofa as it's warm in here and nobody wants to move. Lad is watching some absurd nonsense called "The Walking Dead", which is completely unsuitable for Young Lad but luckily it's all filmed in the pitch dark and nobody can see the fake gore anyway.

Talking of fake, dinnertime's family debate was about whether Donald Trump was actually proving to be Quite A Good President. I kid you not, Readers. There was a lot of heated arguing, and eventually a compromise was reached that if he kept off social media and acted with a smidgen of dignity, things would be better. What a boring conversation. I fell asleep under the table, waiting for a bit of shepherd's pie to drop.

Lad is in a bad mood tonight, as the "Beast from the East" was forecast today and he was absolutely sure that his school would close. The Beast from the East turned out to be Light Snow from Below, and the three flakes that fell did not cause his school to shut. He is very angry about this, and feels hard done by.

Well, Readers, one of the main characters in "The Walking Dead" is taking so long to die that everyone else has lost the will to live. Do get on with it. Such drivel, and still all in pitch black so we can't see what's going on. Or isn't going on. I'm off to my chair for a kip, as I'm absolutely cream crackered from trying to keep warm today.

On my Instagram feed (yep! got the lingo!!) there is a silly video of me trying to get comfortable in my chair last night. If you're desperately bored, you could watch it. It only lasts a minute – it did actually go on for three minutes but you have to trim it down to 60 seconds. (Lad had to do this for her, obviously.) I've no idea how you access my Instagram account. Really, what's the point?

CHAPTER SEVENTY-THREE

Beast from the East

February 28th

Today I lacked enthusiasm somewhat to leave the house and go for a long walk in several inches of snow. I tried hard to disguise myself as the red fleece on the sofa, but unfortunately my nose was sticking out and I was spotted.

So, the snow finally arrived with a vengeance, and bldy inches of the stuff was dumped during the night. When I needed my comfort break this morning, I had to DASH down the garden, under the bushes for cover, and then try to find a suitable spot on the lawn. This was very, very difficult and I went round in circles for ages, trying to find somewhere my bottom wouldn't actually come into contact with the snow. Then I dashed back to the house and straight back to bed. It was traumatic.

Just as traumatic was Lad and Young Lad's wait to see if their schools were open. Young Lad showed a bit more willing, by having a shower and putting on his uniform, whereas Lad took the less positive option of staying in bed with a coffee. Ping by ping came through the emails and messages bringing those words of pure joy; "school closed." Young Lad ran round the lounge cheering, and Lad stayed in bed. Only one person seemed less than pleased about this. She is such a killjoy. Poor He, on the other hand, went into work extra, extra early to clear paths and make everywhere safe. He has been out in the cold again ALL day. He and I are both exhausted tonight. So, an unusual day with nearly everyone at home, and piles of freezing cold snow everywhere you look. Hideous.

Would you think there would be some respite from all the ridiculous walking in these conditions? Well, you would, wouldn't you. Scott of the Antarctic didn't say, "Come on Rover, it's beautiful out there, a couple of miles will do us good." Actually, I think Scott of the

Antarctic ate his dogs because his forward planning was abysmal. Or was that his horses? Hmm.

Well, of course I was dragged out into the morning sunshine and taken down to the river. I have to say, it was pleasant to see hundreds of children out sledging down the one very slight hill, and there were lots of dogs watching. One of them was Rocco the Inspirational Three-Legged Dog who was even more Inspirational than usual as he was coping with the snow on his three legs. The snow made some of the other chaps rather frisky, and as if it wasn't bad enough going out in the first place, some of them wanted me to play with them!

I did make a quick dash for the houses where they often put bread out for the birds, but the snow was so deep I couldn't find any. Irritating. The trouble is with this weather, one minute it's blue skies and sunshine and you could be quaffing schnapps at Val D'Isere, but then seconds later Storm Norman blows in and you are blindly groping around in a blizzard trying to stay alive. This is exactly what it was like at the river this morning. Thankfully once the blizzarding thing started, we headed home.

On the way back I picked up a particularly attractive stick. Something went wrong, though, and I ended up with a large piece of stick wedged in my mouth. I just couldn't get the darned thing out, and it was stuck at a funny angle behind my teeth, so I couldn't shut my mouth. I looked ridiculous. Once home, I was given a carrot to chew on, and this did the trick.

As well as Lad and Young Lad's company today (I use the term 'company' loosely here), we also had The Friendly Electrician round to do a job. This was nice as he pays me compliments and says how handsome I am, which is something that rarely happens in this house. Occasionally during the morning, I wandered upstairs to check on the quality of his craftmanship and sniff through his toolbox. There were no sandwiches in it, which was disappointing. I can, however, report that his wiring is to a high standard and he will be allowed back one day.

Lad surprised us all by getting up soon after 8am and starting some studying! This really was worrying. It all made sense a bit later, when he asked to be driven to a town far away to hang out with his mates. It had to be explained gently and calmly to Lad that this wasn't a great idea. He accepted this without question. I think.

Lad has, at least, done some studying today, as well as a fair bit of time on the Xbox with his friends. Young Lad has done no studying. Young Lad, too, has enjoyed lots of time on the Xbox, but to be fair, he did don layers, coat, hat, gloves and boots this afternoon and go out sledging with his friends. This is a Normal and Healthy pastime for Young Lad, and he kept it up for two hours. Lad was persuaded out for, ooh, fifteen minutes.

I was dragged out for a second walk this afternoon to watch the sledging. Lad threw some snowballs for me and I played along for a while, jumping up and catching them, then eating them in case there was any food inside. There wasn't. So I became bored of that game. Readers, you have no idea what hard work it is walking through deep snow that comes up to your elbows. I am exhausted tonight, and have been snoring loudly through Look East. He had to tell me to be quiet, as it was important to watch the weather forecast so we all know what to expect tomorrow.

My dear friend Pippa was two years old yesterday. Her loving Pack Leader has made her a Liver Cake – yum – and has just texted to say would I like a piece, or will it make my flatulence play up. Honestly, the indignity of it. Is there anyone who doesn't discuss my intestinal comings and goings? It's so rude. And yes I do want a bit. Please.

Well, Readers, who knows what tomorrow will bring? Lad and Young Lad are praying their schools are shut again, but She's told them not to hold their breath. I feel like I could sleep for a week, as it's a well known fact that cold weather makes you tired.

A note to the Friendly Electrician; please put something to eat in your toolbox next time you pop round.

CHAPTER SEVENTY-FOUR

Siberia

March 2nd

I did not enjoy my walk today. I sat down on the path and asked politely if we could bldy well go home now as I was bldy frozen. It was minus two with a windchill factor that made it feel like minus ten. How absolutely ridiculous to be out for an hour's walk in that. The river was actually frozen over, and that NEVER happens, so there was no sign of the Bastard Swans. Good. I'd like to say we walked under clear blue skies and winter sunshine, but no. It was grey and chucking down with Frozen Rain. What is Frozen Rain, I hear you ask? I, too, thought this was just snow, or if push comes to shove, hail. But no. There is something called Frozen Rain, and it differs from snow in one basic way. It hurts.

There were very few other dogs were out with their Pack Leaders in these conditions. In fact there was only one. It really beggars belief that anyone would drag their poor dog out in this. Mind you, it was quite funny when we set off, as She was carrying a bag of shopping for LovelyDor down the road in one hand, and had me on my lead in the other hand. Readers, the pavements were treacherous. It was so tempting to run fast and watch her ski behind me, desperately holding onto the bag of shopping, and finally crash to the ground, but there was nobody around to watch, and really that sort of thing needs an audience. There was a bit of a dicey moment round the corner at the bottom, but sadly She stayed upright.

So on we ploughed through four foot snow drifts, battling through gale force winds and Frozen Rain. None of my friends were down there, not one. They were all on their sofas at home. But surprisingly, the snow did make me feel a little frisky at times, and I did break into a run occasionally! Well, twice. We started heading into Far Field, but at that moment a Full Scale Blizzard started so we wimped out and headed home. Blow me down, the one other dog out there turned out to be some maniac big labradoodle thing that wanted me to play. Normally I would have refused, but I felt so sorry for us being The Only Dogs Out In These Conditions, that I joined in! Yes, Readers, I played!

I was dragged out yesterday in the freezing cold, too. It had been a stressful start to the day at 6.30am, waiting to find out if Lad and Young Lad's schools were open, or closed because of the snow. This saga went on for an hour and a half, and ended with disappointment for Young Lad, as his school was open, and happiness for Lad as his wasn't. Young Lad slammed a door and whinged a lot as he put his school uniform on. Lad sat down in his pyjamas with a cup of tea. Young Lad was then taken to school through a blizzard, and She needed a coffee with Loadsakids to recover from all this. Loadsakids was enjoying the whole teenagers/school/snow scenario just as much as She was, and they stared into their cups without talking for a while. Then rocked slowly a bit.

Lad startled me, Readers, yesterday morning by starting some Revision by 8.30am. This was wholly unexpected, and turned out to be because he wanted to go "sledging" with his friends in a town far away. Now, Readers, the general public had been warned not to travel unless Completely Necessary, due to the bad conditions. Lad seemed to think that going sledging comes into the category Completely Necessary, and asked if She would take him. She said no, rudely and unreasonably I felt. So Lad, in a tremendous show of Determination and Resilience, caught two trains to the town far away, taking an hour and a half, and the same back again. This, to me, is a an example of the British Spirit, not Complete Bldy Stupidity as he was told. I'm not the only one in this house who is underestimated and misunderstood.

Young Lad, who had dutifully gone into school, was allowed to choose the menu for dinner last night. He chose Harry Ramsden's and Aunt Bessie chips. Plus, and this was the deal breaker, it had to be eaten on the sofa, not up at the table. This is normally not allowed until Friday night as it is Common, but Young Lad was indulged as he'd had to go to school. The one I felt sorry for again, Friends, was He. He went to work ridiculously early yet again, to clear the snowdrifts out the way, and then clear them again when they all blew back. He has not had a good week, and deserves that bottle of wine tonight. Doubtless her friend Gordon will pop round too.

So this morning started with yet another will they/won't they open cliffhanger, until the schools decided whether they would open. Young Lad's school did, and Lad's school said they would open too. This displeased Lad, who had hoped for another day of train rides and sledging. There was a calm and sensible discussion for about half an hour that Didn't Involve Any Shouting At All, as to whether Lad would be going into school. Lad's point was that the bus might take a long time and it would be difficult to get there. Lad seemed to have forgotten his marvellous feat in getting two trains back and forward to a town much further away yesterday, which rather blew his argument out of the water.

In the end, She lost the will to live and gave in, somewhat childishly removing his phone and the Xbox controller so that he had to do some work. This was all rendered meaningless by Lad's school making a late decision to close, anyway. Happy days.

So it was just Young Lad, yet again, going to school. Those that made it in were rewarded with a free Pain au Chocolat and some Team Points. I would have just wanted the Pain au Chocolat. You'll be pleased to know that Lad spent his day at home well, working very hard on his revision all about X and Y chromosomes. I lay across his books for half the morning to help. He said he couldn't have done it without me.

Well, Readers, as Winter draws to a close and Spring arrives (yes, really) it's a good chance to reflect on the last few months. The shark jigsaw still hasn't been finished, and there are still two Airfix models that haven't been made. But on the plus side, Young Lad has discovered Energy, and the cupboard under the stairs has been cleaned out! Who knows what the next few months will bring!! Meghan Markle's wedding, for one thing. I'm still working on the route to Windsor.

CHAPTER SEVENTY-FIVE

Sunday Lunch

March 4th

Oh dear, I was wrong. Winter hasn't drawn to a close. It's pouring with freezing cold rain now, Readers, and what was left of the snow has gone. It really is a grim, grey afternoon, and I'm jolly glad it's too wet to drag me out for a second walk today. I did have a lovely walk this morning before it started chucking down, and frankly that's quite enough for today.

Anyway, Lad has just put me in the bath – I wasn't best pleased – as I rolled in some cack this morning and was very muddy. I really don't see what the point was; I'm only going to get filthy again tomorrow, but I suppose it gave Lad a break from his revision. Plus he had to clean the bathroom afterwards and has been spraying Viakal like his life depends on it.

So today started well – a bit of a lie-in, He didn't have to go to work and nobody had to get up early. A leisurely start to the day, just how I like it. Lad needed to lie in a bit longer than everyone else, of course, but He, She and Young Lad took me out for a family walk this morning. Young Lad did everything possible to get out of doing this, but they Stood Firm. He was bribed with a cheese sandwich to take with him, as he was moaning he was hungry; this confused me a lot, as I normally trot down the road facing the way we're going, but today I had to sort of walk backwards so that I could stare at his sandwich and be ready to snatch a bit if it dropped. This gave me a neck ache, Readers, and was very ungainly.

I didn't see many of my friends today (I think I'd missed the busy slot), but it was gloriously muddy where the snow has suddenly melted and turned to bog. Oh, I did see Oscar the Border Terrier on the way back, and he jumped up to spatter mud all over her jeans, like he always does. Oscar can be relied on for this, and it makes me laugh as She brushes the mud off, pretending her jeans were filthy anyway. Bastard Swan was back there, gleaming whitely on the river, but was on his own so I can only hope the other Bastard Swans got stuck in the river when it froze. Young Lad finished his cheese sandwich and didn't give me any, so I ran off in disgust.

Readers, in attempt to look like a normal dog-walking family they took the long pink ball flinger thing with them. This never ends well. I pandered to them by chasing the ball a couple of times, but I find this quite dull so what I do is run off into the bushes and drop the ball somewhere. Then they spend half an hour swiping with the long pink ball flinger thing to try and find it, and never can. It's amusing. He always gets very cross about the loss of a tennis ball, and She says ohwellwealwaysfindanotherone. I wanted to turn left and go over the bridge to Top Field today, but Young Lad refused, saying it was too far, and they didn't have any more sandwiches with which to bribe him. So we went to Far Field instead, where we did indeed find another tennis ball that someone else had lost, proving her right, but it was pretty shoddy and not of the same standard as mine.

Once home the Sunday morning peace was shattered by the arrival of Lovelyneighbourontheright's cockapoo, as we looked after him while they were out. He doesn't seem to understand the very simple premise that if I wanted someone to jump on my head repeatedly, I would tell them. I got very cross with him after a while, and snapped. He even tried to jump on my head while I was doing the pre-wash of the dishwasher; this was most annoying. In the end, the cockapoo was shut in the lounge with Lad and Young Lad, and they were told to play with it. Lad couldn't as he was revising, and Young Lad was very busy on his phone, so the cockapoo entertained himself by running up and down with slippers, socks and other items of footwear. He was taken home just before Sunday Lunch was served.

Now, Readers, as you know there have been many interesting and intellectual discussions at the dinner table recently, and today was no exception. We've moved on from Is Trump Proving To Be a Good President After All, and today it was all about whether Young Lad would like to do something called the Duke Of Edinburgh Award Scheme when he's a bit older. It was explained that this is Fun, and Educational, and Character Building, plus it looks good on your CV, whatever that is. Young Lad thought for a nanosecond, and then asked, "does it involve much walking?" to which the answer was yes, so he has politely declined. I quite agree with him – it sounds like organised fun and those sorts of things are hideous. He and She were rather disappointed and asked him to give it some thought. We all know how much thought he will give it.

Yesterday was quite marvellous, Readers, as I had two long walks. Now normally this would annoy me, but the second one was rather special as I met dear, dear Pippa down there and we went for a walk together. Pippa was pleased to see me and jumped on me very hard; she then ran and crashed into me, knocking me flying to the ground where I rolled over helplessly. It was hilarious. She's such fun. We romped our way up through Top Field, where She said, "ok, we'll leave you here and head home," but I was not having that, Readers, and ignored her. She had no choice but to follow us up through the woods for another long walk. I was very upset at the end, when Pippa and I had to go home in different directions, and I sat down and refused to move. Only the thought of Pippa's birthday cake (made with liver and cream cheese) tempted me to my feet.

It was rather stressful last evening. Lad had gone to a town far away to meet his friends and go to the cinema. Now, the cinema is in a shopping centre, but Lad and his friends had some difficulty finding an exit when they came out of the cinema. The shopping centre was closed and there appeared to be no means of leaving. This must have been very worrying for them and the other people who had just exited the cinema. Luckily Lad and his friends are very resourceful and managed to attract the attention of a Security Guard (they didn't have to do much, just stand around with their hoods up) and they were escorted to a hidden exit. This meant Lad was quite late getting home, and She couldn't get her friend Gordon out as She had to drive to the station to pick him up. I then picked a fight with her, as I had chosen my spot on the sofa for the evening, and not left her any room. She tried to squeeze in and bodily push me further over but I wasn't having this, either, and refused to move an inch. Sometimes you have to show people who's in charge.

Well, Readers, after Sunday lunch it is Sunday tea which involves lots of home-made things, and moaning about spending the wholebldyday in the kitchen. Apart, that is, from the hour spent with Young Lad on his homework, finding out about the features of a town in the Middle ages, and describing a picture of a bombsite. Both of which will stand him in good stead in the future.

I've no idea what the week will bring, Friends, but I'm bound to be dumped with Pippa and Ebony at some point. I look forward to this, as I'm not bored with them.

CHAPTER SEVENTY-SIX

Bribery

March 5th

Readers, it was Rush Hour down at the river this morning. I've never seen so many dogs and Pack Leaders out at one time. This deeply affected our pace per mile, as we had to keep stopping and chatting to everyone; this was highly sociable and is more important than the exercise quotient. I don't see why it was necessary to add on an extra half mile to make up for the slow pace, but there you go.

Actually, something marvellous happened today. I overcame my racist, xenophobic problems, Readers! Teddy the Australian Labradoodle was down there, and his Pack Leader had her friend with her, the one with the skin colour and American accent that I don't like. Normally I bark ferociously at him, to show how brave I am, and I don't care if it hurts his feelings. Today, Readers, the man with the skin colour and American accent that I don't like had a cunning plan. He held out his hand with some food in it. Astonishingly, my fears of Dark Skin disappeared in a flash! I know! I courageously ran up to him, and gently took a treat from him, without snarling or biting his hand off. This was clever thinking on his part, and on the way back from our walk we bumped into them again; I bounced up eagerly, to have another snack. I ignored him as soon as I'd eaten it, mind, but still! I'm sure many of the world's inter-racial problems could be sorted out with a small biscuit.

Two Bastard Swans were on the river, so unfortunately they hadn't met their end under the ice when the river froze last week. Chuck was down there, looking as gorgeous as ever, and we had a lengthy sniff of each others' backsides, as the cold wind has dropped. I was marched round Top Field, and then Far Field as well, to the tune of "Top of the World," by the Carpenters. Readers, something dreadful happened in Far Field. Instead of just thinking it, She started singing out loud. I know! I was absolutely mortified and had to look round quickly, checking there was nobody else in Far Field that might possibly have heard. The shame of it. Thankfully after just a few bars of this retro classic She realised She was singing aloud, and stopped – also quickly looking around to see if anyone had noticed. Dear Lord, Friends, it was awful. Anyone walking past would have thought She was out from Care in the Community for the morning. I hope that never happens again.

On the way back we bumped into Nicedogwalkerlady and her husband, and the three hundred brown labradors although there are a few less now, as the Council have changed their Rules apparently. How ridiculous. Then we saw various other people who all called my name and made a fuss of me, telling me how handsome and slim I'm looking. I would say verging on the under-nourished, actually, but nobody seems to care. Barney the Oh So Adorable Beagle leant against her legs and looked lovely as usual, and then jumped up, wiping mud all over her jeans. Good. I had to get straight into my chair for a sleep when we got home, as I was exhausted.

There was a bit of a result during Sunday tea last night. Young Lad was having another piece of Chocolate Fridge cake on the sofa, and I decided to sit next to him. Despite being shouted at and told to GetOffTheSofa! I stood my ground, and then as they pushed me bodily to the floor, I launched myself over Young Lad's plate and snatched the Chocolate Fridge Cake. It was rather nice, I have to say, with just the right balance of dark chocolate, cream and biscuit. Plus the saltiness of the butter. I don't care that it is very unhealthy; if Lad and Young Lad deserve a treat on a Sunday night, then so do I. This appallingly decadent delicacy had only been made because Lad had done so much revision yesterday, and Young Lad had managed two lots of homework and a dog walk. Normally it would have been banana tea bread. I know which I prefer.

I was dreadfully bored this afternoon, Readers, while everyone was at work or school. I felt I had no option but to root around in the cupboards – unfortunately there is nothing of interest in the cupboard under the stairs, now that it's been cleared out, but I had a good look anyway. Then I opened the food cupboard with the silly Screwfix catch that didn't work – by the way, this still has Velcro strips on it, and looks ramshackle – and in the absence of anything else to do, pulled out the carrier bags and chucked them on the floor.

I made a very pleasing mess with the carrier bags, distributing them all over the (dirty) kitchen floor. When Young Lad came home from school he had to clear it all up. How he laughed.

Do you know what, I'm feeling really rather insulted tonight. We had a visitor this evening, a Nurse Friend, and I was sitting in my chair looking sad as usual while she was here. She said she had been dealing with clinically depressed patients today who had a similar look about them, and then suggested that they give me some of Lad's medication to cheer me up. Readers, everyone fell about laughing. It was rude and unnecessary. I can't help it if my resting facial expression is suicidal. Honestly, there is just no respect here. Tomorrow will be better as everyone is out all day, so I'm being shipped off to dear, dear Pippa's house. Nobody there will make comments about my emotional state.

There are lots of horrid scented candles lit tonight – not, for once, because of my smells, but because She opted to make a hearty, warming fish pie for tea. This was before She thought about Nurse Friend popping round, so now a Yankee Candle is doing its best to fight against the pong of salmon, cod and mashed potato. The candle isn't winning, Readers, I can tell you.

Young Lad actually managed to follow more than one instruction tonight when he came in, and fed Gingercat and I, changed out of his school uniform, closed the windows and THEN went on the Xbox. Well done, Young Lad, this is excellent progress. Oh and don't forget he had to clear up the carrier bags, too. No wonder Young Lad is now lying down on the sofa.

Readers, it has been announced that 2500 ordinary common people are being invited into the grounds of Windsor Castle for Meghan's wedding! How do you get one of these tickets? Please let me know ASAP!

CHAPTER SEVENTY-SEVEN

Cream Crackered

March 7th

Good grief I was bored today, Readers. Well, in the hour and a half that I was left alone after they'd all gone to work/school. I'd been given my Kong 'filled' with a scrape of left-over Shepherd's Pie, but this only kept me entertained for a pathetic two minutes, so I had no choice but to go through the cupboards. Firstly I pulled out the carrier bags again, and threw them on the kitchen floor, and then to my joy, found a new packet of cream crackers. I took these upstairs for a change of scene, and munched through them, leaving three in the bottom of the pack. This was good of me and shows that I am not greedy. I didn't even leave any crumbs on the stairs, but do I get any thanks for this? Of course not. Once I'd finished those, I was still bored so I went to the back porch for a look round. Readers, it was disgraceful out there. We have run out of recycling sacks it seems – to be fair She has tried to get some more but the local Recycling Sack Collection Point hasn't had a delivery for ages and have also run out. Now, what would you and I do in this situation? Yes, exactly. We would neatly stack the boxes, tubs, yogurt pots and plastic bottles in a black sack, or perhaps a large cardboard box, until such time as there is a delivery of Recycling Sacks. What do my family do, in their usual slovenly way? Chuck it all in the back porch. Honestly, it looked like one of those TV programmes about hoarders, where the local council pest control people have to go in and sort it out. Shabby, isn't it. So I thought of myself as the local council, and helped out by moving some of the mountain of detritus out of the back porch, and into the lounge.

I attractively placed the recycling around the lounge floor. This was most creative of me. The Weetabix Minis box took quite a lot of ripping up, I can tell you, but the Alpen muesli box is made from much thinner cardboard and is easier to destroy. I added into the mix a pasta packet that I'd found behind the cream crackers. I hope She wasn't banking on that pasta for tea tonight. I'm sure it has helped them, by removing some of this from the back porch, and might spur them on to doing something about thebldymess.

Do you know, I managed all of the above in ninety minutes? Thankfully, Ebony's Pack Leader then came to rescue me from my boredom, and I had a marvellous day at Ebony's house, where I was as good as gold. She had the good sense not to take me home until fairly late, so I didn't have much opportunity to play up before they got home. Ebony's Pack Leader is wise, like that. Yesterday was equally lovely, as I was at Pippa's house for the day and again, behaved impeccably.

Young Lad has been to Indoor Cricket Training tonight in a freezing cold sports hall. I would not have enjoyed that, but luckily Young Lad did. He's had a rather sedentary week if you ask me, as Lunchtime Basketball was "off" today, as was after school football. This only leaves walking home from school, and cricket. He was given a lift home from school. Which only leaves cricket.

Young Lad was quite disappointed again yesterday. You will remember the farce that was Food Technology – the Fruit Salad last week, whereupon they weren't allowed to chop up their fruit, so had to spend an hour eating it. Well, Readers, the Expensive Fruit had been replenished ready for Food Technology yesterday. Young Lad was so excited. However, this time the teacher said, "We are now one lesson behind everyone else, so you'll have to make your fruit salad at home and take a photo." This was disappointing again, for Young Lad. One does wonder why making a Fruit Salad at school is proving so challenging. Anyway, He and Young Lad spent a happy twenty minutes in the kitchen last night, peeling and chopping until Young Lad had FINALLY made a bldy fruit salad. There was a huge sigh of relief all round, and a very untidy kitchen. Young Lad was exhausted by his efforts and lay on the sofa eating his huge fruit salad. All of it. I think He was disappointed that he didn't get any as reward for supervising, and I certainly was offered sweet FA.

Lad had a long day at school yesterday as he had to stay behind to do Art. Now, for his GCSE in Art he has chosen a really rather wonderful subject for his drawings. Me!! The thing is, I am incredibly handsome and photogenic as many of my nicer Readers have pointed out – and Lad has realised that he's more likely to get a Top Grade if he uses a subject like myself. His drawings are pretty good, yes it has to be said, and he has a little talent, but to be honest, I think a lot of it is down to the subject matter. The only thing I've objected to was the need for photos of me with my mouth open. Now, my mouth doesn't stay open for long, so it's quite tricky to take a picture of it – dear Lord, did he faff around at the weekend cajoling me into showing my teeth. It was very tiresome. Anyway, what a thrill!! I'm the subject of Art GCSE. That sounds very important to me. Tomorrow Lad has to stay late at school for his Maths Tutor. This is a Top Week for Lad, and I suspect he feels quite blessed.

CHAPTER SEVENTY-EIGHT

Red Splodges

March 9th

Well, Readers, I've had a busy couple of days. Yesterday they all went to work/school yet again, which annoyed me. There has been nobody here of a day since Monday – unbelievable. So I decided to make a bit of a stand. They left at 7.30am yesterday, and by 7.32am I had finished the teaspoon of tuna mayo that had been squashed into my Kong. I wandered around looking for something to do, and settled on emptying the bathroom bin.

Now, something very unfair happened. Ebony's Pack Leader came to collect me, but she crept in very quietly and I didn't hear her. I didn't even hear her come up the stairs, and I certainly didn't hear her come into the bathroom because I had my head in the bin at the time. Readers, She made me jump. I was very upset that Ebony's Pack Leader had caught me in the act of misbehaving, as she normally has a very high opinion of me, and so I had an extremely guilty look on my face. Ashamed, I was led down the stairs and off to Ebony's house where I behaved impeccably for the rest of the day.

Once home again in the afternoon, I had a look through the food cupboard. The tins looked boring, but I found a carton of chopped tomatoes, and thought well why not? So I dragged them into the lounge, ripped into the carton with my sharp canines, and ate all the chopped tomatoes. A bit bland, if you ask me, and I think She should buy the ones with basil in for some flavour.

The thing is, Readers, that it's hard to rip up and eat a carton of chopped tomatoes without making a mess. Despite my best efforts at cleaning up – and I did try – there were quite a few orangey red splodges over the lounge carpet. I didn't realise how much I had dragged them around, actually, and managed to red splodge the length of the lounge/dining room. Never mind, I thought. She'll see the funny side of it.

Young Lad was home first, and he found the red splodges, plus the Tesco own brand Shreddies type thing box that I tore into pieces, too. Young Lad told me off, and cleared up all the cardboard. Young Lad didn't, however, think about getting some bldystainremover on the splodges. Young Lad was very busy going on the Xbox. Then He came in from work, and told me off again. Then She came in from work, and did, of course, see the funny side of many stains across the carpet. I think that was laughter I heard, anyway. I would think it's quite relaxing, after a long day at work, to be on your hands and knees half the evening with the Vanish.

By the way, Friends, this all gave me an idea for a new game. You see, I suspect those chopped tomatoes had been bought specially for a nice Spag Bol or Lasagne next week. So I thought, won't it be funny if I carefully remove an essential ingredient from the food cupboard every so often, and watch the panic as the gourmet meal plan goes up the spout? This will be amusing. Thinking on one's feet is an important skill, and it will do them good to practise.

I was quite tired after all the hard work with the chopped tomatoes and the Shreddies box, so slept a lot in my chair last evening. Lad revised Chemistry until gone 9pm, poor Lad – though it does worry me that Chemistry gets so much more attention than any other subject. I haven't yet seen him doing Economics Past Papers, for example. Maybe they're even more dull. Young Lad had nearly fallen asleep on the sofa, after the exertions of Wednesday night, plus staying up to watch a bit of Champions League the night before. So he was shipped up to bed and I wasn't far behind, I can tell you.

Today, there was a new routine in the morning, due to my bad behaviour with the bathroom bins yesterday. Ebony's Pack Leader suggested that I should be dropped at their house as Young Lad and She leave home in the morning, to minimise opportunities for naughtiness. Young Lad took me down the road at 7.30am, and when I saw Ebony's Pack Leader, I sprinted as fast as I could with my tail wagging. Young Lad wasn't expecting this burst of speed, and I dragged him along behind me, horizontally. I think his feet lost contact with the ground at one point, but at least he didn't let go of me. Well done, Young Lad. I had a lovely day at Ebony's, again, and behaved impeccably. Until I got home in the afternoon. This time I emptied the bedroom bin all along the landing and also had another go at the bathroom bin. It is totally their fault for not closing the doors. Or emptying the bins.

Well, it's Friday night and hoobldyray She is saying. Young Lad likes Friday nights, as he lays on the sofa all evening watching Masterchef or Police Interceptors. Lad likes Friday evenings as he eats sweets, drinks rubbish and talks rubbish on the Xbox all evening. This is his downtime. He likes Friday evenings as He has some lovely wine and reads the paper. I like Friday evenings because it's Pizza on the Sofa night and I get the odd carrot stick. I'm not allowed any pizza crust tonight, as I've done a lot of stealing this week and am overweight again. How rude.

Good grief, Masterchef is ridiculous. "Susan has made a game, fig and leek pie, with pomegranate mango molasses....." What the heck? Pretentious nonsense. Come on John and Greg, tell them to get a grip. Fray Bentos all the way for me.

I need to update my regular Readers about Nana aged 86. She has managed not to crack any more bones, and has today been seen sprinting up her long garden to her greenhouse. No crutches, nothing. Then she went for a walk down her long, steep, uneven drive and back up again. This is pretty good going and I am very proud of Nana aged 86. Hopefully I'll see her soon, though I tend to have problems with my anal glands whenever I go to see her. It's not deliberate. Honest.

Thank goodness it's Saturday tomorrow – hopefully I'll get a bit of a lie in. I'm fed up with the alarm going off at 6am.

CHAPTER SEVENTY-NINE

Pardon?

March 10th

I had a problem with my ears, Readers, during my walk this morning. Up in Top Field, I had a lot of difficulty hearing her as She screamed at me to hurry up – there were some interesting smells right in the middle of Top Field today, fairly rank admittedly, but they interested me. I was so absorbed in finding the source of the smells that I didn't notice She had stomped all the way round Top Field and was back at the beginning waiting to move on. However loud the bellowing was, I just couldn't hear it. Strange. Then later, near the river, the same thing happened! I was concentrating so hard on the manky odour on the flooded field (I suspect some raw sewage lies not far beneath) that I failed to hear my name being barked at with me. Many times. When we got home, She rushed to ToysRPetsRVetsRUs or whatever it's called, and bought some ear cleaning stuff to try and improve things. I doubt it will.

But really, an excellent day today. I had a lie-in, as I'd hoped and boy was that nice. Lad had to get up much earlier than usual for a Saturday, as He and Lad were going to Wet Sham again. They left here at 12.30pm, so you can see how early Lad had to stir from his room. Poor Lad. Young Lad and He went into town before this, to do some shopping for Mothers' Day, and then Young Lad went back into town again this afternoon to hang out with his friend. He was given some money as a treat, to buy a sausage roll or such like in Dreggs, but preferred to spend this on some sort of silly points for his Xbox game. What a waste. I would have loved a Dreggs sausage roll. But what a lot of movement from Young Lad on a Saturday! Two trips into town. By car, both times, it has to be said.

I had a lovely long walk this morning, as mentioned earlier – I didn't see many of my friends but was dragged for three miles. I pretended I was really tired when we got back, and lulled her into a false sense of security.

When She dropped Young Lad in town this afternoon, I dashed upstairs and found Lad's school rucksack in his room. Rummaging through, I was delighted to find some leftover packed lunch and ate that, chucking the foil wrapping over the floor. Then I found the remnants of a bag of sweets, and threw that around so that the sugar went all over the place. I went back for another look in his school bag, but it was difficult to see with all his school work in there, so I pulled out all the sheets of paper and dumped them on the floor as well. Success! Right at the bottom of his bag was an old, stale Hobnob bar thing. I took it downstairs and tucked it in the corner of my chair, to have later. Not bad for the twenty minutes She was out the house.

Readers, I had to laugh this morning. There has been Frantic Hoovering of the bldyfilthy house, and I was very amused by this. In the lounge, the hoover didn't seem to be sucking anything up. Puzzled, She had a look up the nozzle thingy, and guess what? It was full of uncooked penne pasta! That must have been from the day I threw the packet of pasta round the lounge, and someone has helpfully tidied up by hoovering it all up, so the hoover was completely clogged and it took a long time to bang every single piece of bldypennepasta out of it. It was very funny.

Then I was dragged for a second walk this afternoon as we are on a Weight Loss mission. It isn't working for either of us. This was a much more fun walk, Readers, as I bumped into dear, dear Pippa and she knocked me over, jumped on me, sat on my back and lots of fun things like that. I chased her, and she chased me, and I snarled and snapped, and we had a splendid time. We walked another two miles, so that is Five Miles today, Readers. Unnecessary. I am absolutely exhausted now, and fit for nothing tonight.

By the way, you know the carton of chopped tomatoes that I ate? Not great for the flatulence problem. Also some interesting little presents for her to clear up in the garden this morning. You really wouldn't think that chopped tomatoes would cause this much gas, but I think they are packed with fibre, wherein lies the problem. You live and learn. And any new supplies of chopped tomatoes will be purchased in a tin.

The assistant in ToysRPetsRVetsRUs or whatever it's called, apparently has a Beagle. There was some discussion about a) how badly behaved we are and b) a world record attempt at gathering together the largest number of Beagles in one place ever. This sounds a marvellous idea. I don't want to go, though, as I like to be the Only Beagle In The

Village, as my Regular Readers will know. All that braying and appealing big brown eyes will get on my nerves, to be frank.

An update on the Recycling front. Some recycling bags have been obtained at long last, and the recycling has been bagged up properly. I then dragged it all out and ripped up boxes in the garden. This was fun. It has taken quite a while for all the little bits of Cap'n Birds Eye fish fingers cardboard box to be picked up. The recycling sacks have now been tied, which is what should have happened in the first place. Shoddy. So as you can see, I've had a busy day even without the five mile walk. He and Lad are due back from Wet Sham soon. They will be sad. Wet Sham lost 0-3 at home. This is very poor and rather disappointing, so I expect there will be an atmosphere. I'll just sleep through it.

Good Lord, I'm exhausted.

CHAPTER EIGHTY

What Goes Around

March 11th

Appalling, Readers, appalling. In the previous chapter there was a pithy comment about the pasta all over the lounge floor which had been hoovered up, rather than picked up, therefore clogging up the hoover. Well. This pithy comment was on the assumption that it was He, Lad or Young Lad that had hoovered it up. But no! It was Ebony's Pack Leader, who out the kindness of her wonderful heart, had tried to clear up my mess. How ungrateful, Readers, and how rude to besmirch the unblemished character of Ebony's Pack Leader. I hope she never again bothers to clear up any chaos that I've caused – it will serve them right.

But there was karma in the air today. Ebony's Pack Leader was away at something called Crufts, so we took Ebony out for a walk with us. Initially She said Ebony was to stay on the lead as she has been known to run off, but up in Top Field, pity was taken on Ebony, who looked sad that she could only walk slowly and not run. It'll be ok, She thought, I'm sure Ebony will come back when I blow the whistle, She said. Ebony had heard about the snippy Pasta comment last night on the blog, and decided to stand up for her Adored Pack Leader. Also, she saw a pheasant in the field next door, so took off like the wind and didn't look back. "I'm sure Ebony will come back when I blow the whistle." Nah. "Shout sausage?" Nope. "Scream lookatthistastysnack?" Nein. Swear very Loudly and Badly, and run desperately through knee high mud and weeds in welly boots for HALF AN HOUR? No. And so, Readers, this is what happens when you slander somebody. You spend your Sunday afternoon panting and sweating as you run uphill in the vain hope that you might catch up with a young, fit Bearded Pointer who was on a mission.

Ebony finally slowed down to pick up a rabbit carcass, and ran off with the head, just as She, He and myself got tantalisingly close. Off we went again, charging through the countryside, one of us dangling rabbits ears from our mouth. A desperate and ungainly lunge was made, with more bad language, and Ebony was finally secured. Ebony and I looked at each other and cracked up. It really was very funny.

We were marched back, both very muddy, and Ebony was delivered home with profuse apologies for the state of her. And for whatever the rabbit's head does to her bowels. A top afternoon, Readers, and well deserved.

Dear Lord, it really has been a day. Being Sunday, we looked after Lovelyneighbourontheright's cockapoo puppy, and being Sunday, it jumped all over my head and wanted to play. I told it what I thought of this. Then Gingercat got involved – he had been happily sitting in front of the telly, as he likes to do as it annoys everyone, and the cockapoo puppy went bouncing up and jumped up at him. Gingercat doesn't tolerate this kind of jolly behaviour any more than I do, so thumped him. Cockapoo puppy didn't quite get the message, so it erupted into a full-on fight, which Lad had to end by separating them. Young Lad very helpfully stood and watched. I suspect this is what he does when there are fights at school. Although possibly he films them on his phone. So eventually Cockapoo puppy went home, and peace was restored. On the plus side, the cockapoo puppy did manage to find a soft rugby ball that Young Lad lost several weeks ago, so Young Lad was very pleased.

Other than that, it's been a Homework afternoon, with Young Lad writing about a poem called Charlotte Dymond by Charles Causley, and learning facts about Britain. I ask you. Lad has been doing some Maths which makes a refreshing change from Chemistry, but I find them all very humdrum. I can't remember the last time Lad or Young Lad learned anything useful, such as how to get chopped tomato stains out of the carpet.

There was a break during the afternoon, Readers, when they all went out because it was Mother's Day. After much discussion, they went for a cream tea somewhere, and it might have been nice to invite me along, but nobody did. I like the sound of scone, jam and cream, or the massive wedge of chocolate cake that Young Lad had, but no, I was left at home. And all the doors were shut so that I couldn't bldygetuptoanything. It was boring. Then, because it was Mother's Day, a trip to SparksmeanMarks was made on the way back from the cream tea, as She didn't want to bldycook tonight. What an attitude.

Now, SparksmeanMarks have this excellent thing called Dine In for £10, Readers, which gives you a main meal, side dish, pudding and bottle of wine for er, let me think, £10. What value, and the best part of this is that these are all ready meal type things that lazy busy people bung in the oven, so there are lots of plastic trays involved. Though I suspect SparksMeanMarks might have to re-think this, since David Attenborough (he's in his nineties you know) brought the world's attention to the problems of plastic.

Friends, I have some bad news. I have been told that She is working all week. I know, I feel exactly the same. It is dreadfully irresponsible and downright selfish to work all week. It makes my eyes fill just thinking about it. But while I'm in my chair tonight, I'm going to have a think about what I can get up to. There has been a lot of tidying up and cleaning this weekend, but I don't remember anyone emptying the upstairs bins, so I'll start there and work down.

Don't worry too much about me, Readers, as yet again Pippa and Ebony's Pack Leaders are stepping up and showing the love and responsibility so lacking here. So I will have fun and wonderful Company, but not with my own family. (I hope Ebony has recovered from being shouted at in that awful fishwife-like way across the fields this afternoon.)

CHAPTER EIGHTY-ONE

Rock Cakes

March 13th

Well, Readers, a busy couple of days. I had NO opportunity to play up when everyone went to work/school yesterday, as Ebony's Pack Leader turned up to collect me before She and Young Lad had even left home! So there was no bin-raiding, cupboard-emptying or recycling-ripping yesterday morning. Bah.

Then, at the other end of the day, I was left at Ebony's house until late because Young Lad was the first person home, and therefore meant to pick me up. However, Young Lad "forgot" despite two text messages reminding him, to which he answered, "ok!" His short term memory was extremely short yesterday, and by the time he'd typed "ok", he'd forgotten what the instruction was. Poor Young Lad. So I stayed at Ebony's until He got in from work and even had a second walk with my dear friend! She was very cross when She found out about this aberration on Young Lad's part, and banned him from the Xbox today in the hope that it might help his short term memory problems. This seems unkind. Anyway, I had a lovely day with Ebony yesterday, and there was no horrid fishwife shrieking at her as she bounded across the fields in search of rabbit carcasses.

There was a half-hearted attempt at a roast for dinner last night, to make up for the indolence on Mother's Day. This is always a good choice from my point of view, due to the gravy and sloppy plates in the dishwasher. Then there was a Quiet Hour after tea, in which Lad did yet more revision, and She asked Young Lad repeatedly if he had any homework to do. Young Lad repeatedly said no, but didn't bother to check. He loaded the dishwasher with my help, and then went to watch Eastenders or some such nonsense on the other TV. It was all very peaceful, until Young Lad remembered, after an hour and a half, that he did indeed have homework to do.

It turned out this was to collect together the ingredients for today's Food Technology lesson – in which the giddy height of Rock Cakes was to be reached. Young Lad had to be told, calmly and quietly, that 8pm the night before Food Technology is NOT the time to announce that he needs 250g of unsalted butter. Young Lad needs to learn about Time Management, much like the rest of the family. And thankgod Tesco opens at bldy7am.

Readers, there has been a welcome lull in the Nordic Scandi Noir Drama Dreary type stuff lately – honestly, I was sick to death of it. But no longer – they've found yet another production from Danish TV with a lot of Darkness and Subtitles. Give me strength. So I slept through that and was jolly glad when it was bedtime. Actually, I was so exhausted from my day at Ebony's that I was in a VERY heavy sleep when Lad tried to put me in the garden before bed. Readers, I was highly irritated at being pushed off the sofa, and I growled and whinged at him. Unfortunately it was in a rather high-pitched silly voice, where I was so sleepy, and didn't sound very masculine at all, so I don't think Lad was frightened. Lad just said, "Russell MOVE", so I growled a bit more and wrinkled my nose to show him who is in charge.

I was SO close this morning to half a croissant. So close, Readers. Lad was, as usual, multi-tasking slowly by eating his breakfast and getting dressed at the same time – he didn't have time to finish his large Lidl croissant, and chucked the end of it in the bathroom bin. What an appalling waste, I thought to myself, and made a mental note of where it was. I sat by the bathroom door and stared hard at the bin, willing the croissant to levitate through the air towards me. It didn't. And then, to my utter annoyance, She put the bin in the bath and pushed it right up the far end, so that I couldn't reach it. I mean, how many of you have your bathroom bins in your bath of a day? Exactly. Golly I was annoyed. I deliberately went downstairs and walked all over the kitchen floor that had just been washed to make a point.

On the upside, though, when She and Young Lad left for school/work, I was thrown a rawhide chewy shoe. I haven't had one of these for months, as nobody ever remembers to buy them, so this was a treat. It does, in fact, keep me busy for about ten minutes, which is 9.5 minutes longer than the Kong.

When Pippa's Pack Leader Male came to pick me up for daycare, he found me upstairs. I had decided that I would start from the top of the house and work down, and I do keep to my word. Unfortunately there was bugger all to do upstairs. I had opened a cupboard in the kitchen and chucked the tin foil on the floor, but that is all I managed to do.

Disappointing. Anyway, it was a top day at Pippa's house with her jumping all over me and a splendid walk – this culminated in me rolling in some cack, over and over again. I stink.

Readers, I've had a right result tonight. Young Lad was STARVING and couldn't possibly wait the fifteen minutes until dinner was ready, so decided to eat one of his Rock Cakes. He sat down with this on a plate, on his lap. Friends, you should never take your eyes off your food. I don't. With one graceful leap, like a salmon rising from the stream, I snatched that Rock Cake and ran off with it. I can tell you, Young Lad's Rock Cakes are a TRIUMPH. Absolutely delicious, and well worth the bldy trip to Tesco at 7.20am for the unsalted butter. Oh, it was divine, just melted in the mouth. Needless to say I was shouted at and told to get in my bed, but I'd do it again in a flash. Mmmm. I'll be dreaming of that tonight.

Lad started an interesting discussion at the dinner table tonight, by saying he wants us to move house to another town, so he can be nearer his friends to hang out. This was talked about calmly and gently, and nobody said don'tbesobldyridiculous/haveyouanyideawhatthatwouldcost or anything like that. It wasn't a long discussion.

Oh dear God, the second episode of the Scandi Nordi Noir thing is going on.

Ebony's house for me tomorrow, Friends, as none of my family give a monkey's yet again.

CHAPTER EIGHTY-TWO

Toast

March 15th

A right result this morning, Readers. Young Lad again took his eye off the ball, or his food in this case, and I ran off with his breakfast. Before he even realised it had disappeared from his plate, Young Lad's rather nice toast was dragged under the dining room table and eaten. It was just the right level of crispy on the outside, soft inside – though I would have preferred a topping such as Nutella or a good quality marmalade, but I don't get asked. There was a plaintive cry of "oh no!" from Young Lad when he realised he'd lost his chance to eat, but it serves him right for looking at his phone instead of his breakfast. I loved it. A top way to start the day.

Things were still looking up when they all left for work/school. I was thrown, for the second time this week, a rawhide chewy shoe thing, to try and keep me busy until Pippa's Pack Leader arrived. Two treats in a week! It took nine minutes to eat the chewy shoe thing, and I spent the rest of the time looking through cupboards. My new delivery of food arrived yesterday, and I KNOW She's put it somewhere safe, but I just couldn't find it anywhere. This was very aggravating and wasted a lot of my time.

I was disgusted by the state of the house, frankly, as I looked round – Lad is having terrible problems with his coordination again, and struggles to bend down to pick up the four towels, pyjamas, school shirts and underwear from his bedroom floor. Poor Lad. I think it is a balance disability. It may be hereditary, as Young Lad is beginning to develop the same problem. The bathroom needs a good clean, in truth, and as for the kitchen.... well, this selfish attitude of going to work every day comes at a price. Thank goodness I went to Ebony's house yesterday, and Pippa's today, as conditions there are much better.

There was no writing for my book achieved last night again – I did warn you things would be slack this week. She and Lad had to go to The

Very Important Place in London yet again, which involved more pleasant travelling in the bldy rush hour and moaning about being bldy tired when they finally arrived home. Dinner was a scant affair of hash browns, fish fingers and baked beans – where is the nutrition in this, I wonder? What an appalling plate of processed rubbish. She said they were bldylucky to even get that, and sat down herself with a healthy tuna sandwich.

Young Lad had been dumped at a friend's house after school, yet again, and then went to Indoor Cricket. He enjoyed this very much, but does tend to exaggerate the "injuries" sustained every week, which is rather tiresome. He went to collect Young Lad from cricket, as She was busy testing those gourmet skills with the hash browns, and then we had a peaceful end of the evening, He, Young Lad, Lad and I – all sitting on the sofa eating processed freezer food and watching football (Chelsea/Barcelona – gripping stuff, apparently. I don't know, I was asleep). In a fit of pique because football bores her rigid, She was watching GPs Behind Closed Doors in the other room. Dear God.

I had a marvellous day at Ebony's yesterday, and thoroughly enjoyed myself. This new routine, Readers, whereby Young Lad or She walk me down to Ebony's house as they leave for school/work, is working well. To be honest with you, and I know this might sound harsh, I couldn't wait to get in the door at Ebony's – she was standing in the kitchen wagging her tail at me, and I ran straight in, not even looking back at my Pack Leader. She said it was like when you leave your precious babies at Nursery, and they can't wait to see the back of you. Anyway, a super day again and I was jolly tired by the evening – they don't have the monopoly on that just because they'd been to school/work and then London. It can't be that exhausting – I know for a fact that Lad and She had lunch in Costalotta in London, because there was a discussion about how outrageous it was that they were only given two small pats of butter with their toast, and how She had to virtually hold the barista at gunpoint to obtain a third one. Really, Readers, if your biggest gripe in life is that the barista in Costalotta Holborn was a tadge stingy with the butter, you're not doing badly.

So on to today, and a lovely day at Pippa's house. I was impeccably behaved as usual, and had two cracking walks. Now, you all know jolly well that there are a few groups of people that I'm not altogether taken with. I bark menacingly and loudly at: Old people. People in wheelchairs or with walking sticks. People with dark skin. People with foreign accents. Large groups of children. Fishermen. And today, I met a new group of people that I Don't Like. Pippa agrees with me, and we both went a bit mental when these people knocked on her door. They were far, far too nicely dressed for my liking, and their shoes were shiny. Their suits and ties were immaculate, and their teeth were very white. I just couldn't take to them, Readers. I believe they are called Jehovah's Witnesses. They'd better not come knocking on my door again, that's all I can say!

Poor Lad had his Maths Tutor after school again tonight, so pity was taken on him as catching the bus home would mean a very long day. So he was given a lift. Young Lad, on the other hand, had to walk ALL the way home from school. It's the first time this week, to be fair, as various friends' relatives have given him lifts every day.

Dinner tonight was a fraction better than last night – spag bol, broccoli and carrots. Oh and two slices of garlic bread found at the bottom of the freezer. Nice sloppy plates for me, so I was happy. Readers, the Dinnertable Discussion never fails to amaze me. Tonight we were back to the Donald Trump; Is He Ok After All? debate, followed closely by Is There Going To Be A War With Russia? which THEN turned into a lengthy discourse about What is The Point Of War Anyway? Sheesh. Why can't they just talk about the Kardashians like most people? It's rather pretentious and very dull – and most of these conversations are started by Lad. Young Lad only really talks about the fight he saw at school at lunchtime, and how fast they all legged it when they saw Mr Newman coming. I don't see why they need to talk over dinner at all - what a ridiculous concept! Just eat!

Well hurrah, it is Friday tomorrow. It's been a long week, Readers, in which I've barely seen my family. I can only hope things improve next week. Another day at Pippa's tomorrow, praise be, and then my own family might deign to spend some time with me at the weekend. Don't hold your breath.

CHAPTER EIGHTY-THREE

Spaghetti Confetti

March 17th

Evening, Friends. Another interesting day yesterday – when they all left for work/school I was given a silly plastic "dog puzzle", in which you are supposed to leave treats and it will take your dog all morning to find them. This is blatantly not true. All you have to do is pick the toy up, bang it on the ground hard, and it all falls apart. Ergo, treats fall out. What a major design fault – some idiot was probably paid generously for this idea.

So I was quite bored after breaking the puzzle apart, and had a look through the cupboards. Then I remembered my new game; Let's remove important ingredients from the cupboard to spoil the gourmet menu plan next week! So I dragged out the packet of spaghetti, which was half full, and clearly there for a planned bolognaise or Pasta Bianco (Jamie Oliver). I chucked it on the lounge floor, where it shattered into lots of tiny pieces, and ate most of them. I did find some bits that I'd missed tonight, which is always a result the day after. Honestly this game is fun. So there goes the quick spaghetti dish for next Tuesday. Hee Hee.

Pippa's Pack Leader came round to collect me for daycare, and found the mess I'd made. I had also thrown carrier bags over the kitchen floor. Anyway, I had a splendid day at Pippa's house and made myself at home. He picked Young Lad up from school and they were home nice and early, it being Friday, so we all settled down and waited for She to come home with the usual pizzas and Friday night treats.

It wasn't quite the usual Friday evening though, as She went out to the cinema with Loadsakids, as they both bldy well needed a laugh, and Lad was on the Xbox, so it was just He, Young Lad and me on the sofa for the evening. Very pleasant I must say. And a lie-in this morning, which I needed badly.

But what do you know! When I went outside for my early comfort break this morning, it was snowing again. This is ridiculous. I had more than enough of that a couple of weeks ago, and it is now mid-March, for the love of God. The daffodils are out! It has snowed in a rather pathetic powdery neither-one-thing-nor-the-other type of way all day, and it is BITTERLY cold again. Down by the river there were very few dogs out this morning, and for good reason. But of course we had to do the three mile power walk, due to the lack of power walks this week, due to being at work all the time. Three miles in windchill minus six, Readers. It wasn't fun.

At lunchtime Lad had to be driven to a big town a little way away for a friend's birthday celebration. This was a surprise for the friend, and nobody had any idea what was going on. Lad was rather concerned about the dress code, which stipulated no hoodies or joggers. Lad only has hoodies and joggers. Or school uniform. Eventually he found a pair of jeans, but was still stumped by the no hoodie rule. He has worn a hoodie, but not put the hood up. See what he did there? Clever. Anyway, whilst we were on our way back from the river in minus six degrees, Lad rang to ask if there was a setting on the tumble dryer to get clothes dry in 15 minutes. She was rather short with him, I feel, and unnecessarily harsh in her words. Well, I hope Lad has had a lovely time wherever he is. He needs to be picked up at 11pm, and it is snowing heavily plus there is a night-time road closure for roadworks, so that could be entertaining.

Young Lad has had a busy day doing, er, one piece of homework. He felt that was enough for one day, and has left the rest for tomorrow. This is not good Time Management, and he may regret this. To be fair, he did try to do a second piece of homework, which involved listening to Mozart and commenting on timbre and pitch, yawn, but it proved tricky listening to Mozart over the noise of rugby matches on the telly.

There has been a lot of activity in the kitchen all afternoon, as it is Grandma's birthday tomorrow, and we are going there for lunch. She has been in the kitchen most of the afternoon making a Chocolate Baileys cheesecake (yes, that old chestnut again) and a huge lasagne. Can you imagine the state of the kitchen afterwards, Readers? Quite how these are going to be transported in the car with all of us (including me) tomorrow, I do not know. But it bodes well for a good spillage and something for me to clear up. Especially if the roads are slippery. I look forward to it.

Thankfully, as it's Saturday, there was no dinner round the table tonight, and therefore no Dreary Dinner Table Debates. Honestly, it all gets a bit much. The discussion about Wet Sham's mismanagement and what needs to be done went on for forty minutes the other day; interminable. If only The Wet Sham Board, Vladimir Putin and in fact all world leaders would listen to Lad, the planet would be a better place. He knows so much! He's very underappreciated, like myself.

Oh dear Lord. The Scandi Nordi Noir thriller thing is on telly tonight, so there'll be an hour of Sinister Music and Danish musings. Young Lad and She are looking forward to cuddling up and watching this. I can only hope there are some snacks to make it bearable. I know I've finished all the little bits of spaghetti from the carpet under the table, so I could do with something. Though I did have something of a result this morning – He gave me my breakfast at 5.40am when Gingercat wanted to come in, and then She gave me breakfast at 6.30pm when Gingercat wanted to go out! Sweet! Two breakfasts today! I was given half a dinner tonight, which is just cruel in this temperature. Plus I had no titbits from their meal – after all the bldycooking of Cheesebldycake and bldyHugeLasagne, there was no energy left for nutritious home-cooking, so the cheaper version of Harry Ramsden's it was. The batter isn't quite as good, if truth be told.

I'll let you know if the huge lasagne and cheesecake end up all over the car. I would think it's likely.

CHAPTER EIGHTY-FOUR

Custard

March 19th

While they were on the school run this morning, Readers, I had a look through the food cupboard and found a carton of custard, which I threw on the lounge floor. I also spotted a plastic bag with some carrot ends in, ready to give the rabbit next door, so I ate those and chucked the plastic bag in the lounge as well. I positioned things nicely all over the carpet.

Now, please note that I did NOT rip open the carton of custard, to blend nicely with the chopped tomato stains (see previous chapter), but will I get any thanks for that? Of course not. She huffed and puffed while putting the custard back in the cupboard, so I thought it would be funny to get it out again this afternoon, while She was on the school pick-up. I threw in one of her socks for good measure. It was funny, Readers. It made me laugh. I've been in one of those moods today – you can't help it, sometimes.

When I came home from my walk I was really, really muddy and I waited until her back was turned, and legged it up the stairs. She thought I was being a good boy in my bed in the kitchen. Wrong. Young Lad's sheets and duvet cover had been taken off for washing, so there was just his fluffy 13.5 tog duvet on the bed. It looked warm on this chilly day, so I jumped on and walked up and down until I found the right spot for a kip. There was some shouting and sighing when the state of the white 13.5 tog duvet was realised, and I was pushed off rather firmly.

Now, we learned something today, Friends. Young Lad's 13.5 tog duvet doesn't really fit in the washing machine, even if you shove it in and put your full weight against the door until it clicks. Yes, in theory the machine does fill with water and strange sounds can be heard, but there is no room for proper washing and certainly no room for spin cycle. I tried not to laugh when She took the duvet out and it was saturated, and so heavy it was barely movable. There was some valiant struggling down the garden path, and an effort worthy of a Russian weightlifter to lift it above her head and hang it over the goalpost. Too funny. It's still sopping wet and will be until July.

I had a good walk this morning – there was still a lot of snow around on the ground, and I really have had enough of it now. The only good thing about it is that I can't be seen, especially in Far Field where, as you know, I blend in completely. It's really amusing watching the panicky screeching and puzzled squinting around, trying to spot me. Sometimes, I stand still and camouflage myself so that any Pack Leader with dodgy eyesight over the other side of the field can't see me.

It was a beautiful day, with a blue sky and sunshine, but so so cold, Readers. This can't be right for the middle of March. The wind was glacial, and my ears kept flapping out which is both undignified and painful. Nicedogwalkerlady and her husband were down there with their brown labradors, and they told me to keep up the good work in terms of my poor behaviour at home. I also saw dear, dear Chuck and his coat looked better than ever – so shiny and full. He really is in marvellous condition. It's all due to Greek yogurt, apparently.

Now Chuck and I do like to appreciate each other's backsides, but we don't always time this right and it sometimes coincides with one of us lifting our leg. One has to duck out quickly from this position, otherwise one gets an unusual kind of shower. Chuck's Pack Leader had a name for this, but I didn't really understand. Anyway, I digress.

I was marched at full speed for 3.2 miles today, and our speed/distance quotient was quite good as we didn't stop to talk to people much. How sociable. Over the bridge and round Top Field, we stomped in time to, "Saturday Night at the Movies" by The Drifters. Who cares what picture you see? That's awful grammar, by the way. Then we went through Far Field as well, so it was a good long one today. I was exhausted.

But back to yesterday! I went for lunch at Grandma's house, as you know, and I was really, really hoping that the huge lasagne and Baileys chocolate cheesecake would go flying across the car when He braked. Sadly they didn't. I had a lovely time, as the Derby Chicks were there and had bought me a large rawhide bone thing. This kept me quiet for ages. I did pop into the dining room while they were having lunch, but Lad was holding forth at the dinner table about Russia, Wet Sham's management mistakes, and all the other things about which he knows so much. Honestly, there is no escape from it. So dreary. I could only put up with the conversation for so long, and went back to an armchair in the lounge for a kip.

I'd been told off when we arrived for going straight out in the garden for a comfort break. Apparently this is impolite, to deposit things on Grandma's snow-covered lawn the minute we get there. What's a chap to do? At least it was easy to find, and it wasn't my fault that the poo bags had fallen off my lead and were somewhere in the car.

Well, Grandma was very pleased to try the Baileys chocolate cheesecake at long last, having heard so bldy much about it. Plus she was very understanding about the ripped paper on her birthday present – that's what happens if you put it in the boot with me.

Once we came home, Young Lad and Lad had to knuckle down to their homework, and I went out for my long walk. This was fab, as coming back from Far Field I spotted dear, dear Pippa in the distance and I ran like the wind to catch up with her. Oh how we romped, leaping over each other, or, in fact, mostly Pippa leaping on me. How she knocked me half way across the field, and how we laughed. It is a wonder my bones are still in one piece, but I do love her. Once home, Young Lad had to listen to Symphony No.40 by Mozart and write all about the texture. timbre, dynamics and pitch. Readers, this was a learning experience for us all.

Lad is working hard tonight on, you guessed it, Chemistry revision. He is cross and shouting what the heck a lot, as he didn't think alkali shows as purple on the Universal Indicator, and feels they've got it wrong. In fact, Lad has got it wrong, but he may struggle with this as a concept. Young Lad is watching Rookie Blue, now that Chicago Fire has finally been exhausted, and it is fairly peaceful. His duvet is now on the hall radiator, sopping wet, and the summer 7.5 tog duvet is on his bed tonight. Poor Young Lad. Lad has just shouted, "ah, formulation!" I am concerned that he is developing Tourettes or some such thing. Poor Lad.

I'm off to visit Sicknote tomorrow. I've been told to be more sociable than I was last time.

CHAPTER EIGHTY-FIVE

Surprise

March 20th

Oh it's too funny, Readers. My new game is just brilliant. Tonight's dinner couldn't be spaghetti-based as I had eaten all the spaghetti, so in a cunning plan, a curry was cooked. It smelled good, and there were poppadums and naan bread to go with it, but Oh Dear!! Where's the rice? I'm sure there was some rice in the cupboard/whereisthebldyrice? Not on that shelf, or that one, and surely not behind the cereals, it never goes there......no, Readers. There was no rice. And I think we all know why, don't we? I told you, this is a top game.

Oh, I chuckled to myself in the lounge as I heard her banging through the cupboards looking for the bldyBasmati. Friends, She even texted Lovelyneighbourontheright to see if she had any rice to spare, in order to save the curry. Just in the nick of time, an old and very out-of-date bag of Sharwoods noodles was found and substituted for the missing grains. Young Lad wasn't impressed and said it tastes better with rice. Hee hee.

Apart from that I've been pretty well-behaved today. During this morning's school run I did open the kitchen cupboards and have a look through, but decided not to pull anything out today. I went for a kip on Young Lad's bed instead. Then I had my morning walk, which was lovely as the sun was shining, and there were lots of friends down there. I wanted to take my time and have a good sniff everywhere, but She said we were on a tightbldyschedule and kept shouting at me to hurry up. It wasn't very relaxing. Dear, dear Chuck took my mind off all the shouting, and we wandered along together for ages. Chuck's Pack Leader is very funny and there is always a lot of laughing and sniggering. I don't understand any of it; neither does Chuck. We only did two miles this morning, due to the tightbdlyschedule, and I have to say that made a welcome change. I had a sleep when we got back whilst

Frantic Hoovering was done yet again.

Then it was time to visit our friend Sicknote, and her Brown Labrador. I had been told to try harder on the socialising front, and Readers, I did my best. I'll admit that there was a brief pause on the socialising front when we arrived, as I ignored Sicknote completely and ran into her kitchen to hoover up anything on the floor under the table. (There wasn't much). This is rude, it seems, and one should always say hello first, before running off to look for food. I do the same at Nana age 86's house. Anyway, I also stood up at Sicknote's kitchen worktop to look for food, and licked the front of one of her cupboards as there was something tasty on there.

I felt I was being far more charismatic and engaging than on my previous visit, when I was in a mood and just went to sleep. During lunch I sat and whined and grizzled, begging for food, which was highly sociable of me, and barked grumpily at the Brown Labrador when he looked at my rear end. See how hard I tried? Then I stood on a chair in Sicknote's front window and barked ferociously at anyone walking past. I had a lovely walk over the fields, but She spoiled my fun by putting me on the lead once it was established there might be large deer in the woods. I don't have a good track record with stags. Anyway, it was a lovely day and made a nice change. It would have been perfect if I'd been allowed to chase a deer, but there you go.

Young Lad had a good day at school, and is looking forward to next week's Food Tech lesson, which is Fruit Crumble. If it is anything like his Rock Cakes, we are in for a treat. Young Lad is allowed to choose any fruit to put in his crumble. Various things have been suggested, but he thinks he'll opt for apple. Some would call this playing safe, but I like Young Lad's thinking. If it ain't broke... He can't even be persuaded to stick in a blackberry or two. I'll let you know how it turns out, if anyone drops any.

Lad has mostly grunted tonight but I think it was morse code for "I've had a super day at school, thank you for asking, how was your day?" I am lying half across Lad's lap this evening, helping him with his Biology. The Chemistry Tourettes from last night seems to have calmed down, which is a relief. Poor Lad. It's hard for him to concentrate, as he is busy thinking of schemes to make money, at the same time as revising. Lad is very clever at doing more than one thing at once. I do feel a bit sorry for him, though, as I know for a fact that leftover curry and noodles have been put into a tupperware box for his lunch tomorrow. I hope he doesn't open it on the bus, that's all I can say.

An update, Readers. Now, I haven't mentioned Homeless Guy

outside Sainsbury's for ages, partly because he wasn't there for quite a while, and partly because She's been parking at Tesco to avoid shelling out on Dreggs coffee for him. Nice. Well, he is back outside Sainsbury's, I'm glad to say, and the other homeless people that had stolen his pitch seem to have gone elsewhere. Yesterday he seemed to be overflowing with coffee and hot drinks, so She gave him some money instead. He doesn't look very well and it is so bitterly cold. Some deep soul-searching needs to go on, if you ask me, about the avoidance tactic of going to Tesco. Shameful.

He is upstairs having a warm bath to recover from yet another cold day outdoors. Thank goodness He had a nice hot curry to come home to tonight. Shame about the rice! I'm exhausted after my morning walk, then going out visiting, so I expect He will join me on the sofa soon and we'll both be asleep before the end of Eastenders.

It's Wednesday tomorrow, Readers, which is always problematic – tomorrow I have an assortment of arrangements for my entertainment. Lovelyneighbourontheright is going to let me out in the morning, then Pippa's Pack Leader is taking me for a walk at lunchtime. However, you and I know full well that this leaves several hours for me to find something to do. Watch this space. I hope they leave me that soppy Keep Your Dog Entertained for Thirty Seconds puzzle again.

I doubt there'll be a very nice mood here tomorrow, Friends, as Wednesday's are always Labour Intensive and Scheduled Tightly but the good thing is that Young Lad has his last Indoor Cricket session tomorrow night. It will then be outside Cricket training, and I go along to this which is fun, as there is loads of birds poo on the ground at the cricket club, which I tidy up for the groundsman.

CHAPTER EIGHTY-SIX

Having A Kip

March 22nd

Gingercat and I tried to have a sleep yesterday, when everyone was at work/school. We had prowled round the house after they left, and found that the door to Young Lad's bedroom wasn't shut properly, so we made ourselves comfortable. Gingercat preferred the yellow blanket, whereas I settled down under the duvet and Manchester City blanket.

The bed looked such a mess because, if you remember, I had made the 13.5 tog duvet filthy the other day, so poor Young Lad has a thin summer duvet on, with blankets piled on top. Very elegant. Gingercat and I had been heavily asleep, when Lovelyneighbourontheright came in to let me out, and surprised us. We were woken up very suddenly and were rather bleary-eyed. Gingercat actually said something quite rude.

Anyway, prior to this I had been through the cupboard in the kitchen and chucked the carrier bags on the floor, then dragged the tin foil into the lounge and dumped it on the carpet. It was something to do. Thank goodness Lovelyneighbourontheright came to let me out and break up the morning, as it was a VERY long time until lunchtime, when Pippa's Pack Leader took me for a walk. The rest of the day was uneventful until tea time, when it all became hectic as it was Wednesday Evening. The usual rubbishy dinner from the freezer was cooked; She says it is just possible that fish fingers are the best invention ever.

Young Lad was at Indoor Cricket which was a Fun Match this week, but poor Lad had still not made it home from school at nearly 7pm! There was much worried text messaging and phoning him, to find out which ditch he was lying in, but no answer from his phone. This was concerning. Eventually Lad turned up, having had his phone confiscated for Improper Use during the day, and the confiscator had forgotten to give it back and gone home with it. This was annoying, but better than the lying in the ditch scenario. Lad was very, very cross about it all but I feel there is a lesson to be learned in there, Readers.

When Young Lad finished cricket, pity was taken on him for having a long day at school followed by Energetic Sport, and pity was also taken on Lad who had had a Crap Day and was so very late home. Not usually known for such spontaneity and generosity, She stopped at the chip shop on the way home and bought them a £1.60 portion of chips. To share. And He fancied some too, so they were shared three ways. Though nobody shared any with me of course! Oh no. I was secretly pleased to note that they weren't the best quality chips, if we're honest, and lacked any sense of crispness whatsoever. Flaccid and uninteresting might be a better description. Serves them right.

Today started in the usual way. Gingercat began yowling to come in at 5.40am, which meant whoever let him in managed to go back to bed for a very unsatisfactory twenty minutes until the alarm went off at 6am. I think Gingercat does this to wind them up. Then there was the usual stressy hour of trying to get everyone up, showered, fed and out the house. Lad is finding it harder and harder to put his feet on the floor in the mornings, and move to an upright position. This often takes a full 40 minutes. I worry for Lad. Young Lad is far better at this, as it then gives him lots of time to sit on the sofa before leaving the house.

Anyway, we tried the new routine of Young Lad walking me down to Ebony's house as they left home. I don't like this. I feel very panicky that I can't see Pack Leader, who is loading up the bldycar, and I drag Young Lad back up the road towards her. I can only stop panicking once Ebony's Pack Leader is out on the pavement in the freezing cold, and I can see her. Then I run like the wind down towards her, dragging Young Lad behind me once more. This wakes Young Lad up, ready for the day ahead.

I had a smashing day with dear, dear Ebony and rolled in the most enormous pile of poo I could find. It didn't seem to be the normal fox kind, and Ebony's Pack Leader can only think it is elephant poo. I stank. Poor Ebony's Pack Leader had to clean me up, which she does with kindness and a gentle touch. Later we went out again, and Ebony and I played with a ball – Ebony was more successful at this than me, as she understands the concept of dropping the ball so somebody can throw it, and also doesn't try to stick two balls in her mouth at the same time. I learned a lot from her today. When I came back home, my family were still out, so I went through her coat pockets and found some Polo mints. I ate them, and threw the wrapper in the lounge. My breath smells nice, even if the rest of me doesn't.

They were all late home, as Young Lad had football after school, and then had to walk to his friend's house to wait for a lift. Lad had his Maths tutor after school again, so pity was taken on him (that's twice in two days), and he was picked up to avoid the long bus journey. So it was jolly late by the time they got home and fed me – I was at the front door waiting for them, and barked loudly to show my displeasure. Dinner involved slightly more effort tonight (I should think so too) plus there has been some baking. I can smell shortbread, as we are going to visit Nana age 86 on Saturday, and bread pudding to use up the rock hard French stick that's been lying around all week. The bread pudding will be rubbish as there weren't enough raisins, but I'd still eat it. Not that I'll get the chance. The kitchen is filthy again, as you can imagine.

BUT, Readers, there was nearly a very sublime moment! While a feeble effort at tidying up the kitchen was made, something fell out of the fridge. Guess what it was? That's right! HALLOUMI! A blooming lovely big chunk of Halloumi cheese came flying out of the fridge and down to the floor. It bounced on the open door of the dishwasher – Halloumi is quite rubbery, you see – and it was about to bounce into my mouth but it was intercepted just at the last moment. Oh I was so close, so close to a big chunk of Cypriot sheep/goat squeaky rubbery cheese. I was gutted, Readers, gutted. It's not like me to miss out on something.

I'm quite tired after my day with dear Ebony, and I'm back there tomorrow. I imagine we might avoid the part of the field that had the elephant poo in.

CHAPTER EIGHTY-SEVEN

Nana

March 25th

Readers, this is likely to be an epic chapter, so please pour yourselves a glass of something and settle down. There is bugger all on telly anyway.

Nana aged 86 is no longer 86! She is now Nana aged 87. Yesterday was her birthday, and we all went down to take her out for lunch. I had a WONDERFUL time, apart from the five hours of driving – but I slept through that. (The language in the car, Readers, when they saw a sign saying "One and a half hour delay, Junction 29 to 1a." And to be fair to the Transport people, they were bang on. It was a delay of exactly 90 minutes, on top of a two hour journey. That is impressive accuracy. But was this appreciated? No. Non-stop huffing and sighing as we sat in a traffic jam.)

However, once we arrived at Nana aged 87's, things really started to look up. There was a frantic ten minutes of shouting for everyone to go to the toilet and get back in the car, but I quite enjoyed myself in the garden, and let them get on with it. I have to say Nana aged 87 wasn't over-thrilled to see me, especially as I ignored her when I arrived and raced to the cat food bowl. But really, Nana aged 87 looked marvellous, very pretty and one would never know she was of such Advanced Years.

Then, Readers, they went out for lunch. To a carvery. Now I think I would quite like a carvery, but did I get taken along? Oh no. So I was left at Nana aged 87's all by myself.

Well. What's a boy to do? They left me with TWO bones, in the hope that I might spend a couple of hours eating them. Nah. One was a soppy chew thing and one was a bone filled with tripe – I know you're jealous. I waited till the car had pulled away, then took them both upstairs. It was an Error of Judgement, Readers, on their part, not to shut all the bedroom doors. I needed somewhere to bury my bones, after all.

Now, it is never good practice to bury more than one bone in the same place. There is the danger that a rival dog might sniff them out and then you're scuppered. It is always wise to bury multiple bones in multiple places. And so I did. It is also important that you bury your bones very deeply so that a Rival Dog can't find them. To that end, I completely trashed two beds in Nana's house, ripping off all the sheets and blankets or duvet, so that I could bury my bones a long way down. I was very pleased with my handiwork and was feeling quite smug about how well hidden they were. Nana aged 87 was Not Pleased when she found the state of the bedrooms after we had left, but to be honest, it will give her something to do, tidying them up again.

Then I popped downstairs for a look round the kitchen. I could smell some bread, so I stood up at the work surface and eyed up the extremely old wooden bread bin. With a bit of a stretch and some jigging about, I could just get my claw under it, and dragged it towards me with all the things that were on it/in front of it.

Readers, try to imagine what happens when you drag a bread bin off the work surface, and send it crashing to the floor. It made quite a mess of the kitchen and I fear the bananas that ended up under the bread bin may be a little bruised. A cup was smashed to pieces in the process - it really did look like someone had ramraided the place. Anyway, I found half a loaf of Hovis and took that off to the dining room to eat – it filled a corner. I didn't stop to think whether Nana aged 87 might have any other bread or whether I'd just eaten her week's supply. Oh well. I also pulled a punnet of grapes off the side and took those to the dining room, but they were black grapes, and I prefer green. I hope she buys green grapes in future. So I dumped them on the floor.

This really was a splendid way to spend a couple of hours, and serves them right for not taking me to the carvery. Apparently they had a lovely meal, and Funnygit her brother was called a tart by the waitress, as she brought the food round (as in "are you the tart?" "YES!" they all shouted). Nana aged 87 had a lovely time with her entire family as all her grandchildren were there. Quite incredibly, they managed to have yet another Dinnertime Discussion about Russia/MI5/whether England will go to the World Cup/general politics etc etc. Dear God. How dreary. I'm glad I wasn't there, in some ways, as I was happy trashing Nana aged 87's house, though I would have liked the Beef and Gammon. Thankfully, they all came back to Nana's house for tea and birthday cake, but of course there was lots of shouting at me beforehand. I had to sit in the garden and put my sad face on for five minutes. Then I tried to sit on their laps, but people said I smelled, and I was pushed off. Still, it was a lovely day, and I don't think Nana aged 87 will ever forget it.

Today I have been dragged for TWO walks, totalling five miles, because I didn't have a proper walk yesterday and spent most of it asleep in the car. This is rather ridiculous, and I found the second walk quite hardgoing. I had also rolled in two loads of fox poo this morning, and another one this afternoon, so I've been bathed as well and moaned at a lot. I bumped into lots of friends down there, and even saw The Friendly Electrician and his lovely wife. Their dog was nice and clean, but he smelled the fox poo on me, and thought what a cracking idea, so he found some and rolled in it too. How they laughed.

She was bldyknackered after the hideous journey yesterday, and the priority seemed to be getting Gordon out the cupboard when they got home (He had a nice glass or two of red, to settle his nerves, too). Friday night was the usual Slovenly Pizza evening after a week at work. I was SHATTERED on Friday evening, Friends, as I'd been at Ebony's house all day. Not content with walks, they are now trying to teach me better ball skills. It's exhausting. I snored and snored on Friday evening, comatose in my chair.

The day had started well. She and Young Lad left the house at 7.29am. Ebony's Pack Leader came to collect me at 7.35 am. In those six minutes I had pulled everything off the shelf in the kitchen cupboard, dumping carrier bags and tin foil everywhere. Pretty good Time Management, yet again.

Skilfully I arranged the clingfilm, tin foil, greasproof paper and a tin of Heinz beans on the floor, adding a slipper, a sock and an Adidas trainer for effect. This is called a Collage. I was quite pleased with this, and had finished by 7.34am.

This afternoon has been fairly peaceful, as He went into work for a couple of hours, Lad and Young Lad did homework all afternoon and She did the cleaning. Plus walking me again, and giving me a bath. The bathroom has been cleaned twice today. This is, if nothing else, thorough.

I've been told that She is working all day tomorrow, so doubtless I'll be shipped off elsewhere. I suppose I should cherish the five hours they spent in the car with me yesterday.

Happy Birthday Nana aged 87, and sorry about the state of your house.

CHAPTER EIGHTY-EIGHT

Sun Worship

March 27th

Yesterday was lovely, Readers, quite lovely. The sun was shining, and for once there was less nip in the air. I was dumped at Ebony's good and early for the day, and had a marvellous time. As well as lovely walks, I decided to have a kip in the sun, in Ebony's garden.

However, I was rather put out by the level of my discomfort. At this point in the day I was forced to lie on a hard surface,which was not conducive to a good sleep. I put up with it for a while, but really it wasn't good enough. Thankfully, Ebony's Pack Leader realised this was not good hospitality, and soon brought the cushion out for me. This made all the difference. I was now clearly comfortable, and able to sleep properly. Sadly there was no room for Ebony on the soft cushion, and she was still on the floor - but, as I've said before, I am the guest after all. I had a lovely time, lying in the warm sunshine on a cushion, and having a doze.

We had two walks yesterday, Readers, and I struggled a little on the way back from the second one. Then, would you believe, She came home from work and said She might take me out for another walk after tea, as the Hour Has Come Off and the Evenings Are Lighter! I gave her a look that told her what I thought of this ridiculous idea. Thankfully She had toomuchbldywork to do. Honestly.

Young Lad was the first one home last night, having "walked home from school." Yes, Readers, he was given a lift by someone's Grandma again. So Young Lad was home nice and early, and settled down on the Xbox with nobody to nag him. It was halfway through the evening when Young Lad realised he had Food Tech today, and quickly announced all the ingredients he would need. Young Lad has not learned his lesson from last time, but luckily all the ingredients for his apple crumble were in the house, so there was less swearing. Lad came home from school and worked hard all evening on his revision, poor Lad. He did intersperse this with discussion over which new hairstyle to try, so I'm not convinced his mind was on quadratic equations all the time.

It was omelette with jacket spuds for dinner last night, as there seem to be a glut of eggs in the fridge. Everyone seemed to like this dinner, and there was very little on the plates for me to pre-rinse in the dishwasher. Disappointing. After the Quiet Hour of homework (dull), Young Lad and She watched Masterchef again – more pretentious nonsense. Someone even cooked a biryani and put a pastry crust on it. Is it a pie? Is it a curry? For the love of God. He finds Masterchef boring, which surprises me as He likes eating food quite a lot. So He watched Eastenders in the other room.

Readers, I didn't have a good night. I had to ask for two Comfort Breaks in the night – nicely spaced out at 1.10am and 3.20am, so that I could deposit quite a lot of things on the lawn. I'm not sure what I ate yesterday but it didn't agree with me, and that rarely happens as you know. There are four people in the house at night, but only one of them manages to hear me whining and gets up to let me out. Strange, isn't it? She was not best pleased, after the 1.10am and 3.20am excursions, to be woken by Gingercat at 5am, yowling to come in. There may be a case for getting the hearing tested of He, Lad and Young Lad. Anyway, I needed to drink a lot of water in the night and just didn't get a good night's sleep. I'm very tired today.

Young Lad had an awfully heavy school bag this morning, Readers. Not only did he have his PE kit, but also all the Food Tech things. Realising that four huge cooking apples just weren't going to fit in the box, one had to be ejected. It was a terribly heavy weight for Young Lad to carry all the way to school. Oh wait, he was given a lift from a friend's Dad. Thankfully She had a day off today, and could collect him after school so that Young Lad didn't have to carry an apple crumble all the way through the town. Poor Young Lad. But Readers, the Crumble was as much a Triumph as the Rock Cakes! I tasted a bit, when some of the topping fell off onto the floor. Marvellous. Young Lad is a talented cook.

I was left with a Kong this morning, filled with a couple of teaspoons of leftover fish pie. Nice. She popped over to a big town nearby, and sat in John Lewis, which hasn't happened for quite a while. The over-priced coffee seemed to go before even half the newspaper had been read, and there was some debate as to whether to try asking for a refill. On the balance of probabilities, this was considered likely to be turned down and anothersoddingtwopoundstwenty was NOT going to be spent. Still, it was a pleasant hour, gazing out at the very clean, nicely ordered products that We Will Never Be Able To Afford or Fit Into (it appears one must be very streamlined to shop in the hallowed halls of JL.) It did smell very nice in there, though, and all was right with the world and safe. Temporarily. The main purpose of the visit to the big town was to track down the Hair Styling Products requested by Lad – I did tell you his mind wasn't on his work last night.

Later in the morning we had a nice walk in the drizzly rain, down by the river. We stomped along to the rhythm of Wuthering Heights by Kate Bush, and I was mightily relieved that there was no singing out loud of that particular tune. Can you imagine? I didn't see many friends, as it was raining and most of them were at home in the dry. Even the Bastard Swans weren't out.

There was a traumatic moment for me, when I saw a Lady with a carrier bag. Now, this normally means there are treats in the bag, for a dog. This Lady didn't have a dog with her and was simply on her way to the shops, via the scenic route, but I didn't realise this, and felt sure there were dog treats in it. So I ran alongside her and gazed adoringly at her, making firm eye contact, and gesturing to the bag. I could see that she had something in her hand as well, and felt sure it was a Bonio biscuit. Finally she got the message and bent down to show me what it was. It was a Marlborough Light. Disappointing.

Readers, I feel I ought to update you about poor Nana aged 87's house. I did, indeed, leave it a little on the trashed side, but luckily Nana aged 87 saw the funny side and so did her Friend What Helps Out, who had to help sort it all out. They found the bone I had buried in one of the beds, which is a pity, as I was saving it for my next visit. Oh well.

CHAPTER EIGHTY-NINE

Penne Pasta

March 29th

I love this game, Readers. Today I went through the food cupboard carefully, choosing which Essential Ingredient to remove, and decided there was a good chance it would be Pasta Bake on the gourmet menu tonight. So I dragged the half-full bag of Penne Pasta into the lounge, and ate it on the sofa. A few bits fell down between the cushions, so I will be sniffing those out this evening. It was extremely crunchy, and quite hard to swallow in bulk, but I persevered and eventually the bag was empty. It will be very funny when the food cupboard is opened tonight, in anticipation of cooking Pasta Bake.

This serves them right for leaving me alone for over three hours this morning, while they were all at work/school. Thankfully dear, dear Pippa's Pack Leader took me for a walk, but I had been very bored up till then. Pippa's Pack Leader chuckled when she saw the empty Penne Pasta packet. My plan has worked, because there has been much huffing and puffing about what to bldycook for bldydinner and they had to have jacket potatoes. I laughed to myself.

Yesterday was a good day, as I was taken to dear Ebony's house again, and couldn't wait to get there. I was exceptionally well-behaved all day. My stomach was better – I know many of you will have been concerned – and this is a good thing, as we didn't want Ebony's Pack Leader having to clear up anything like what I left on the lawn in the middle of the night the other night. When viewed in the daylight, you would have thought there had been an explosion in a bronzing lotion factory. Sorry to be crude, but that's the way it was. All shiny and glittery, with a strange texture. There has been much pondering over what on earth he'sbldyeaten to produce such items, and Ebony's Pack Leader (who has the edge on intelligence, to be honest) has worked it out. Whilst basking on their garden chair in the sunshine the other day, I stuffed myself silly with birdseed. And there you have the strange texture.

I wasn't altogether thrilled about my second walk of the day today. Reader; it was POURING. I was drenched and I feel this is Neglect. Just because She has missed our Power Walks this week it was quite unnecessary to wake me up (I was dead to the world on the sofa) by saying in that silly pseudo-excited voice, "Shall we go for a WALK?!!" My face clearly gave an answer in the negative, but no notice was taken and I was dragged out. It was foul – pouring with rain and chilly. Ridiculous. On the way back I saw poor Ebony, who was also being taken out in the Pouring Rain. What is wrong with these people? There would be less need for hearty Power Walks if She would lay off the Cadbury's mini eggs.

Guess what?! Some post arrived for me today! It was addressed to Russell Beagle, which makes me sound very grand – rightly so. It was a present from one of my blog readers, of a very stylish dog poo bag receptacle, for me to use when I go up to the Royal wedding. What a brilliant idea! I really can't have my manky old cloth one, with a bit of velcro that has seen better days, when I meet Meghan Markle. I bet her beagle has a Good Quality Poo Bag Dispenser. Thank you very much, dear Friend, you made my day.

You'll be pleased to know that Lad has finally settled on a new hairstyle and went to the Barbers. He looks much better without curtains, if you ask me. Today was the Last Day Of School before the Easter Break, which means of course that there is a House Party to attend. Lad's plans are rather vague but they involve friends' houses, pizza, a House Party and Hanging Out tomorrow. It will be nice to see Lad tomorrow night, when he has all these plans out of his system. His plans will then have to change to Heavy Duty Revision as the bldy GCSEs are only a few weeks away. Poor Lad.

Young Lad is pleased Lad isn't here to argue with him tonight. Young Lad has finished school for Easter today, too, and is looking forward to a couple of weeks on the sofa. One of his friends has suggested hanging out in town on Saturday, but Young Lad isn't sure he has the energy for this. He needs to conserve his strength, as next term he will have cricket training at school, football training at school and club cricket training on a Wednesday night. This will be exhausting. There might even be some matches. Plus that heavy school bag on Food Technology days. Poor Young Lad.

He has finished work for a couple of days, too. This is excellent news, as there will be no alarm clocks going off at 6am, and I'll get extra walks. He is more patient when he takes me, and doesn't walk at a silly frantic pace the whole way. I will, of course, still need a comfort break at about 6.20am, approximately 40 minutes after Gingercat has yowled to be let in, and She's just got back to bldysleep. I'm not sure why this is so annoying. There will be some chocolate in the house over the weekend, it being Easter, so I'll be keeping a close eye on where they put it. Chocolate doesn't cause the Tanning Lotion Explosion effect, unlike birdseed.

Tomorrow morning, She is going out for coffee with LovelyDor down the road. Neither of them have invited me. I know for a fact that dogs are allowed in Barstucks, as I've been there before, but do I get asked along? Of course not. I'm getting a bit fed up with this going out and not inviting me.

I'm also not sure I like the clocks going forward. It is now light until 7.30pm, which means I can see out the window in what appears to be the rush hour in our road. I've just had to bark hysterically at a black poodle going past the house, followed by a disturbing greyhound. And then the window cleaner came round for his money! It's too much, and I'm exhausted.

CHAPTER NINETY

Easter Jubilation

March 31st

Today's march through Top Field, Readers, was to the rhythm of "Easter Jubilation." I doubt many of you know this jaunty hymn, as it is probably a modern trendy Easter song that your primary school didn't use way back in the day (unless you went to one of those progressive schools in the 1970s, where the teachers wore jeans and you sang a Groovy Rock version of The Lord's Prayer in assembly). Anyway, I was glad there was no singing aloud of this seasonal song, and actually that hasn't happened since the awful incident of the Carpenters that day, so hopefully it was a one-off. If She starts singing trendy hymns aloud on our walks, I am definitely leaving home.

Readers, there has been so much rain that the river has burst its banks. Parts of the fields were flooded, and a tricky time was had negotiating it all. More of that later – our walk started well today, as we immediately bumped into a Young Pug called Gus. Now, I hadn't met Gus before and I did find him somewhat intimidating to start with; it was the commanding way he stood in the middle of the path and wouldn't let me past. I stood uncertainly for a while, hopping from foot to foot, as I was bldy scared and unsure what to do, and yelling " Ohforgod'ssake manupRussell!" didn't help. Eventually I took my chances and inched past Gus the Pug. He chased me and I ran for my life. But the good thing was that Gus was distracted by the smell of smoky ham in the "treat" bag in her pocket, and jumped all over her jeans with his filthy Pug paws. She laughed and said don't worry they were dirty anyway to the apologetic Pug owner, but they weren't. They were clean on, which is just plain stupid when going for a dog walk. This is Poor Planning. So Gus the Pug plastered her legs in mud, which was funny.

Further on, we met NiceTallLadywiththeStaffie. There was the usual dull discussion of how badly behaved we both are, and how they wouldn't be without us, blah blah blah. Eventually we trekked on over the bridge and into Top Field, where I failed to find any cack in which to roll. This was disappointing and unusual. Coming back along the path, we met the Nice Lady with the Long Hair and brown labrador. (Why are there so many brown labradors everywhere? I fail to see the attraction.) Nice Lady with the Long Hair stopped for a chat and said she now reads my writing – has she really got nothing better to do? It does worry me. But it's nice of her, thank you.

Readers, I had real trouble due the burst banks of the river. I had to think about how I was going to get across this part of the field. I'm not one of those dogs that throws themselves into water (that'll be the brown labradors), and I really had to consider my options at this point of our walk.

Eventually I worked out my route across the flooded field, and stopped for a drink en route. I was shouted at for this, as there is some thought that this floodwater might not be very hygienic in the drains/sewage side of things. For Goodness' Sake. We walked briskly for three miles through the sodden fields and mud, as there is a need for upping the Exercise Quotient at the moment. Three little words, Readers: Hot. Cross. Buns.

Yesterday She went for a coffee with Lovelydor down the road and they even splashed out on some toast and a bacon roll. I would have liked either of these options, but wasn't invited. He took me for a lovely walk in the morning, without any of the nagging and shouting at me, and it was at a much more sensible pace. Then we had a Quiet Day at home as it rained incessantly, until of course She decided I needed another walk and dragged me out again in the pouring rain (Exercise Quotient issues).

Well, Young Lad, He and I had tried to have a quiet day at home, which wasn't easy with the Frantic Cleaning going on. Lad was away staying with friends, after the Party of the Night Before. He had a very nice time, and they went to bed early as they were so tired... at 2am. Poor Lad. Lad decided he needed picking up from his friend's house in the evening, to which there was some huffing and puffing as it is a 40 minute drive each way. On the way home, though, Fish and Chips was bought for tea, as this is traditional on Good Friday. Fish and Chips definitely makes Friday Good, if you ask me. Not that anyone does. I whined and begged, and eventually had a couple of small chips. Generous, aren't they?

Young Lad did very little yesterday. Well, it was raining. Today, though, Young Lad has been out! Yes, after resting sensibly yesterday, he had the energy today to hang out with his friends in town. For an hour and a half, a whole ninety minutes. Well, it was raining again and it's much nicer on the sofa on days like these. Plus he had put the shopping away earlier, so that counts as a busy day for Young Lad.

I wasn't very popular this morning, Readers. I had a little problem with my digestion and was making some shocking smells again. The lounge stunk. I don't know what I've eaten this time-it's a mystery to me. It seems to be a little better tonight, and there is no need for all the Yankee Candles to be lit.

There has been lots of baking going on today, and the kitchen is in its usual state. Admittedly, Shortbread does smell divine when it's in the oven, and I did manage to clear up some crumbs from the floor, but my word the mess! Dear, dear Ebony has been helping out on the baking front today, as well. Her Pack Leader made a nice carrot cake, and turned her back for a second, which it is never wise to do near Ebony.

It's a classic schoolboy error to leave a carrot cake on the work surface, and turn your back. Ebony was simply checking the consistency for her Pack Leader, and making sure the texture was spot on. It was. Now they only have half a carrot cake for Easter Sunday tomorrow. Ebony was shouted at, Readers. Poor Ebony.

Lad has been revising all day today, and is now firmly attached to the Xbox for the evening. There has been a discussion about some Family Time tomorrow, it being Easter Sunday, though She has thought better of suggesting Church to Lad and Young Lad, knowing that this won't go down well. Instead, Readers, I have heard the words HartyFartyForest for a family dog walk! I couldn't believe my ears – I haven't been taken back there since I chased that stag for twenty minutes! Oh please, please take me to HartyFartyForest tomorrow – there are loads of cow pats, fox poo, and stags!! What a wonderful idea. I will let you know how it goes.

Well, it's the last day of March and really, Readers, that brings my winter of discontent to a close. Of course, it will be no surprise if we have a blizzard tomorrow instead of Spring Sunshine, but let's hope for the best. It's been a funny old winter, with plenty for me to moan about and a few nice bits in between. Mostly the nice bits have involved people other than my family, whom I do love dearly, but seem lacking in appreciation of me. Who knows what the summer might bring? Spending more time with me? Lad deciding on a hairstyle and finding a clever money-making scheme, whilst nailing his GCSEs? Young Lad moving off the sofa more regularly and organising his Food Tech ingredients earlier than the night before the lesson? Well, I wouldn't put money on any of the above. We can only hope that life in my house becomes more organised, time efficient and Beagle-friendly over the summer months. Watch this space.

Golly, I'm exhausted.

A VERY IMPORTANT MESSAGE

Long ago, Readers, when Lad was just a Young Lad, he was Very Poorly Indeed with something called a ruptured brain aneurysm. I'm told this is even worse than full anal glands. Lad's life was saved at Great Ormond Street Hospital, referred to in my book as An Important Place In London. Lad is still under their care, seven years on,and it is thanks to this amazing place that he is able to hold such wonderful Dinnertime Debates, and knows so much about everything.

A contribution from every sale of my book will be made to Great Ormond St,in recognition of their incredible work. So stop thinking you are funding a worrying Costalotta habit by buying this, and put your hand in your pocket.

Thank you so much.

Russell

CAST OF REGULAR CHARACTERS

The Humans

He, She, Lad and Young Lad
My family, who don't spend enough time with me

Pippa's Pack Leader
Ebony's Pack Leader and Pack Leader Male
My friends, who do like spending time with me

Loadsakids
Often to be found in Costalotta with She, comparing notes

Young J and his Pack Leader
The reason for my blog - to cheer them up in hospital. It did

The Evil Vet
There are several of them and She says they're nice

Sicknote
Suggested I came to live with my family. Thanks a bunch

Colleagues 1 & 2
Long-suffering souls

Chelsea Girl
Earliest and most enthusiastic blog fan

Nana aged 86
Loves having me to visit. Does like a chat

Lovelyneighbourontheright
With whom Young Lad and I are frequently dumped

LovelyDor
Friend down the road, with whom YL and I are often dumped

Pretty AD
An attractive lady, whose beauty has an obvious effect on me

Grandma
Loves me, cooks nice food

Nicedogwalkerlady and her husband
Always at the river with brown labradors

Batch
Technical genius behind my book and v clever man

Teddy's Pack Leader's Friend
Chap down by the river who has some features I don't like

Funnygit
Her brother. Thinks he's funny

Homeless Guy outside Sainsbury's
Has moved pitch a bit. Nice chap

The Costalotta Baristas
Patient, smiley and ever-ready with the cheapest coffee

Sir David Attenborough
He's in his nineties, you know!

Meghan Markle
Beagle owner. There are no words

The Animals

Pippa
Biggest, longest, bounciest Golden Retriever ever

Ebony
Biggest, longest, nuttiest Bearded Pointer ever

Chuck
Stunning Blue Border Collie

Lexie
Black Lab, usually has a large stick in her mouth

BarneyTheOhSoAdorableBeagle
Gentle and sweet. Annoys me

Rocco the Inspirational Three-Legged Labrador
Inspirational and amazing. Also annoys me

Oscar
Border Terrier who always plasters her in mud. Funny

Chloe
Huge Golden Retriever that doesn't like me

Teddy the Australian Copper Labradoodle
He's NOT a Cockapoo!!

Mr Squibb
Spaniel. Chases me

Next door's Cockapoo
Bounces all over the place. Annoys me

The Bastard Swans
Beautiful but evil

Gingercat
Lives with me. Over-indulged

The Stupid Starlings
Keep me supplied with food from the bird table

29435298R00148

Printed in Poland
by Amazon Fulfillment
Poland Sp. z o.o., Wrocław